Handling In-Flight
Emergencies

TAB
PRACTICAL
FLYING SERIES

Handling In-Flight Emergencies

Jerry A. Eichenberger

TAB Books
Division of McGraw-Hill
New York San Francisco Washington, D.C. Auckland Bogotá
Caracas Lisbon London Madrid Mexico City Milan
Montreal New Delhi San Juan Singapore
Sydney Tokyo Toronto

pbk   3 4 5 6 7 8 9 FGR/FGR 9 0 0 9 8
hc   2 3 4 5 6 7 8 9 FGR/FGR 9 0 0 9 8 7 6

Library of Congress Cataloging-in-Publication Data

Eichenberger, Jerry A.
        Handling in-flight emergencies/byJerry A. Eichenberger.
            p.   cm.
        Includes index.
            ISBN 0-07-015093-1 (pbk.)   ISBN 0-07-015092-3 (h)
        1. Airplanes--Piloting.   2. Aeronautics--Safety measures.
    3. Emergency management.   I. Title.
    TL710.E44   1995   95-32255
    629.132'5214--dc20   CIP

Acquisitions editor: Shelley IC. Chevalier
Editorial team: Robert E. Ostrander, Executive Editor
                        Norval G. Kennedy, Book Editor
Production team: Katherine G. Brown, Director
                        Ollie Harmon, Coding
                        Brenda M. Plasterer, Coding
                        Janice Ridenour, Computer Artist
                        Rose McFarland, Desktop Operator
                        Nancy K. Mickley, Proofreading
                        Jodi L. Tyler, Indexer
Design team: Jaclyn J. Boone, Designer   PFS
                    Katherine Lukaszewicz, Associate Designer   0150931

This book is dedicated to the memories of the following aviators who have flown their last Earthly flight:

E. Arn	K. Morgan
D. Brunton	R. Moss
H. Burkes	W. Peoples
R. Caldwell	L. Purtee
H. Door	R. Schilling
J. Doyle	W. Sprinkles
R. Drake	R. Weir
G. Jennings	C. Wilson
W. McCracken	W. Wiltberger
C. Roberson	R. Carnahan

R. Robinson

Contents

Introduction

GENERAL AVIATION IS AN EXTREMELY SAFE METHOD OF TRAVEL AND IS THE source of countless hours of sport to those who participate in it. In this age of the business jet, corporate flight departments are achieving safety records that rival those of the major scheduled airlines. Flying personal airplanes, singles and light twins, can reward the pilot and passengers with a degree of freedom that cannot be equaled by any other mode of transportation. In the hands of a competent aviator, flying personal airplanes will contain a degree of risk that is acceptable to all but the most phobic of folks.

Lightplanes do have inherent risks that are not as prevalent in heavier aircraft, but the risks can be managed by any pilot with the proper training and mental attitude who wants to attain and maintain the necessary proficiency. This book will deal with the darker side of aviation: the emergencies and other gremlins that can befall anyone who flies. The foolish deny that things can go wrong; the wise study the potential for problems, avoid those that can be, but learn to deal with both the avoidable and unavoidable.

A theme that will run throughout this book is that if emergency procedures are truly learned, and then practiced, they cease to be emergencies and simply become additional procedures. This is the goal of most of the better training facilities that teach pilots of airliners and corporate jets. When the lightplane pilot is trained to the same standard and then assumes the same professionalism toward flying, the risks associated with aviation shrink tremendously.

If you are a pilot who feared emergency training when you learned to fly, hopefully you have overcome that hesitancy since you got a license; if not, you need to. Enough of the right kind of training can remove most of the fright about things that typically cause lightplane accidents, but never confuse lessened fear with lack of respect. Respect for the potential for emergencies should sufficiently motivate us to train to handle them so that the fear recedes, and competence takes over.

Reading and digesting this book is only one small component of a well-trained pilot's education. No amount of reading alone will get the job done. Practice with a competent flight instructor who understands how to handle in-flight emergencies, and who has developed procedures to cope with them, is the most important part. Some of the ideas and methods discussed in this book can be practiced solo, and most of them should be fine-tuned only with an instructor on board the airplane.

Don't add risk to this or any other aspect of your training by going out to teach yourself. You might be able to safely practice a procedure by yourself after you've learned how to do it from an instructor who knows what's going on. Read the suggestions in this book for what they are, only suggestions. If you or your instructor disagree with any of them, that's fine. Do only what is comfortable for you and then only after you've thoroughly discussed it with a flight instructor in whom you have confidence. There is seldom only one way to deal with any problem, whether it be an in-flight emergency or some other event of concern.

Once you have geared your thinking toward the formerly unthinkable, received the training required, and melded it all together with a desire to achieve real proficiency and an attitude of professionalism, you'll have gone most of the way toward *Handling In-Flight Emergencies*.

1
Attitudes

REMEMBER THE OLD SAYING "THERE ARE OLD PILOTS AND THERE ARE bold pilots, but there are no old bold pilots"? In my experience in general aviation, which dates from being a teenager in the early 1960s, nothing could be closer to the truth. A pilot's attitude toward flying will do more to make herself or himself safe or dangerous than anything else. This is so because with the right attitude, any pilot will recognize the limitations of both aviator and machine.

Most all of the endeavors in which we engage have accepted standards of levels of performance that are considered satisfactory. When a person performs to those levels, he or she is not negligent because he or she has met the required level of skill and care for that activity. But there is another higher goal to seek. We can never achieve perfection in anything we do, whether it's as a parent, child, practitioner of our profession, or as a pilot. But the reality that we can't be perfect should not prevent us from trying.

General aviation, in the words of a popular photo and saying, is not inherently dangerous. That is a true statement, with certain givens. One of the assumptions behind the safety of aviation is that the pilot of the aircraft will be competent and safety oriented and will possess the proper attitude about the entire affair of flying. All certificated pilots were required to demonstrate the legal minimum level of competence during the written, oral, and practical exams they underwent to get their licenses and ratings.

In training, all were taught to be safety oriented. What the system of pilot training and licensing can't do is control a person's attitude. In my mind, once a pilot gets a certificate, attitude makes all the difference in the world from then on in one's flying career.

A safety-minded pilot will constantly seek to improve her flying knowledge and skills for as long as she sits in a cockpit. Just maintaining the competency level that had to be demonstrated to pass the tests for whatever certificate that a particular pilot holds is not the answer for a safety-conscious aviator. The answer is constant improvement, not maintaining the status quo. Every airline pilot has to pass a proficiency check semi-annually or annually. All pilots of jet aircraft, whether in commercial or private operations, must do likewise. Virtually all corporate flight departments require recurrency training of their flight crews, again normally done on an annual basis. Flight instructors must show the FAA every two years that they are competent to continue to exercise the high privileges of their certificates.

Yet any pilot who is flying piston-powered equipment normally considered as a lightplane is only required by the federal aviation regulations to undergo a biennial flight review. While the regs dictate that this review, uniformly known as a *biennial flight review* (BFR), must consist of at least one hour of ground discussion and one hour of flight instruction, the real content of the review is left up to the instructor who administers it.

I've seen many certificated flight instructors (CFIs) who have allowed the pilot undergoing the review to set the agenda for it. While it's certainly wise to tell the BFR instructor about any areas in which you feel weak or where you'd like to concentrate during the review, run like a scared rabbit from a CFI who just rides along during a BFR and who shows any disdain or cavalier attitude toward the requirement.

Unfortunately, one flight review every two years can never achieve the level of recurrent training that any pilot should want or even needs. There is no area of human endeavor that cannot profit from continual practice, and when practiced, every person engaged in a job, profession, or hobby will improve in the performance of it. Most pilots of lightplanes consider their flying to be more of a hobby than an occupation. Regardless of everyday work, few of us would consider two hours of training once every two years to suffice. Few occupations harbor the potential for disaster that the recreational use of lightplanes holds.

Sadly, if you read aviation accident reports, you'll come across many instances every year where a pilot was confronted with an emergency that resulted in serious injury or death to someone, a result that probably could have been prevented if that pilot had only undergone enough training to deal with the situation.

How many private pilots have ever experienced an engine failure? The answer to that question is always positive because few modern engines do fail, except for pilot-induced causes. The reliability of engines makes most pilots give little thought and practice to a successfully executed forced landing. I've suffered through three occurrences of either total or partial engine failure in small airplanes. You shouldn't ignore the possibility of engine failure either, even if you've never seen a cowling jump up and down after an engine swallows a valve, or if you haven't yet seen a motionless propeller on the front of your airplane. If you have the right attitude about practicing forced landings and fly accordingly, you'll probably make it through such an experience with nothing more than a fast pulse.

There is no excuse for a pilot rated only for VFR operations to continue flight into instrument meteorological conditions (IMC). Yet this is still the leading cause of light-plane fatal accidents because the pilot had the wrong attitude. The pilots who I have known to do it did not come out of the other side of the weather in one piece. Beyond flying, they didn't play Russian roulette or engage in other suicidal behavior. Possibly they thought that for some reason or another they were immortal in an airplane. If that were the case, they proved themselves wrong. But worse yet, the outcome also proved that they didn't have the skills to extricate themselves from that emergency, even if it were of their own making.

Any pilot can get lost. In the old days before reliable electronic aids to navigation, we used to jokingly say that the only people who hadn't gotten lost were nonpilots and liars. Modern navigational gear has certainly lessened that problem, but the most prevalent side effect of the rarity of getting lost has become the fact that "being unsure of your position" is a real emergency to all too many pilots. Again, a correct attitude about learning how to navigate with a chart, compass, and clock will make the failure of navigation radios an inconvenience instead of a time of fright. Even when truly lost, a competent pilot will solve the problem through deliberate trained action rather than maybe by chance alone.

Other elements of an airplane's equipment can and do fail. Modern dry-vacuum pumps have a failure rate much higher than their older and heavier ancestors, the wet pump. Every pilot who has an instrument rating had to demonstrate rudimentary partial-panel skills during the flight test for the rating. How many pilots could do an instrument approach at night in turbulent air to minimums 10 years later? I would venture not many. Have you given any real thought to this possibility if you fly instruments? If not, and if you haven't kept a sharp edge on your no-gyro instrument flying abilities, you need to modify your attitude about the subject.

We've all seen pilots who lose their cool when the communications radios go silent. Can you remember what to do without reviewing the *Airman's Information Manual* (AIM), especially if you're IFR, when you suddenly find yourself unable to talk to anyone? Again, attitude about training and then getting it on a reasonably frequent basis is the answer to making radio failure into a nuisance instead of an emergency.

Certain emergencies can never be made into the inconvenient. Life is full of risks, some of which can be totally managed. Some risks can be only partially eliminated. You can only hope that you never encounter a few risks, such as the prospect of ditching an airplane over open water; however, with some training in the subject, even this most dire of emergencies can be handled in a manner that your chances of coming through it alive greatly increase.

One pat answer will never enable even the most careful and well-trained pilot to deal with every possible gremlin that might appear in the course of a flight. It's been said that you can't teach judgment to a person. I disagree with that cliché, because judgment is developed through training, practice, and attitude. While an instructor can never be totally sure that a pilot has good judgment in all situations, no one will ever gain proper judgment without a dedication to achieving it. If all of the instructors to whom a pilot is exposed demonstrate a high degree of judgment in the course of flight training, they'll be leading and teaching by example. If the instructional pros show a dedication toward developing and then using the degree of judgment possessed by a good pilot, so will most of their students. Again, it's a product of attitude.

A vital part of a good pilot's judgment and attitude is mental preparedness. Hopefully you'll gain some of that from reading the following chapters in this book and also through obtaining some flight instruction and then some practice in the areas that can be safely practiced in an airplane. Don't forget that approved simulators offer a great training environment, particularly for emergency procedures. While you'll never practice coping with an engine fire, jammed controls, or selected structural failures in a real airplane, those emergencies can be demonstrated in a first-rate simulator.

As you develop and modify your attitude and flying judgment, you'll naturally become a safer pilot. But one of many beneficial by-products of attitude and judgment is the proper confidence that can be gained that in turn makes your flying more enjoyable as you learn to deal with the in-flight emergencies that might someday beset any pilot. All of us enjoy doing anything more when we can do it well. Did you ever see a kid playing an organized sport who didn't enjoy it more when he or she was one of the better players on the team?

While we can't all develop superior athletic ability without the basic skills that come from nature, almost anyone can become a safe and proficient pilot. Thankfully, we long ago discarded the notion that a good pilot had to be a superman and a perfect physical specimen. While, as in all things, some people will achieve a higher level of skill than others, attitude, training, and practice will produce a safe pilot out of almost anyone who wants to learn to fly right.

Remember the attitude that is taught at most airline training departments:

If emergency procedures are learned well and practiced often, they cease to be emergencies and simply become additional procedures.

Adopt the same approach, and you'll be served well.

2
Engine failure

T HE FIRST EMERGENCY WITH WHICH WE'LL DEAL IS THE FAILURE OF THE
engine in a typical single-engine lightplane. Engine failure is not the leading cause
of fatal accidents in general aviation, but when you ask most pilots what emergency
they consider the most dire, a good number will immediately respond by saying that
they think most about the engine quitting.

Every candidate for a private pilot certificate is required to demonstrate the ability
to set up the airplane for a forced landing during the checkride. Certain flight schools
and freelance instructors teach students the word "emergency" connected with a simulated engine failure. I've seen many a student who thought that this was the definition
of an emergency. Certainly it is one, but as you'll see through the succeeding chapters,
it isn't the only ill-timed or unexpected event that can befall a pilot.

Before discussing how to deal with a stopped prop, let's examine a few of the
causes of engine failure and see if we can do anything to prevent it.

FUEL MANAGEMENT

Without a second's worth of doubt, the major cause of all engine failures has nothing
to do with the engine itself—it simply doesn't get an adequate supply of clean fuel to
burn. It is correctly perceived that the engine really burns air, and we just add enough

fuel to the air to make the mixture combustible; however, we all know that air by itself won't burn. Some sort of fuel has to be added to make the fire. Other materials, such as water, dirt, and the wrong type of fuel, don't burn either.

Fuel management, or maybe better put, fuel mismanagement is a pilot-induced event. When the level of mismanagement gets to the point that it causes the engine to quit running, that is also a pilot-induced problem. What we'll try to do is eliminate all of the emergencies that are created from pilot action or inaction and then learn to deal with them if we fail to prevent them. Many an airplane has been found after a forced landing with fuel in a tank, contaminated fuel in all of the tanks, or no fuel in any tank. Only one person is responsible for those sad states of affair, and that person was sitting in the left-front seat.

Fuel contamination

Before discussing running out of fuel altogether or mismanaging an otherwise adequate supply of gas, let's begin with the notion that the fuel in the tanks has to be free of contamination. That's no news to about every person who has a pilot certificate in his or her possession because every student is taught from the beginning of flight training to ensure that the fuel in the airplane doesn't contain water. We were all schooled to drain the fuel sumps, right?

But the way a good number of pilots check for fuel contamination does little if any good. As a compromise to modern concepts of general aviation as a business tool and to keep pilots from spilling a little gas on their clothes, many manufacturers have gone to a fuel drain in the engine compartment that pours fuel onto the ground when you pull up on a small handle near the top of the cowling. This is the only fuel drain installed in many airplanes that can be conveniently used by the pilot.

Unless you have an NBA player's physical size and arm reach to put a cup underneath the cowling while you pull the handle, you probably can't do anything more than pull the handle and watch a stream of fuel splatter on the pavement underneath the airplane. And in a good many of the airplanes so equipped, there are no drains in the wing tanks, again to keep the process of checking for fuel cleanliness simple and convenient. If you're a renter pilot, you're pretty much stuck with what your club or FBO has available in rental aircraft. So you've got to deal with and improve on this situation. If you own an airplane, this subsection describes how matters can be improved at little cost.

If anyone is flying with you, ask him or her to pull the handle inside the cowling while you catch a supply of gas in a strainer cup that is transparent. Your passenger will most likely enjoy being part of the program, and you can use this time to explain what you're doing, how you are safety conscious, and why this step is important (Fig. 2-1).

Then examine the contents of the cup very carefully. Don't just give the drained fuel a casual once-over and pour it on the ground. Really look at it. See if it's the right color for the octane level that your airplane needs. Feel it. Jet fuel is chemically very close to diesel fuel or kerosene and will have a slippery oily feel. If a load of jet fuel is

Fig. 2-1. *A helpful and interested passenger helps the pilot who is checking an under-cowling fuel drain.*

in your piston-powered airplane through someone's obvious error, the engine will probably run long enough for you to taxi out, take off, and maybe climb a few hundred feet as the fuel already in the lines from the tanks to the engine is consumed. Then the world gets very silent.

Look for water in the fuel because it's heavier than gasoline and will sink to the bottom of the cup. See if there are any little bits of debris either floating in the sample or sinking to the bottom. They could be pieces of a failing fuel bladder, tank sealant, or just dirt that got into the fuel from the refueling delivery system. In any of these events, your flying plans are over until the airplane is defueled, the problem rectified, and then refueled.

My practice is to take at least two samples of fuel because if there is any meaningful amount of water in the gas, the first sample drawn might be nothing but water. Smell the sample. If it's all water, you'll only have a faint odor of gasoline at best. Dump it and refill the cup with another sample and test again. This process takes no more than a minute, yet few pilots go to this extent to see if the engine has the life blood that it needs: clean and proper fuel in the tanks.

Always check for any local airport rules governing proper disposal of fuel to eliminate or reduce pollution. The airport might be atop an aquifer or in a reservoir's watershed.

If you own the airplane, have a drain installed at each tank in addition to the drain on the inside of the cowling. With independent drains for each tank and checking each as carefully as if you just had one, you've protected yourself just that much more. All airplanes used to have a drain at the bottom of each tank and all still should. Figure 2-2 shows sump drains at the bottom of a Cessna's wing tank.

Fig. 2-2. *A fuel drain in the wing of a Cessna.*

The best way to keep water out of the fuel is to fill the tanks after each flight and either keep the airplane hangared or, if it sits outdoors, make certain that the fuel caps seal properly. Weight considerations might dictate that you not fill the tanks after one flight if the next flight will have a close-to-maximum cabin load. Even the smaller four-place airplanes like the Cessna 172 or Piper Warrior suffer from a design compromise that will enable them to carry full fuel or full seats and some baggage, but probably not all together at the same time.

If you must put the airplane away after a flight with less than full fuel, be aware that condensation can form on the inside walls of the fuel tanks and deposit some water in the gas. If the airplane is normally tied down outside and you are going to park it with less than a full fuel load for the next flight, and if there is any hint of rain, put it in a hangar until the next flight. The hangar roof will shed any rainwater that might have leaked through the fuel caps. Furthermore, a heated hangar will reduce the chances for condensation inside the tanks because the airplane is not subjected to wide temperature variations. Lastly, be extra vigilant and thorough in your preflight check of the fuel for freedom from water and other contaminants.

Fuel quantity

How many times has an instructor, book, or other written material tried to convince you not to trust fuel gauges? Yet pilots do it everyday and begin a flight thinking that they have more fuel than they discover they really have. It's time for a war story:

During the middle 1960s, I was putting myself through college as a flight instructor and general airport bum at a small field in central Ohio. In those days, there seemed to be a good deal of fellowship around the airport, and all of the regulars became friends. One of my students decided that the least expensive way to continue his love affair with airplanes was to quit paying rent and buy one (which is still a good idea today). He looked around, pored through stacks of issues of *Trade-A-Plane*, and finally located a Cessna 140 that appeared, from the ad, to be in decent condition and at a price he wanted to pay. The trouble was, it was in New Jersey, over 400 miles from our airport. We mounted an expedition to take four of us to the East Coast. The group included the soon-to-be proud new owner of the 140, one licensed pilot who already owned a 140 and was competent to bring it back, and a buddy to accompany me on the 3-hour flight back.

Then we had to find an airplane to get us all there. My student and the other fellow who was to come back with me were stalwart skydivers, and somehow they talked their skydiving club into letting us use the club's Cessna 182 for the trip. I had flown this 182 quite a bit dropping jumpers. There was one minor snafu with it: The gas gauges didn't work. We never really cared in skydiving operations because we never went anywhere except straight up and back down to the same airport; we simply refueled it after three loads of jumpers.

One afternoon we fueled the 182 full and had an uneventful trip to New Jersey. We arrived just at sunset, unloaded all of our baggage, figured out where a motel was, and called a taxi to get us there. I told the linecrew to fill the tanks full because I intended to leave early the next morning and get back to Ohio before noon. Because it was dark by then, I didn't watch the airplane.

The next morning dawned bright and sunny. The new owner of the 140 paid for it, and he and his buddy fired up and started back. My friend and I did the same thing, but without getting a ladder and climbing up to the fuel-tank caps, removing them, and visually checking the fuel supply.

Because we left early without any breakfast, my friend and I decided that we could spare 30 minutes to stop at an airport along the way to eat. We landed at a nice field halfway across Pennsylvania. For some reason I asked the FBO to fill the 182's tanks, knowing that even without more gas, I still had plenty to get home.

When the bill came for the fuel, I was shocked to learn that the airplane took all but 8 gallons of its total capacity. I forget now what the unusable fuel was in that model of 182, but I suppose that we had about 5 gallons of usable gas left when we landed. The FBO in New Jersey hadn't put a drop in. I was shaken to think about the prospects of a forced landing in the mountains of central Pennsylvania. It's true that the Lord looks out for fools and drunks; I'm glad that we hadn't been drinking to really test His patience.

No matter how large a bother, get a ladder, climb up onto the wings, or do whatever is necessary to eyeball the tanks of your airplane and see how much gas you have. Many high-wing aircraft are equipped with steps and handles to ease the job of getting up to a point where you can peer into the wing tanks without the use of a ladder (Fig. 2-3). If you own the airplane, splurge for the small cost to have them installed.

Fig. 2-3. *The step and handle installed on a Cessna to enable a person to check the fuel tanks and caps.*

Manage the gas that you do have

Typical lightplanes with more than one fuel tank have one of three types of fuel selectors. Most Cessnas (172s and others) have a selector that enables the pilot to choose four settings: OFF, BOTH, or only the LEFT or RIGHT wing tank (Fig. 2-4). Most Piper, Beechcraft, and Mooney products eliminate the BOTH option and compel the pilot to choose one tank or the other (Fig. 2-5).

Fig. 2-4. *A Cessna fuel selector with four positions.*

Fig. 2-5. *A fuel selector with separate positions for each fuel tank.*

Cessna 150s and 152s have a selector that only has two positions: ON and OFF (Fig. 2-6). In these popular trainers, you can't select which of the two wing tanks is feeding the engine; they do it together. Because so many pilots have learned to fly in the Cessna trainers, those folks need to concentrate on fuel management techniques as a part of their upgrade training when they begin to fly different airplanes.

Differences in the design of cockpit controls among the products of the various general aviation manufacturers have caused pilots to come to grief several ways. This variation in fuel-tank selectors is one problem that pilots have to deal with as they fly different airplanes. Even airplanes from the same manufacturer have differences that need to be learned, such as the aforementioned Cessna 150/152 and 172.

It takes careful study and constant reminding of oneself to become and stay aware of fuel system intricacies. Renter pilots and flight instructors are the most prone to suffer from fuel mismanagement accidents, but it can happen to anyone who gets compla-

Fig. 2-6. *A Cessna fuel selector with only two positions.*

cent. I'm always somewhat surprised to see how many of these fuel mismanagement scenarios occur with flight instructors and other experienced pilots at the controls.

If you own or routinely fly an airplane that has a fuel selector that requires the selection of only one tank at a time, like most Pipers and Mooneys, you need to develop a system for managing the fuel burn out of the different tanks. In addition to simply making sure that you've selected a tank with gas in it, a good system for equalizing the load in the tanks will help keep the airplane in lateral balance, and therefore in trim, as a flight progresses. I owned a Piper Comanche 180 for about seven years; two fuel tanks held 30 gallons each for 60 gallons total fuel. For cross-country flights, I would always taxi, take off, depart the area, and initially cruise on the left tank.

I used the left tank first for two reasons. The main reason was that I did most of my cross-country flying solo on various business trips around the Midwest. Because the airplane was already left-side heavy with only one person it in, burning fuel out of the left tank helped restore lateral balance as the fuel weight decreased due to consumption.

The second reason: I could readily see the fuel cap on the left wing, and the cap on the right side was visible only by squirming around a bit. If any fuel were siphoning out of the left tank as a result of a loose or defective filler cap, I'd likely notice it right away and return to the departure airport to fix the problem. During the climbout, I would always hunch over to the right and get a "look-see" at the right tank's cap to make sure that it was sealed tightly too.

Every good pilot notes takeoff time. If you don't routinely do it, start. I would fly the first hour of a trip in the Comanche on the left tank, then switch over to the right tank for the next two hours. This technique kept the airplane in lateral trim because:

- More fuel was used out of the left tank in the first hour of a flight.
- Extra fuel is consumed in a takeoff at full power.
- The climb to cruise altitude was performed at a power setting still quite a bit above cruise power.

The extra power used in the first hour of flight wasn't as much as two hours in cruise, but it wasn't too far off.

After cruising on the right tank at a lean cruise power setting for two hours, I'd go back to the left tank for the next hour. Because few lightplane flights take over a total of four hours, this technique worked well for me in that airplane for all of the years I flew it. Plus, the end of the flight occurred using a fuel tank that I already knew had good fuel in it, and was only about ⅓ empty at most when I had switched back to the left tank for the last hour.

Few lightplanes have the endurance of a Comanche 180, which will burn only about 8 gallons of fuel per hour at a high altitude with the mixture properly leaned. With the total fuel capacity of 60 gallons, that airplane could remain aloft for about seven hours, which is longer than about anyone's comfort range. Even using a VFR reserve of one hour remaining fuel, I could fly for over six hours; I'd naturally go back to the right tank after using the left tank for the first hour, two hours on the right tank, and then one and a half hours on the left side. The right tank still had about 12 gallons in it when I'd switch to it after having then flown a total of four and a half hours. Those 12 gallons would take me another half hour, when I'd be landing with well over an additional hour's reserve still on board.

If you fly a Cessna that has a selector with a BOTH position, you can leave it there and forget switching between tanks if you want to, but be sure that you observe any contrary directions in the pilot's operating handbook (POH). Some Cessna POHs either recommend or require that the fuel selector be changed from the BOTH position to a single tank position at certain altitudes.

Total time in the air and knowledge of the airplane's consumption rate solve most of the fuel management equation. Some of these airplanes with a fuel selector position for both tanks seem not to burn fuel equally out of both tanks when the BOTH position is selected; I have never figured out why. When that happens—and if the airplane gets out of lateral trim because of the ensuing imbalance in the unequal quantity of gas in each wing—you can revert to using just one tank at a time for a specified interval to restore balance. Go back to the BOTH position for descent and landing.

Obviously, follow the manufacturer's recommendations if a POH prescribes a different method of fuel management among the tanks as equipped on that aircraft.

Engine maintenance

You eliminate the great majority of engine failures when you become determined to ensure fuel cleanliness, quantity, and management. Even though the modern lightplane engine is a marvel of reliability when properly fed and maintained, it can quit for mechanical reasons, albeit rarely. A good number of these failures can be taken out of the statistics if you diligently maintain the engine.

Most pilots aren't mechanics, and neither am I. But if you learn just a little about the basics of how a lightplane engine runs and more importantly why it won't run, you'll put yourself in better stead to keep yours spinning happily away. Safe flying is a product of knowledge, practice, and attitude. If you really don't know anything about how the engine works, knowledge is lacking. Fix that situation. I'm not advocating that every pilot needs to be a mechanical wizard; I'm certainly not one either. But you do need to know enough to manage the engine properly through all of its regimes. I know of no pilot who flies well and with confidence who doesn't understand some basic mechanical concepts and why the POH recommends the procedures that are stated in it.

Every engine goes through an annual inspection, as does the airframe. If the aircraft is used to carry passengers for hire, the same inspections must be done at intervals of 100 hours operating time in addition to the yearly requirement. If you own your own airplane and don't use it commercially, you might well fly for more than 100 hours between annual inspections, which is when your mechanic gets a thorough look at the engine. Carefully consider whether safety would be enhanced by subjecting your airplane to 100-hour inspections even though they aren't required by the regulations. I've always done that in every airplane that I've owned. My three engine failures all occurred in other people's airplanes, not my own.

The best way to assist your mechanic in keeping your engine in tip-top shape is to keep an ongoing diagnostic record of how your engine operates. In addition to giving the mechanic some valuable data, you'll get to know the engine better. Observe and record how much fuel it consumes and how much oil it burns between changes; if you normally add oil before a routine change, record how often and how much. Record the cylinder head temperatures in normal cruise at the power setting(s) you like to use. Note what the differential drop in RPM is between the magnetos when you do the mag check before each takeoff. Also, check how many RPMs the engine declines when you apply carburetor heat.

If you have a fixed-pitch propeller, steal a glance during the takeoff run to see what RPM the engine is turning during the run before lift-off. You could do a *static runup* every few flights. Hold the brakes tight and run the engine at full throttle for a few seconds while noting what RPM it develops. But be careful about full-power runups. Be certain that the ground underneath and for several feet around the nose of the airplane is totally free of any loose objects, even small pea gravel. Foreign object damage (FOD) will chew up a propeller, skin up the paint on the cowling, and is a needless consequence of a carelessly performed full power check. Be sure that the area behind the airplane is clear. Don't run the engine at full power if there are other planes in the runup area or if there is anything behind you for at least a hundred feet, maybe more. Be sure that the brakes will hold, and pay attention to whether they do.

If the airplane has a constant-speed prop, notice if the engine turns up to redline on the tachometer during the takeoff run, and see if the manifold pressure is up to ambient atmospheric pressure. If these conditions aren't present, it doesn't mean that something is for sure wrong, but a mechanic should check it out. Often a slight adjustment to the prop governor will set things straight, but there could be some other cause for the apparently low power output.

If any other engine-operation parameters change, find out why. If the oil temperature starts climbing measurably above recent indications, something is going on that you should know about. The same goes for the cylinder head temperature or if the peak exhaust gas temperature starts changing quite a bit.

Let your mechanic know about any changes in the RPM indications during the mag or carb-heat checks. An engine that starts burning more fuel or oil should be checked by someone who can find out why. As is often the case with our physical bodies, if you detect a problem with an engine early, that problem can usually be remedied at far less cost than if early symptoms are not discovered or ignored.

Engines don't cure themselves if they start to get sick, even if the symptom temporarily goes away. One of the few people I knew well who died as a result of injuries suffered during a forced landing had plenty of warning of impending problems.

He was planning a trip from Ohio to Florida. During three local flights before his vacation the engine had unexplainably run rough. Each time it would run rough for only a few minutes and then resume smooth operation. He did nothing about it and never had a mechanic diagnose the situation or attempt to find out why. All went well en route to Florida until he was over the mountains of eastern Kentucky. When the engine did quit for good, he was over inhospitable terrain and was severely injured in the accident that followed. My friend lived about three weeks before succumbing to those injuries.

To make matters all the worse for those of us who were close to him, he was the same fellow who bought the Cessna 140 in New Jersey whom I had taken out there to get his airplane. The airplane didn't let him down; he let it down by not finding out what was wrong when the engine gave plenty of advanced warning that something untoward was going on.

Don't let something like that happen to you. If the engine in your airplane starts displaying warning signs that its health is declining, find out why immediately. Don't put it off until the next annual inspection. If you've kept a record of the operating characteristics of the engine, you'll most often be able to spot a problem before it results in engine failure. And as a side benefit, the fix will most likely be much less expensive than if the condition were allowed to go on and probably worsen. In the language of aviation, this kind of worse means more costly.

ENGINE FAILURE

Discussions about engine failure will explore four different events:

- Failure of the powerplant during takeoff.
- When the engine packs it in after takeoff but while the airplane is still close to the ground, which might well be the most dire of the various scenarios.
- Engine failure during cruise flight.
- Progressive failure, which means the engine obviously has something drastically wrong with it but for the moment it is still producing some power.

Engine failure during takeoff

Takeoff puts the maximum amount of stress on a lightplane's engine that it endures in all of the normal phases of flight. The amount of power that the engine is asked to produce goes from idle to maximum-rated power in only a few seconds. As this demand is met, the temperatures and internal stresses rise dramatically, and the change rates are great. The pilot might be asking the engine to do more than it's capable of if the POH recommendations concerning warm-up haven't been followed. Even when everything is done by the book, you're taking the engine from a lazy idle to maximum output in a very short period of time.

My three engine failures in lightplanes were of the progressive variety, thankfully. The most recent experience was on takeoff and occurred just a few weeks before this was being written. It occurred immediately after takeoff and prompted me to give some thought to the training we've all had about dealing with engine failures, especially during takeoff. Let's dissect takeoff engine failure.

The initial part of the takeoff run naturally occurs well before the airplane has reached flying speed. In the typical lightplane flown from a reasonably long runway, there is still plenty of room left before reaching flying speed to abort the takeoff and stop on the runway.

As soon as you apply takeoff power (which is full throttle in almost all lightplanes), quickly assess the state of the engine. Is it producing the proper RPM and manifold pressure? Is the rate of acceleration in speed normal? Is it running smoothly, or is there any roughness or hesitancy? Is anything abnormal as compared to all of the other takeoffs you've performed?

If the answer to any of these quick questions is in the affirmative, retard the throttle right now, and abort the takeoff. This assessment can be made, with a little practice, long before the airplane reaches lift-off speed, and generally you'll be finished with the questions before the airplane has rolled more than a few hundred feet at most. Unless you're performing a short-field takeoff under real conditions, you'll have plenty of room to stop on the remaining runway.

If you are taking off from a short field, you've got another factor to consider. Would it be better to abort and perhaps run off the end of the runway attempting to stop, or should you continue the takeoff, fly the pattern, and land back at the same field? There never can be an absolute answer, but if I were in serious doubt about the health of the engine and really concerned about whether it would fly the pattern, I'd probably shut down, stop as best I could, and maybe bend a little metal by running off the end.

If there aren't any life-threatening obstacles at the end of the runway, this fact would work in favor of aborting the takeoff. Remember, impact forces increase exponentially with increases in speed at the time of the impact. Even if you can't get fully stopped before running off the runway, consider the speed at which you'll likely encounter the first obstacle. If you hit a normal farm fence or bounce through a ditch at 20 knots, it's highly unlikely that you'll suffer any physical injury.

The variables are just too numerous to set out any hard and fast rules about aborting takeoffs from really short fields. The risks inherent in doing so vary with the conditions that you'll face at the end of that runway if you do run off and how fast you'll be going at the time. Maybe these risks ought to be factored into your decision to operate from a critically short runway in the first place. You can also walk the runway to find out what awaits you at the end if you have to abort the takeoff, and depart the runway.

You could easily do a little experiment that can give you some peace of mind; always watch for landing traffic, clear the runway as soon as safely possible, and be courteous to any pilot conducting a normal takeoff. At a normal airport, begin a takeoff, accelerate to your usual rotation speed, chop the power, and see how quickly you can stop the airplane without skidding the tires during the braking effort. Note where the airplane stops, and measure it from the point where you applied takeoff power. This distance is what pilots of larger airplanes refer to as the *accelerate-stop distance*. Add a safety factor of 50 percent of the measured distance to account for the fact that during your experiment you knew what was coming and didn't experience any elapsed time for a decision about whether to abort or continue. Make that ensuing number your minimum acceptable runway length. If you abide by that rule, you'll operate with a degree of takeoff safety akin to that used by turbine and large aircraft.

Engine failure right after takeoff

If the engine calls it a day after you've rotated and broken ground, you still might have enough runway left upon which to do a successful landing. Don't discount this possibility if the engine quits while you're really close to the ground.

Several factors have to be considered. The obvious one is the remaining length of the runway beneath you. From the altitude at which the engine quits, you quickly have to analyze how much space you need to glide down to the normal flare point and execute a landing. Again, there aren't any hard and fast rules for this call; it's all a matter of informed judgment.

Keep in mind the same point made regarding aborting a takeoff from a short field. If there are no meaningful obstacles at the end of the runway, you might be able to get it down on the runway, dissipate most of the speed, and depart the runway surface without hurting yourself or damaging the airplane too heavily. A wise pilot will analyze every takeoff and every runway from which it's made and think about the options available before snap decisions have to be made in the midst of a real-life emergency.

Pilots of retractable-gear airplanes have another issue to consider: when to raise the wheels. My practice is to leave the gear down until I no longer have enough runway left to land on if the engine starts misbehaving. Rarely will the runway be so long as to make that rule result in leaving the gear down for an absurdly long time after the airplane breaks ground. If everything is going routinely with the departure, your risk in raising the gear after climbing several hundred feet isn't very large, even if some pavement is still underneath you.

We still see some pilots who seem to think that their macho factor is increased by retracting the landing gear as soon as possible after they become airborne. They'll probably get away with it for quite a long time, but if they fly long enough, the day will come when they'll wish that the wheels hadn't been packed away so soon. Once in a while we see accidents where this technique is used and the airplane settles back down onto the runway either due to a premature rotation or some turbulence close to the ground that causes the contact with the runway.

When the departure has progressed to the extent that there isn't any runway sufficient to land on straight ahead, a whole bunch of new factors enters the picture, and new decisions have to be faced.

When I learned to fly airplanes in the middle 1960s, every instructor whom I encountered and all of the volumes of written material I read gave only one piece of advice:

> If the engine quits before you reach pattern altitude, or very close to it, land straight ahead, and accept whatever obstacles you're faced with, and *never* try to get back to the runway.

Today we're starting to see some moderation in that stern rule. For sure, there is an altitude at which some degree of turn can be made to avoid an obstacle directly in your path. It would be silly to plod on with no turn whatsoever and plow into a building when a 10° or 20° heading change performed from several hundred feet high would take the airplane clear of the structure and result in a landing in a decent field.

We can't dictate or teach judgment in a vacuum. What we can do is try to identify the elements that a pilot ought to consider in various situations to try to improve the process and outcome of using one's judgment. Until you know all of the facts to consider, you can have the best innate judgment in all of aviation, but your decisions will be potentially faulty.

Turning back to a runway from which you've just taken off can be a dicey affair. The risk of a stall/spin accident is very high, and the presence of that risk is why we have been traditionally taught not to consider going back. If you want to follow the age-old advice, few can be critical of your judgment. But every pilot should realize that there are combinations of circumstances that might well permit a safe turnaround. The first is altitude.

In a moment we'll describe another experiment that you can perform to analyze the questions inherent in the decision of whether to attempt to get back to the runway after an engine failure occurs during the initial climbout after takeoff. Certainly, you first have to be high enough to realize that the engine has quit, get the nose down from climbing to gliding attitude, and decide whether to turn and which direction to make the turn. The ultimate goal is to end up going in the opposite direction with the wings level and the airplane high enough above the ground to have adequate room for a flare and landing.

Before experimenting to find out where this magical altitude is, we need to think about how to glide down after the engine has quit. The POH for your airplane probably has a speed quoted for best glide. The best glide speed specified in a lightplane POH is what glider pilots call the "best L/D" speed, which means *best lift-over-drag* speed. This speed will result in the best *distance* over the ground during a glide, but it is not the speed that will keep the airplane aloft the longest period of time.

You also need to know something that isn't published in most POHs: the *minimum-sink* speed. An airplane's minimum-sink speed is usually obtained at a very slow airspeed, often around 5–10 percent faster than stalling speed. Minimum-sink speed is the speed that will result in the least rate of descent and therefore the *longest time aloft*, but minimum-sink speed will not produce the best lateral distance over the ground during the glide.

Conceptually, these speeds are the reverse of two speeds you're used to seeing: best angle of climb and best rate of climb. Best-angle (V_X) gives you the most altitude gain in a given distance over the ground and is the converse of best L/D when you think about gliding. Best rate of climb (V_Y) results in the most altitude gain in a given period of time irrespective of the distance traveled over the ground. Minimum sink speed is V_Y's opposite when gliding.

Turning around after takeoff will take a given amount of time because rate of turn is what counts, and that's measured as a function of time. To have the most time in which to execute the turnaround, you need to be gliding at the minimum sink speed. Using minimum sink speed will result in the least altitude loss during the turn back to the runway because the turn is consuming ticks on the clock, irrespective of distance.

The turn should be made into any crosswind that is present to prevent being blown away from the runway's extended centerline during the turn. If you mistakenly turn away from a crosswind, you need even more altitude and time to complete the course reversal. Turning away from a meaningfully strong crosswind will probably blow you so far away from the runway as to put the success of the maneuver in serious doubt.

I've done the experiment that follows in every airplane that I've owned so that I had the knowledge before the need arose of when I could consider going back to a runway and when I had no choice but to either land straight ahead or at best make only a slight turn to avoid an obstacle. Regardless of whether you own or rent the aircraft that you fly, do it yourself.

First, get the airplane into the normal configuration for the initial climb after takeoff. In most lightplanes, this will be full power, flaps up, and gear down. At a safe altitude, stabilize the airplane in a climb at the airspeed you normally use for the initial climb after takeoff. You should know at this point that if your habit has been to climb at V_Y or faster, every minute during the climb is taking you farther from the runway.

If you normally climb at V_X or at a compromise speed between V_X and V_Y, you will be gaining altitude while staying closer to the runway than if the airspeed is at V_Y or faster. Climbing at either V_X or somewhere between V_X and V_Y has a downside, though. It will take longer to gain a given amount of altitude while you stay closer to the runway during the climb because you're climbing at the maximum angle of climb; hence, you're vulnerable to an engine failure at a lower altitude for more time but for less distance from the runway. Some pilots are more comfortable gaining altitude as quickly as they can, in terms of time, and climb at V_Y initially. Others want to stay closer to the runway for a possible turnaround. Use *your* judgment, and do what's best for you. Also, climbing at V_X or close to it results in a more exaggerated noseup attitude, which reduces visibility over the nose.

When you have the airplane in climb configuration for the experiment, select an altitude that you can remember for a few minutes, such as 3,000 or 3,500 feet, and chop the throttle. Do nothing for at least 3 seconds, and even better, wait 4 seconds because many human factors studies have shown that it takes this long to recognize that the engine has failed and for the pilot to start to deal with it.

Simultaneously get the nose down and start banking into a turn. This part sounds easier than it is. First, what is the best bank angle to use during the turn? If you bank too steeply, the stall speed increases rapidly to an unsafe point, increasing the risk of the dreaded stall/spin accident. A bank that is too shallow will waste valuable time because the time spent in the turn is a direct function of the angle of bank, which determines rate of turn.

Probably the best compromise is a bank angle of about 45°, which still is not in the realm of greatly increased stall speeds, but the turn will progress quickly. Much steeper than 45° will increase the sink rate and the stall speed too much. ***Be absolutely certain that the turn remains coordinated.*** The largest factor in inducing a stall/spin accident is trying to "push" the turn around by adding too much rudder pressure in the direction of the turn. If a stall does occur when you're standing on the rudder, the airplane will snap into a spin in the blink of an eye; the real thing will almost always be too low to effect a recovery.

After you begin the turn in the experimental maneuver, get the pitch attitude at a point where the airspeed is about 10 percent above the stall. In most modern airplanes, the stall warning device (a horn or light) will activate at about this point. The stall warning device should be sounding or flashing intermittently during the turn to indicate that you are maintaining the airspeed just about at the right value for achieving minimum sink speed.

If you aren't proficient at flight at minimum controllable airspeed, don't even attempt this maneuver. The risk of a stall/spin accident is always high, and flying this slowly this low to the ground while turning and with your heart pounding should never be tried by any pilot who can't control pitch attitude and the resulting airspeed as second nature.

Carry the turn slightly more than 180°. If you go around only 180°, you'll be off to the side of the runway because the turning maneuver will cover some ground to the side of the runway corresponding to the direction in which you made the turn. If there is a strong crosswind, and if you remembered to turn into it, perhaps 180° will do; otherwise, make the turn about 210°.

Level the wings and subsequently lower the nose a little to get back to a more normal, faster gliding speed from which you have a better chance of executing a normal flare and landing. Execute a flare, and see what altitude is shown on the altimeter. Whatever altitude was lost during the experimental procedure indicates the absolute minimum altitude that will be used up in a turnaround.

But leave more room for error, fright, confusion, and all of the other events and emotions that you'll have to deal with in a real engine failure. Increase the altitude *loss* as shown on the altimeter by at least 50 percent to give yourself a safety factor. The resulting total altitude should be the *lowest* height from which you'd even consider trying to go back to the runway.

Consider one last set of factors. If you fly a fairly heavy airplane, like a Cessna 210 or Piper Saratoga or other such airplane with a high useful load, you have to be cognizant of the effects of gross weight upon the altitude loss that you determined in your experiment. You probably did the test alone or with maybe one other person on board and with less than a full load of fuel. If a real engine failure happens when the airplane is substantially heavier, two things occur. First, the minimum sink speed increases because the stall speed increases at heavier gross weights. Second, the rate of descent will also increase. Don't try it for real unless you know how to handle the airplane at full gross weight.

Turning back to a very short runway probably won't work. You'd likely be high enough by the time that you started to get turned around that you would not have enough runway beneath you to get down, flare, land, and brake to a stop. There isn't any absolute number that will give you a minimum runway length where a turnaround stands a reasonable chance of success, but I wouldn't try it unless I had at least 3,000 feet of total runway, considering the performance of most lightplanes; more that 3,000 feet would be wise for a heavier airplane.

This isn't an easy maneuver. It should never be attempted during an actual takeoff by a pilot who hasn't practiced it at a safe altitude or who is apprehensive about it. Don't forget that at many airports you don't need to turn all the way around in order to reach a safe landing area. Maybe a 90° heading change will carry you to a field where a safer forced landing could be accomplished. Analyze the situation before every take-off and be ready to act accordingly.

The experiment will probably reveal that the lowest altitude from which to think about returning to the runway is at least 600 feet above ground level (AGL) and often much higher. Glider pilots are taught the turn-back maneuver if a tow rope breaks or the towplane engine fails at low altitude. They learn to turn around and get back to the runway from an altitude of 200 feet AGL. *Never try it from that low in an airplane; it won't work.*

Training yourself to decide whether to attempt a turn back to the runway will achieve at least some of the proficiency needed to make that crucial decision. Remember that before you can ever use this maneuver in a real life engine failure, you first have to have excellent piloting skills, particularly in airspeed control and turn coordination. If you are lacking, you are asking for a stall/spin into the ground, which is almost always fatal. For the less-than-really-proficient pilot, the best options are landing straight ahead or making slight turns at the most.

Engine failure during cruise

If the engine fails during cruise flight, you've got more time to think over the options and perform the necessary piloting tasks compared to right after takeoff. But the extra time doesn't mean that you can be less proficient or sloppier doing what needs to be done.

Pilots enjoy the many options of planning and flying the cruise portion of almost every flight. All too few consider the prospect of an engine failure when analyzing the available choices. Yet that possibility should be a part of every pilot's thinking, and proper planning for the day when the engine quits can add to the survivability of the event.

Choose routes and altitudes that give you some outs if the powerplant prematurely decides that it has labored enough for a given day. Don't fly over inhospitable terrain if a short detour can avoid it. Do you really need to venture out over the water, out of gliding distance of land to get where you want to go? Or will staying over land add only a few minutes and just a few more miles to the flight? If the answer to that one is in the affirmative, it's a no-brainer in a single-engine airplane.

If you fly over canyons, forests, lakes, and mountains, will the planned routes remain over safe landing sites as much as possible? Many pilots don't take the time to read a chart to determine the terrain that will be beneath a proposed route of flight and then consider when a little alteration in the supposed routing might result in their being within gliding distance of more tolerant landing spots.

Few aviators consider the airplane's gliding performance when selecting cruising altitudes. Most airports in the Midwest where I do most of my flying have field elevations around 800 to 1,200 feet MSL, unless you take into account the string of mountains that runs from the Northeastern United States, southwesterly to Georgia, where elevations naturally get a few thousand feet higher.

Far too much flying is done in my area at 2,500, 3,500, and 4,500 feet MSL, depending upon the aircraft's heading. I have never figured out why so many pilots are loath to climb a few thousand feet higher where the air is often smoother; navigation is much easier because you can see farther and radio-reception ranges are longer. I'm not advocating climbing to 10,000 feet to fly 100 miles, but neither do I think it makes much sense to make such a flight at 2,500 feet.

Every increase in altitude also increases the options available to a pilot if the engine fails. Think about the alternatives that you accept or reject when you choose a cruising altitude on any given flight. No doubt a higher altitude will mean that the available choices of where to put the airplane are multiplied, sometimes several fold.

The previous discussion about dealing with an engine failure right after takeoff defined the two different measures of glide performance. Minimum sink speed results in the least altitude lost per unit of time (usually minutes), while the best L/D speed will enable an airplane to glide the farthest over the ground but not at the lowest sink rate.

When an engine fails during cruise flight, most of the time the best gliding range will be achieved if the pilot glides at the best glide speed as recommended in the airplane's POH, and that speed will be the best L/D speed, although not described as such. But there are times when it won't take you the greatest distance.

Best glide speed, as quoted in the POH, assumes calm winds and stable air. Let's take a simple example. Assume that you're flying a popular two-place trainer; its POH gives a best glide speed of 60 knots. If you are headed into a 60-knot headwind and maintain a 60-knot airspeed, you'll descend vertically without going anywhere laterally. Seldom will you be flying in winds equal to your airplane's best glide speed, but you'll fly in totally calm conditions, especially aloft, with about the same frequency. Learn a lesson from the glider pilot; when gliding into the wind, you'll extend the gliding range by adding airspeed to the book's best glide speed.

A good rule of thumb is to increase the gliding airspeed by about one half of the speed of the wind into which you're gliding. If you're headed into a 30-knot headwind, increase the quoted best glide speed by about 15 knots. That will come close to optimizing the distance that the airplane will glide in that wind condition. Remember that winds aloft generally increase as altitude gets higher; therefore, if you're gliding down from a high cruise altitude—you always get the winds-aloft forecast for every flight, right?—adjust your gliding speed as needed to account for changes in the wind velocity as you descend.

The reverse comes into play if you're gliding with a tailwind. Gliding range will increase if you decrease the airspeed during the glide. In the example of an airplane with a calm-wind, best-glide speed of 60 knots, let's assume that the glide ratio under those conditions is 8.5-to-1.0. If you're gliding with a 30-knot tailwind, you can get a ratio of about 13-to-1 if you reduce the airspeed to around 54 knots.

A reduction of only 10 percent in the gliding airspeed yields a gain in the glide ratio of 53 percent. If you're at 7,000 feet above the ground when the engine conks, an 8.5-to-1.0 glide ratio allows you to glide for 11.27 statute miles before ground contact. But when you can increase the ratio to 13-to-1, again from 7,000 feet, you can go 17.23 miles. It would seem likely that you could find a place to make an acceptable forced landing when you are working with a distance of more than 17 miles. You already realize that the distance is a radius, which is closely examined in a few paragraphs.

The biggest difference in obtaining the maximum possible gliding range between gliding into a headwind or with a tailwind is the amount of airspeed change to make from the stated best glide speed in calm winds. When gliding into a headwind, the modification is about one half of the speed of the headwind, but when gliding with a tailwind, just a small reduction in airspeed will produce quite an improvement in gliding range. This ought to show you that if you have a choice of potential sites for a forced landing, you'll have a much better chance of making one that is downwind of your position rather than trying to glide into the wind.

Most lightplanes have glide ratios from about 8-to-1 to 10-to-1, depending primarily upon whether they are the fixed-gear or retractable-gear variety. When the airplane is flown in a power-off glide at the best glide speed, that's about what you can expect. This means that for every foot of altitude lost in the glide, the airplane will progress forward about 8 to 10 feet horizontally. Naturally, if you fly an airplane that folds its wheels, leave them up in a power-off glide until you're ready to land. Most retracts have far poorer glide performance with wheels down than will a fixed-gear airplane because the airflow around open wheel wells and extended gear doors creates far more drag than is present with a fixed-gear airplane, especially if the latter is equipped with wheel fairings.

Gliding range is best thought of as a gliding radius of action. Here is a simple example. Assume that your airplane will glide with a ratio of 9-to-1 and that you're cruising at an altitude of 6,000 AGL when the engine stops. Theoretically, you can travel a total of 9 feet horizontally for every 1 foot that you consume coming down. So, from 6,000 feet you could glide laterally for 54,000 feet, which is 10.23 miles in any given direction, disregarding the effects of the wind and maneuvering. For ease of discussion, let's call 10.23 miles 10¼ miles.

The 10¼-mile range is how far you could glide in any direction, which really means that you could put the airplane down anywhere within a circle that is 20½ miles in diameter. But that circle gets increasingly smaller as your altitude gets lower. That's one reason for cruising as high as practical on any given flight.

Another thing that will dramatically reduce your effective radius of action in a glide is any undue amount of time spent deciding which way to go to reach the best available landing field. I suppose that I constantly pay attention to potential forced-landing sites as I fly along because I've had the experience of using them. During cross-countries, keep an eye on where you'd go if the engine quit "right now." Know the surface wind conditions.

It's not all that difficult to remain aware of the basic direction of the surface wind. Listen to the ATIS broadcasts from airports near your route of flight. Watch the smoke from power plants or factories that you might see as you motor along. You can't determine much from looking at trees or lake waves if you're flying very high, but if you do insist on flying low, you can see what's happening on the surface by looking for those kinds of cues. If you do fly low, your need for this information is all that much more important because your radius of action is already that much less, so the amount of time you've got is likewise decreased.

Before devoting the discussion to the actual selection of a landing site, let's examine a couple of ways that gliding range can be extended, besides leaving the gear up if you're flying a retractable gear airplane.

Some pilots think that a glide can be extended if they stop the windmilling propeller from rotating. That thought is technically correct. A windmilling prop produces more drag than one that is stopped, even though the propellers of almost all single-engine airplanes can't be feathered. But there is a problem in stopping the prop. Unless the engine physically seizes, in which event the propeller will likely stop turning anyhow, you'll have to slow the airspeed dramatically, maybe even to stall or just a little above stall, and maintain that slow speed for a short while to get the prop stopped. The airflow through the propeller will try its utmost to keep it turning, and you've got to reduce that airflow in order to stop the prop.

Similar to so many emergencies, there aren't any hard-and-fast rules about this topic either. If you suffer an engine failure at a very high altitude, you might be justified in spending the time that will be necessary in slowing the airplane down enough to stop the prop. While you're doing that, the rate of descent will increase quite a bit at the necessarily slow airspeeds. Whether the increase in glide performance that you'll enjoy after the prop stops turning will offset the time that you suffered from the increased rate of descent at slow airspeed is dependent upon all of the conditions with which you're faced, primarily wind and altitude. And you'll certainly waste time and altitude while concentrating on getting the propeller stopped instead of finding a place to put the airplane. If faced with the prospect of a forced landing from a usual cruise altitude, I would forget about the prop in an airplane equipped with a fixed-pitch propeller.

It's a different story if the airplane has a constant-speed propeller. When you pull the propeller control toward you and away from the instrument panel, you are changing the pitch of the propeller blades, which also reduces the RPMs of the engine in normal flight.

The prop blades increase in pitch as you reduce RPM, which is done by pulling the prop control aft. When the engine is no longer providing power to the propeller, the drag of a windmilling prop can be significantly reduced if the prop control is pulled all the way back. That brings the pitch of the blades as coarse, or as close to what would be the feathered position, as anything a pilot can do from the cockpit.

When I instruct in an airplane equipped with a constant-speed propeller, I always demonstrate this effect to the pilot, whether he or she is a student or an experienced aviator because few have ever seen how much the glide will be improved. Reduce the throttle until the engine is at idle, then pull the prop control all the way back. You can feel the reduction in drag at once.

You may try this yourself, but do it at a safe altitude and within range of an airport because there is always a possibility that anything mechanical can break. If the prop control jams in the rearmost position, you don't want to have to fly very far before you can land at an airport and get it fixed. With a prop control jammed in the full coarse position, you can't use full throttle, and you might not be able to climb. If you do a proper job of cycling the propeller during your pretakeoff check, you've exercised the control and its cable throughout their range of operation, which should make any problem apparent.

Selecting a landing site

The entire point of this chapter has been and is the fact that you've got to land the airplane someplace. The selection of that someplace is superseded in importance only by keeping the airplane under control and getting there.

We have to assume a few things that are happening during the glide and affecting it. First, most pilots of powered aircraft don't fly gliders, so they're probably in a fix they've never been exposed to before. Regardless of how practiced you are at simulated forced landings, there's nothing like the real thing. That's no excuse for not practicing, but every pilot must realize that real forced landings are different from the comfort of an engine that is only idling, not stopped.

An idling engine is still producing some amount of power. Depending upon your particular airplane, the propeller could be giving out some thrust, or at a minimum overcoming any drag that a windmilling prop would produce. In a real forced landing, the glide performance will be worse than any you've ever experienced before because the engine isn't helping at all, and the windmilling prop has a debilitating effect that you've not seen previously. So plan your glide very conservatively.

Next, there's the effect of the "pucker factor" during a glide. Chapter 1 stated that training and preparation for emergencies help reduce them to the level of additional procedures, and that's true. But another truth is that very few nonprofessional pilots ever train for emergencies to an extent that all of the fear, anxiety, and doubt will ever be removed. Again, that's no excuse for not training, but rather it's just the way things are. Any reduction in those feelings and their adverse effects upon a pilot's performance is laudable and will almost certainly affect the outcome of dealing with every in-flight emergency, not just the failure of an engine.

Panic will kill you faster than anything else. While you probably won't be able to eliminate all fear from the prospect of a forced landing, keep one very important thought in mind. If the airplane contacts the ground under control with the wings level and at a normal landing speed and attitude, you'll most likely walk away from about any forced landing, unless you drive straight into an immovable obstacle like a building or big tree; if you've done that, you really didn't arrive under total control.

Let me take a minute for a commercial touting glider flying. Not every pilot who tries it will fall in love with the sport of soaring, and that's okay, but every pilot would gain an immense amount of increased confidence and skill from taking at least a few dual-instruction glider flights. Most competent power-plane pilots can solo a glider in around 10 dual flights. Once you've soloed a glider, you realize that aircraft land just fine without any power to modulate the parameters of an approach. Better still, you will see that it's not all that hard to fly an approach to a designated landing spot without any engine, and your confidence goes up accordingly. You learn to plan your flight, especially the approach, and manage both the potential and kinetic energy that you have. You also gain an appreciation for using all of the flight controls and techniques necessary to be in total control of the situation and get where you want to go.

Back to picking your landing spot in an instant glider: Plan your glide to arrive over the intended landing site with enough excess altitude to circle it relatively tightly at least once before setting up a traffic pattern to land. This is one element of conservative glide planning, and it also gives you one last opportunity to examine the field closely.

As soon as the engine quits, and as soon as you've gone through the restart procedure mentioned in the POH, accept the inevitable and realize that you've got to land in the best available place. Far too many forced landings have gone more poorly than necessary because the pilot was in denial of this basic fact until most of the options that would have been available had been given away by too much lost time, altitude, and space.

If you're over a large and dense forest that doesn't have any meaningful clearings, all is not lost. Remember that you'll most likely walk away if you keep the airplane under control and land level and right side up at a normal landing speed. Your landing field will be the canopy of the trees, and, if you contact them correctly, they can attenuate much of the energy of impact.

Plan your landing flare to skim the tops of the trees just barely above stall. Don't risk stalling above the trees and getting the nose of the airplane pitched down before contact. That will increase the potential for serious injury to the occupants as the airplane falls nose down through the trees and into the ground. Pancaking into the tree-tops is the desired result and is best achieved by contacting them just above stall with the airplane firmly under control.

If your flight takes you over large expanses of forest, think again about your selection of cruise altitude. If you want to fly low over this kind of terrain, realize the increased risk that you're assuming. Management and control of as many risks as possible are the wisest safety actions any pilot can take, and one way to do that when flying over any kind of inhospitable terrain is to fly as high as practical.

During cross-country flights over most of the mountainous and nonmountainous United States, you'll likely be able to find some sort of forest clearing or clear farm field in which to land, assuming that the airplane's altitude permits a reasonable gliding time after the engine fails. Fields come in all sizes and types, and some are better landing sites than others. If you don't have any knowledge of or experience with farming, it's time for a little lesson.

The best fields are naturally the smoothest, and you need to learn how to find them. Look for fields that have not been plowed deeply, which would have the furrows (sharp ridges of dirt) as a result of deep plowing. You can often find a field that has some sort of grass or grain crop growing in it: alfalfa, oats, wheat, and the like. From the air, they will appear like a large, green lawn, or perhaps they'll be brown, tan, or golden in color if the crop is nearing maturity.

Corn fields are still generally plowed and furrowed, although with the increasing popularity of no-till farming, some might be smooth. The same thing goes for bean fields. A mature corn field is not a primary choice because the combination of the high corn plants and the ears of corn on them will clobber the airplane during the landing. But a corn field is better than some alternatives. Livestock pastures are often used for that purpose because the land is not tillable, which means the pasture might be strewn with rocks, ditches, or gulleys.

Regardless of the type of field chosen, look out for obstacles such as power lines, ditches, and similar threats to a safe landing area. Fences aren't usually visible until you're quite low, so assume that every field's boundary contains a fence row. Ditches that look shallow from the air can be several feet deep.

Power lines are the greatest nemesis to a pilot faced with a forced landing. They can be hard to see, especially if they don't have large towers for support. Few people come through an encounter with a power line unscathed, so be particularly vigilant. If you notice that the landing approach will be hampered by the presence of a power line, you might be wise to change fields, even at the last minute. Never try to fly under a power line, forced landing or not, because you won't make it.

If you have to land in a plowed field, notice the direction of the furrows. Unless the wind is really strong, 15 knots or more, you'll have a better chance of success if you plan to land parallel with the furrows, irrespective of the wind. Landing across the furrows will almost certainly break the nose gear off of the airplane, increasing your chance for injury. Don't be a slave to the wind; it's just one of the factors to consider in deciding where to land.

If available landing sites are few and far between, there is another time when the wind may be ignored, unless it is fairly strong. Take a look at Fig. 2-7. If you find a field like this one—which in itself is a fine landing site, but really only has one way in and one way out—should you ignore it just because the wind doesn't favor approaching it from the direction that is free of obstructions? Probably not, unless there is either a better field within your gliding range, or the wind is strong enough to not allow a downwind landing. If you do a downwind approach and landing, modify your glide planning accordingly. Any tailwind component will lengthen the distance that the airplane will glide and will also appear to flatten the glide angle. Don't forget these effects and end up overshooting the field.

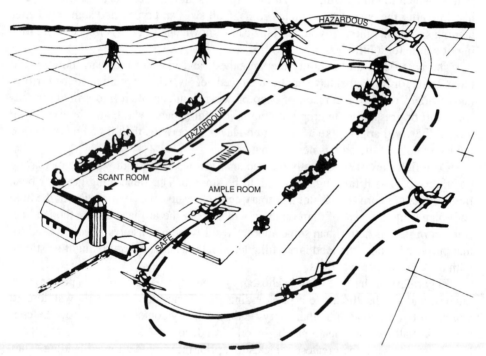

Fig. 2-7. *A downwind landing is sometimes the better choice, but be careful.*

Some pilots have fared well landing on highways, and others haven't. Roads look inviting because most of us are used to landing on strips of level pavement. But highways contain more traps for the unwary than are obvious at first thought. First, there are probably power lines along one or both sides of the road, as well as across it. If the pavement width is narrow, can you put the airplane between two rows of utility poles that will likewise form a narrow corridor? Think long and hard about that one.

Recognize that power lines also cross roads, and you don't want to face the possibility of dealing with a set of wires in the windshield as you get down to within a hundred feet of the ground where you have almost no remaining options. Consider overpasses. Interstate highways and freeways are particularly inviting until you think about hitting an overpass during the last stages of the final approach.

If you're sure that a beautiful strip of pavement beckons and has none of the aforementioned obstacles in your path, should you land with or into the stream of traffic?

The authorities on the subject go both ways, and there's little agreement. Some advise that flying the final approach into oncoming traffic gives the drivers more opportunity to see the airplane and either stop or get off to the side of the road to accommodate the suddenly appearing visitor. Others feel that you're safer landing with the traffic.

I know of only three pilots who have landed on highways; all three did it successfully, landing with the traffic. If I were faced with the decision, I'd go for landing with the flow of traffic. Because the speed limit is 55 mph and in some places 65 mph on rural stretches of interstate and similar highways, your final approach speed will only be slightly faster than the cars are traveling. Drivers will see you coming over them, and the speed differential won't be so great as to threaten yourself and the drivers with a high-speed frontal-impact if you do collide with a vehicle.

Pilot and drivers will have more time to do what will probably be less maneuvering to avoid the other. As a driver, I would rather have an airplane drift over my car going the same direction about 20 mph or so faster instead of seeing one coming straight at me with a combined closing speed of a least 120 mph.

A median strip of an interstate or four-lane highway is seldom a good landing site. It will most likely be festooned with drainage ditches, guardrails, police turn-arounds, and other obstacles to any kind of traffic, whether 4- or 18-wheeled vehicles or 3-wheeled airplanes.

Ditching is a last resort when you can't land on any acceptable terra firma. (Chapter 3 has more information about ditching procedures.) As long as there is any hard place that is not extremely hazardous, I would never choose a river or a lake as a forced-landing site. The exception would be during winter over the northern extremes of the 48 United States or Canada where it would be safe to assume that the water was sufficiently frozen to enable the ice to hold the weight of the airplane. I don't live in those climes and have little experience with them; therefore, I don't think I'd readily make that assumption.

Three instances come to mind where airplanes have gone down into a lake or river. One of them happened many years ago to a friend of my wife who put her Comanche into Grand Lake in northwestern Ohio. Grand Lake is one of the lakes built in the early 1800s to act as reservoirs for the canal system that served commerce and predated the coming of the railroads to Ohio. Most of these lakes are very shallow, although they are large in surface area. After the ditching, the tail of the Comanche stuck out of the water, with the nose of the airplane resting on the bottom. The pilot simply sat on top of the fuselage until a fishing boat pulled up next to her, and she jumped into it.

While performing a wreckage inspection with an expert who was working on one of the legal cases in which I was representing a party, I noticed an intact Beech King Air not far from the wreckage that we were investigating in the salvage yard. I asked the proprietor of the operation the story behind the King Air. He told me that it had gone into Lake Michigan and was retrieved sometime later. Even though the airplane suffered almost no perceptible damage in the water landing, all of the occupants drowned.

Lastly, I remember a case when a pilot ditched a twin-engine business airplane into the Ohio River, which is very deep and can have treacherous currents. Even though the river isn't all that wide, this unfortunate pilot also drowned before he was able to swim to shore. I would not choose a body of water as a forced landing site unless no other options were available.

Unfortunately, there might be times when a lake or river is the only smooth place available to put the airplane. If the terrain is mountainous or heavily forested, I would place a lake higher on the list of acceptable landing sites. Better to land in a lake, assuming that it's large enough, than it would be to face an almost certain accident from trying to land in some inhospitable place just to avoid getting wet.

If a river is your only option as a landing site, you've got to consider whether to land downstream or upstream. Unless the wind speed is equal to or greater than the probable speed of the current in the river, you're better off to land downstream, regardless of wind direction. Remember why we land into the wind in normal conditions: to reduce the relative speed between the airplane and the runway. A downstream river landing accomplishes just that; what matters is the differential between the speed of the airplane and whatever the landing site is. We're so used to thinking about the landing site as being immovable—it always is on land—that we forget the river water is in constant motion. Obviously, if the wind is really blowing, or if the river has little current, then do the normal thing and land in the direction that favors any headwind component.

Pilots of retractable-gear airplanes have another decision to make: land wheels up or down. Take heed of the advice in the POH because most lightplane manuals nowadays recommend landing with the wheels down. Years ago when the military flew piston-powered equipment, performing a forced landing was an option that was often covered in the pilot handbooks for those airplanes. Since the advent of the jet and the ejection seat, few if any military pilots would consider trying to accomplish a forced landing and would instead opt to punch out because jet fighters have such fast landing speeds that bailing out will probably be far more survivable than trying to land in a field.

Pilots who have read the old military manuals or who might have been trained by a former military pilot from the piston days might have been taught to make a forced landing with the wheels up. Even though the piston-engine fighters landed much slower than modern jets, they still had approach and landing speeds far faster than what we experience in lightplanes. At their speeds, chances were that the gear would break off in a forced landing, so the advice was often to leave the gear retracted.

But for our airplanes, most manufacturers advise to make a forced landing with the gear down. See what the POH has to say. If you are landing in any sort of decently smooth field, put the landing gear down. There is an exception to that rule of thumb.

If you have to land across a heavily furrowed or other very rough field, either due to the physical constraints of the area or the wind, you might consider leaving the wheels up to avoid breaking them off during the landing. Breaking the gear off would likely damage the airplane more than landing wheels up. It will also increase the likelihood of physical injury to the occupants of the airplane because the deceleration forces will be higher. Remember that the true objective being served in a forced landing is to minimize the risk of harm to people, not the airplane. Do whichever you believe will serve that motive.

There is one last scenario to consider in choosing the forced landing site. If you can't find a level place to put the airplane and must make the landing in mountainous or hilly terrain, you've got to decide whether to land uphill or downhill. Again, this depends upon the combination of wind speed and the relative degree of slope of the site. If the area is quite rolling or mountainous, you're almost always better off to land uphill. Even though the differential landing speed will be increased by accepting some downwind component, landing uphill reduces the landing roll considerably, and thereby also lessens the time and distance during which you're exposed to hitting something.

If there is a strong wind, or if the angle of slope isn't great, then land into the wind. It's purely a matter of analyzing the conditions with which you're faced and then applying good judgment.

Setting up a landing pattern

When gliding down from cruise altitude, plan the glide to arrive over the planned landing area high enough to circle it at least once and also high enough to set up a normal "traffic pattern" approach. This provides two positive elements for the entire forced landing procedure.

First, you can size up the field one more time, and if you have to change fields, which should only be done as a last resort, you have sufficient altitude that it might be successful.

More importantly, it is virtually impossible to shoot a successful straight-in approach during a forced landing. To have a reasonable chance of making a successful landing, fly a normal traffic pattern as best you can, but keep it tighter and closer to the field because of the decreased glide performance compared to any airplane that you've flown before. If you are able, set up the pattern so that turns will be made to the left because that's what you're used to doing most of the time. Do everything conceivable to eliminate as much "unfamiliarity" as possible so the forced landing can proceed as close to normal as the situation allows. A nearly normal pattern under the circumstances provides the beneficial visual cues to which you are accustomed.

This procedure can be continually practiced. When you are number one to land and flying a traditional pattern, frequently close the throttle to idle and make a totally power-off approach all of the way around the pattern through the landing. Remember that glide performance in a real forced landing will be worse than you'll see in practice, so keep the emergency pattern a little tighter than you do in practice.

Much has been written about the harm that will come to an engine from shock cooling; however, little shock cooling is likely to occur during a power-off approach from a normal traffic pattern. Shock cooling normally happens when a descent is made from cruise altitudes with insufficient power applied to the engine to keep the cylinders warm. The combination of the high airspeeds inherent in long cruise descents and the low power can cool the cylinders more quickly than the metal can absorb the rapid temperature change without warping or cracking.

Making a power-off approach from a traffic pattern doesn't involve the same set of circumstances. Pattern and approach speeds are far less than the speeds at which most pilots make descents from cruise; hence, the airflow through the engine is not nearly so great, and the cooling rate is slower as a result. Also, if you fly the downwind leg properly, you're already operating at reduced power before you bring the engine back to idle. Practicing power-off approaches and landings is a vital part of the proficiency training of every pilot who flies single-engine airplanes.

When you have arrived over the field and given it the last close examination, plan your maneuvering to enter a downwind leg as far upwind as practical. During the downwind leg, monitor your glide performance. If you see that you won't remain high enough to fly a normal pattern, you can nearly always cut the turn to base leg a little sooner than otherwise, and still be able to land in your selected field. Avoid the situation of either making steep turns close to the ground or trying to stretch the final-approach glide. You can't stretch a glide, and you'll either stall in the attempt or land short of the emergency landing field. Making steep turns close to the ground greatly increases the chances of the dreaded stall/spin accident. Keep your turns coordinated and don't get too low before establishing the final approach. You can get rid of excess altitude; you cannot get back what you've wasted.

Establish the final leg of the approach with extra altitude. At the risk of excess repetition, you must keep in mind that the glide angle is steeper than you've ever seen before. On final, it's time to pick an aim point.

The aim point is the point where you're aiming the airplane to begin the flare for landing. It should not be too close to the approach end of the field because you'll need to probably clear a fence, and you need a little extra cushion for that decreased glide performance. Pick out a distinguishable point in the field where you want to start the flare.

As the glide continues, watch how that point moves in relationship to a point on the windshield. If the aim point moves up the windshield, toward the top, you're not going to make it. If it moves down toward the bottom, the present glide angle will result in overshooting the intended flare point. If the aim point remains stationary in the windshield while gliding toward it, you've got it nailed.

Another part of practicing power-off approaches involves learning how to modulate your angle of descent to reach the selected aim point. Airplanes have several control surfaces on them, and you need to begin thinking of the flaps as control surfaces that are used to control what the airplane is doing. All too often we use flaps by rote, and too few pilots use them to accomplish a predetermined objective.

During a forced landing, I wouldn't apply any flaps in a typical lightplane until established on the final approach, and then only when I knew that flaps were needed to reach the aim point. Altitude lost can't be regained, so don't waste it by a premature use of flaps. You also cannot stretch a glide, no matter what you do. Best L/D is best L/D, and you can't change either the design of the airplane or the laws of aerodynamics.

If you do add flaps too soon and see that you won't make it to the aim point, you can retract them somewhat if the airplane is high enough. You're not changing the physical laws, you're changing the airplane. Best-glide speed, as quoted in the POH, and the resulting glide range assume zero flaps in every lightplane of which I'm aware. By retracting flaps that were deflected too soon, you're restoring the wing's shape to a condition that will provide the longest glide. If you do reduce flaps, remember that the gliding attitude needs to change some, so be ready to alter that as well. Don't reduce flaps when you're very near the ground in a last-minute attempt to stretch the glide. That will momentarily increase the sink rate and increase the stall speed, neither of which is desirable down low.

If you're too high on the final, you can do several things. First and obviously, put the flaps fully down to steepen the glide angle. Don't increase the airspeed by diving toward the ground because that will probably increase the distance to touchdown. Instead, slow the airspeed. A slower speed will provide a shorter gliding distance because the airplane is slower than the best L/D speed, and as a result, the glide angle steepens. Don't overdo it and get so slow that you risk a stall or end up with too little airspeed left to flare.

How long has it been since you've practiced slipping? It's an age-old technique to steepen a glide angle and was the way it was done in the days before lightplanes commonly had flaps. Learning to slip is another aspect to pilot proficiency. But as always, read the POH to see if there are any restrictions applicable to slipping your airplane. Some airplanes, notably several Cessnas, can't be slipped with flaps extended because the flaps can disrupt the airflow over the tail during a slip, stalling the tailplane, and resulting in a loss of pitch control. Know all airplane limitations.

If permitted, slipping with full flaps extended will provide the steepest possible descent angle. Be careful, though, because you'll be coming down like a brick, and you could easily misjudge the situation and end up short of the aim point. Extremely steep approaches can easily fool you as to where to begin the flare. If you are coming down at a high rate of descent, you have more energy to dissipate, so keep the airspeed slightly fast, and flare a little sooner than normal.

When you practice power-off approaches, experiment with the different combinations of flap extension and any permitted slipping to get an idea of how much you really can control the angle of a glide. The results will astound you if you haven't done it before.

At all costs, resist the temptation to shallow a glide angle by pulling the nose up. Because the ground is coming up at you at a rate far faster than you're accustomed to, there is a real natural reaction to pull the nose up. A stall is the last thing you want, and further keep in mind that pulling the nose up will lessen the airspeed, which in turn will only deteriorate the glide performance all that much more.

A considerable headwind means the angle of descent will be all the steeper. This is the situation that creates the most temptation to try to stretch the glide. Be aware of what wind does to glide angle. If you blow the approach and see that you'll be short of the "runway," accept the fact and make the best of it. Any attempt to stretch the glide by pulling up the nose will only worsen an already poor situation.

When you get down to the last couple of hundred feet in the approach, be ready to experience a steepening of the glide angle if there is any stiff wind blowing. Normally, wind velocity lessens quite a bit within 200 feet or so off the ground, as compared to the wind at higher altitudes. As you descend through this layer where surface friction tends to slow the wind, be prepared to experience wind shear. Wind shear isn't that great a problem to lightplane pilots under routine conditions because one benefit of piston engines is the ability to accelerate faster than jets, and you can add power to overcome the effects of the lessened wind velocity. A forced landing has no power to add, so the only method of maintaining airspeed during times of rapidly falling wind speeds is to lower the nose, which naturally steepens the descent angle. Don't get caught by surprise.

Plan to actually land as slowly as possible, stalling the airplane just inches above the surface of the field. It's imperative to touch down at the minimum possible speed because you're landing on an unimproved field. If the field is rough, or if you encounter any unseen holes, ditches, and the like, the slowest possible speed at touchdown will be necessary to increase the probabilities of a successful outcome. Impact forces increase and decrease exponentially with increases or decreases in the speed at which you're traveling when you hit an obstacle; therefore, land as slow as possible.

Progressive engine failure

We'll use this term to describe the situation that might present itself when the engine starts running so poorly that it's apparent something is drastically wrong and total failure might happen in a split second.

This possibility presents a pilot with some other decisions to make. Should you stop the engine before further damage occurs? Should you make a landing into the first field that comes into view where it's likely that you can land without destroying the airplane? Should you continue on to the nearest airport?

Progressive engine failure is probably about as common as sudden failure because engines can sometimes continue to run and put out some power after they have suffered an amazing amount of damage or degree of failure. Two of my engine failures were the result of cracked cylinders. The cracking occurred around the base of each cylinder. When that happened, the cylinder was askew from its normal alignment with the piston inside of it, and the result was a tremendous amount of increased friction from the piston's up and down motion. Power fell off dramatically, making me wonder whether level flight could be sustained.

The first rule of thumb for dealing with this kind of an engine problem is don't shut it down unless there is a fire or if the engine is vibrating so much that it might tear away from the mounts. Some power is always better than none and always gives the pilot more options over those present when the world is silent. Forget about whether the engine will suffer more damage. You can always replace an engine. You can't replace life and limb.

If the engine is on fire, it is a serious problem. Fire in aircraft is the worst emergency that a pilot can face, even worse than the loss of control authority of a primary control surface. The only thing more dire would be a structural airframe failure. Read the POH carefully because all modern handbooks have something to say about dealing with an in-flight fire.

If the fire is in the engine compartment, you must immediately shut off the fuel because it's probably fuel that's burning. It's crucial to keep your priorities in order because you won't stay in the air for long if you have a fire out of control. Shut off the fuel, turn off the magnetos, and turn off the master switch. Remove all sources of ignition and fuel to the fire, and get on the ground NOW.

Some POHs recommend diving, where the increased speed might blow out the fire, while others don't make that suggestion. Most POHs will have something to say about removing smoke from inside of the cockpit; if not, try a slip, and open a small inset sidewindow (if equipped) on the "up" side of the slip to likely suck out any cabin smoke. Close all of the air vents, including the heater and defroster, that come through the firewall from the engine compartment because they will probably add to the smoke in the cockpit. Open any air vents that don't take in air from the engine area, such as the vents in the wing roots and at the top corners of the windshield in most Cessnas.

If the engine is vibrating terribly, it might tear loose from the mounts. This problem generally happens when you've lost a piece of a propeller blade and the imbalance that results creates havoc in a hurry. If the engine does tear loose, you run the very real risk that the basic weight and balance of the airplane will change to a point that the center of gravity (CG) is so far outside of the certificated range that the airplane is uncontrollable—not a pleasant thought at all.

If you have any doubt about whether the engine will stay in its mounts, shut it down; otherwise, when things start going south and the continued health of the engine comes into serious question, don't be in a hurry to deny yourself the use of whatever power remains. Just a little power output will increase glide range tremendously, and you might need every foot of that extra distance to reach a suitable place for a forced landing.

Whether to immediately set up for a forced landing or try to make it to the nearest airport is a question of analyzing the situation and using good pilot judgment. There isn't any black-and-white answer to this query. It depends on what's underneath you, and how far it is to the nearest airport, and what's wrong with the engine.

Because you can't determine exactly what is going on under the cowling, and because most pilots aren't mechanics, our guesses wouldn't be worth much; therefore, determine what is happening in terms of situational stability. If the engine's condition suddenly changed but then seemed to stabilize with consistent power output, everything will probably stay that way for a short time. Then again, the situation might change again just as suddenly. Be ready for a total power failure at any moment.

I've always carried the proper amount of insurance on my airplanes so that I wouldn't suffer financially if one got destroyed. With that fact in mind, I've never been hesitant to accept an off-airport landing if that option seemed to have the better chance of successfully saving my neck compared to attempting to remain aloft and landing at an airport that wasn't very close. More pilots have come to grief by attempting to stretch it out and flying toward an airport rather than executing an off-airport landing with perhaps power remaining.

The hardest part of successfully making a forced landing is the fact that under typical conditions forced landings are made without power. A pilot must instantly become a glider pilot and solo that glider to a harmless touchdown without any previous practice or instruction. At least a progressive engine failure reduces the stress associated with crucial parts of the forced-landing scenario. Descent, pattern, and approach segments with at least some power make the entire event more routine.

If the nearest airport is more than a very few minutes flying time away, and if the terrain is suitable for a landing, more often than not I'd opt to land. If you're over dense swamp, rugged mountains, or forests, you might as well go on. The question becomes even tougher over water. Ditching is the worst kind of forced landing, and you're more likely to live through it if you ditch with power. So, over water, I'd again choose the landing in the wet with partial power rather than flying for a distance that I'm probably not going to make.

Depending upon my analysis of the engine's propensity to get me there, I would keep flying if the airport is extremely close. It's probably better to make an off-airport landing under power if engine failure is imminent rather than deal with total engine failure at a time and over a place where the chances of making a passable forced landing are diminished.

Every pilot has been trained to scan the instrument panel as a flight progresses. If you follow this wise advice and notice that something has suddenly gone wrong that indicates imminent engine failure, you're in the same boat as a pilot with a rough engine. If you notice that the oil pressure has dropped to zero, you don't have much running time left. An oil line rupture caused a very serious accident that disabled a surgeon. The pilot noticed it but blindly pressed on hoping to make an airport about 30 miles ahead. He didn't. Instead, he had to put the airplane down in a very hilly area where he survived the crash but with injuries that ended a brilliant career. Perhaps dealing with the inevitable and landing in a suitable field while the engine was still functioning would have saved not only his life but his hands, too.

The declining state of an engine's health presents a pilot with a situation full of variables where the decision of what to do has got to be the product of judgment. Be aware of the consequences of any potential course of conduct, analyze your options, and choose the one that seems best.

SUMMARY

Even though this chapter has centered on engine failures, the inescapable facts are that the lion's share of all lightplane engine problems are directly attributable to the pilot.

If you keep fuel in the tanks, make sure it is uncontaminated, and properly manage fuel flow to an engine, you've eliminated most causes of engine failure. Couple that with good maintenance, an awareness of when things might be going wrong, and the presence of mind to do something about a progressive engine failure before the options are taken away from you, and your chances of ever needing to put these lessons into actual use are indeed small.

3
The VFR pilot
in IFR conditions

THE LEADING CAUSE OF FATAL ACCIDENTS IN GENERAL AVIATION AIRPLANES has been for decades and continues to be continued flight by noninstrument-rated pilots into instrument meteorological conditions (IMC as the weather people call it), or into IFR weather as most pilots refer to it. The reason for this sad statistic has always been a mystery to me.

Most of us who have taken up flying as a hobby or way of making a living were probably first interested in aviation because of the challenges inherent in leaving the surface of the earth and subsequently returning to it in one piece. In fact, a recent survey by a major aviation trade organization proved that supposition to be true. Well over half of the pilots who responded to the survey answered the question of why they first began to fly by saying that meeting a challenge was their primary incentive.

Yet few VFR pilots would ever admit that they intentionally get caught in clouds, on top of the clouds, in haze so thick that there is no discernible horizon, or in other situations where instrument flying skills mean the difference between life and death. Meeting a challenge doesn't equate to suicide. Whether the cause of these events is the old "it-can't-happen-to-me" attitude or the result of ignorance and the inability to see the inevitable coming will always be a question that defies an accurate answer. If there is a majority cause, it's probably ignorance and the desire to press on a little farther, not recognizing that VFR flying is either no longer possible or shortly won't be. Any accident that results in serious injury or death is tragic, but the most tragic of all, particularly to the passengers, are the accidents that are the product of a pilot's ignorance or foolish daring.

The best way to deal with this emergency, which is purely pilot induced, is to avoid it. You might not have a clue that the engine is about to fail or that the alternator or generator in the airplane is about to give up the ghost, but you certainly can avoid stumbling into IFR conditions if you're not rated to fly IFR or not in an IFR-equipped airplane. Any pilot who has to fly solely by reference to instruments without the training and rating to do so has less than an even chance of coming out of the encounter without a scratch.

For the purposes of discussions in this chapter, it is assumed that you're flying in an airplane that is equipped, at least rudimentarily, for IFR flight; the aircraft has the normal complement of gyro instruments, a directional gyro (DG), attitude indicator (sometimes called an artificial horizon), and a turn coordinator (or its predecessor, the old needle and ball). All airplanes have an airspeed indicator and altimeter. If you get in the clouds without these basic gyro gauges, you don't have any chance at all, unless you're instrument rated and have remained proficient at flying with a partial panel.

KNOW THE WEATHER

Practically all of the inadvertent encounters by VFR pilots with IFR weather occur during cross-country flights. Occasionally we'll see a pilot who departs an airport when the weather is below VFR minimums and gets into trouble shortly after takeoff. I'm aware of one such incident where two restaurant employees closed the bar of the establishment where they worked and in the wee hours of the morning decided to go for an airplane ride. The weather was very low IFR with a ceiling of only a few hundred feet. In their inebriated state, they probably weren't able to see well enough to know that the clouds were so low, or they didn't care. Anyhow, the flight didn't get very far until the airplane impacted inverted, actually ejecting one of the bodies from the wreckage. Most pilots don't take off into this kind of weather if they're not instrument rated.

A working knowledge of meteorology is important to IFR pilots because an instrument rating is no cure-all for all of the miseries that adverse weather can visit upon a pilot. Because IFR pilots fly in clouds, their focus is upon the weather conditions that present unique hazards to instrument flight, such as icing, thunderstorms embedded in cloud layers, and the possibilities of the ceiling or visibilities going below the minimums for approaches at their primary and alternate airports.

The VFR pilot needs just as much knowledge about the weather, but his or her concerns are different. If you are a VFR-only pilot, thunderstorms are certainly still high on the list of weather conditions to avoid, but unlike the IFR pilot, the very possibility, or maybe probability, of weather near or below VFR minimums is vitally of concern. Sometimes it takes even more weather wisdom to discover the risks to VFR flight than it does to figure out if an IFR pilot is likely to see the weather go below minimums or create some other impediment to a safe flight.

In the aviation training environment, there is a lot more emphasis put upon weather knowledge during the schooling for an instrument rating than is received by, or required of, the average primary student acquiring a private pilot certificate. While it's certainly necessary for the IFR pilot to know a great deal about the weather, we shouldn't assume that the VFR pilot can stop learning about the subject after obtaining the certificate. How much weather wisdom do you possess? Have you ever tried to improve your own ability to read weather maps and charts and come to an educated estimate about what you think is likely to happen? Have you ever compared your personal forecast with either the official forecast or what the weather really did a few hours later? If you haven't gone through these exercises, it's time to start. During a cross-country trip, when the weather is different than forecast or previously reported, you need to know why and what the likelihood is for further weather deviation from information in the preflight briefing.

You don't train for this to outguess the professional meteorologists, but you learn to take a forecast, realizing that it is sometimes subject to variables that the meteorologist either didn't account for or that developed since the forecast was made, and then use your knowledge to figure out what is probably going to occur when the official forecast doesn't pan out. We all know how often we've seen a blown forecast: when the weather either didn't improve as it was supposed to or deteriorated much more quickly than predicted.

Two of the basic rules about weather forecasting that every VFR pilot needs to know are that weather predicting is much more precise and probable in summer and far less accurate in winter. In the summertime, weather systems work across the North American continent at a much slower pace than in the winter. It can take a week or more for a front to cross the United States in the summer. In the winter, the United States often sees Alberta clipper storms race down out of western Canada, across the Midwest U.S., and go on out to the U.S. East Coast in little more than a day's time.

Winter presents more hazards to continued VFR flight than in the summer. If it starts to rain a little from a safely high ceiling, many VFR flights can be successfully concluded in warm weather. But if the same thing happens in the winter, the precipitation can turn to freezing rain or sleet in an instant. It is virtually impossible to fly VFR in any snowfall, except for widely scattered snow showers that can be circumvented. As a VFR pilot, avoid all snow. Even if the visibility is presently above VFR minimums, it will go to pot "right now" if either the intensity of the snow or the size of the flakes increases. You won't be able to tell if either is about to occur until it does, and then it's too late; you're IFR in an instant.

Part of the theory that training alleviates most emergencies to manageable procedures is applicable here, before examining how to get out of the weather if you're caught in it. Train first to identify the threats that all weather systems pose to your flight, and then train to analyze the threats. You want to be able to decide how much hazard is presented, how widespread it is, and whether you need to stay put and fly another day or launch figuring that the risks are small and easily avoided.

When the weather forecast is questionable, but the current conditions are satisfactory, an IFR-rated pilot can often begin a flight safely with a series of "outs" in mind if conditions turn poor. As a VFR pilot, you don't have the same options. It's one thing for an IFR pilot to expect a 1,200-foot ceiling at his or her destination airport that has an ILS approach, only to be confronted with a 400-foot cloud height. No big deal, he or she can make the approach and land in either situation. For the VFR pilot, the first is scary, but the latter is a life-threatening emergency.

EMERGENCY INSTRUMENT CURRENCY

The concept of currency is familiar to every pilot. All pilots have studied the applicable provisions of the FARs. Most pilots know whether they satisfy the requirements to be legal to carry passengers in the day or at night or in an aircraft that they might not have flown recently. Unfortunately, there are no regulatory mandates for emergency instrument proficiency by the noninstrument rated pilot. In fact, the only recurrent training currently required of lightplane pilots by the FAA is the biennial flight review (BFR).

The conduct of a BFR and the depth of coverage of the subject matters covered are largely left up to the flight instructor who administers it. All that the regulation requires is that the BFR encompass at least one hour of flight time and one hour of ground instruction. One hour of proficiency flying every two years is a paltry amount compared to what is really needed to stay proficient, regardless of a pilot's level of certification or experience. Some flight instructors thoroughly cover emergency instrument flying during a BFR, while others only pay lip service to these life-saving skills.

After achieving a private pilot certificate, an airman can and should practice many of the elements of good piloting without an instructor on board, even in regards to flying under the hood with a safety pilot who is competent and legal (current) to fly the aircraft. Before you corral a friend to go along as a safety pilot during a session of practicing basic emergency instrument flying, get some dual instruction from an instrument flight instructor. A dual lesson or two can uncover any real weaknesses or errors that you might suffer; when the weaknesses are eliminated, you may practice with a safety pilot aboard if you don't want to pay for the instructor's time. Return to the instructor after every few sessions with a safety pilot to prevent developing and reinforcing any bad habits that might develop.

I wouldn't recommend that any pilot start out on a cross-country flight without being thoroughly proficient at emergency flying skills unless the weather is severe clear, forecast to remain that way, and the flight is conducted completely in daylight. I don't think it's safe for noninstrument-rated pilots to fly night cross-countries of much more than 50 miles. Too many things can go sour so quickly at night, like the quick formation of ground fog. To do otherwise is playing Russian roulette, and the chamber with the round in it just might come up under the hammer.

Think about starting instrument rating training as soon as you get the private certificate. While it might be a time before you can either complete the training or build up the flying time and experience to qualify for an instrument rating, any training toward it will enhance your ability to fly solely by reference to instruments and make you that much safer.

THE PURPOSE OF EMERGENCY INSTRUMENT FLYING

When a VFR pilot is suddenly immersed in IFR conditions, there is only one goal that should be in mind and toward which all efforts should be exerted, and that is to get out of there and back into VFR conditions. This simple fact has been lost on more than one pilot who figured that he or she knew enough to forge onward and fly through the clouds for an extended period of time. These scenarios almost always end in disaster. Remember, you're building life-saving skills that are best viewed as rescue techniques. We don't try to teach a drowning person to swim; we train lifeguards to get him or her out of the water. View your instrument flying the same way if you aren't rated for it.

Sometimes there is no immediate escape from IFR conditions, and then a simple 180° turn won't get you back into VFR. You might have to fly on the gauges for a while until your escape route pays off; therefore, every VFR pilot needs to be able to do four basic piloting techniques solely by reference to the flight instruments:

1. Execute a 180° turn maintaining altitude and then fly straight and level until out of clouds.
2. Perform a controlled descent while flying on a constant heading and while turning.
3. Climb straight ahead and while turning.
4. Fly for an extended period of time on a constant heading, do controlled turns, and navigate by electronic aids to navigation all at the same time.

If you can do these four basic tasks without reference to any outside visual cues, you'll be equipped to handle an inadvertent encounter with IFR conditions if you control your fear.

Panic is your worst enemy

This statement is true of all in-flight emergencies but particularly so here. You can survive almost any emergency if you keep the airplane under control. The problem with the VFR pilot in IFR conditions is that the very emergency consists of the high likelihood of losing control. Pilots seldom spiral into the ground or lose basic aerodynamic control of an airplane because the engine or electrical system failed. Basic loss of aerodynamic control kills VFR pilots who encounter IFR conditions.

Recall from chapter 2 that when most pilots are asked which emergency first comes to mind, they will respond with engine failure. As you have hopefully seen, engine failure can be managed to the extent that it shouldn't be life-threatening. I would propose that the worst emergency any VFR pilot can encounter is the sudden need to fly instruments. Such an aviator just isn't ready for any aspect of the occurrence: how quickly it develops, the totality, the feelings of impotence to control the outcome, and the fear that is then generated. Plus the situation might last for some time until the pilot can work his or her way out of the IFR conditions. The longer any scary situation lasts, the easier it is for panic to set in. Again, any amount of training in instrument flying will help with panic. The more you learn, the less you will fear.

VERTIGO

The human sense of balance wasn't designed for instrument flight. We are able to stand upright on two feet, or even on one for that matter, because we have a sense of balance. Primarily, we achieve balance by using two of our sensory organs.

Small canals in the inner portion of the ear are filled with fluid. These are called the semicircular canals. As a body moves, the fluid in the canals moves, and sensory signals are sent to the brain. The signals alert the brain as to the orientation of the body, and the brain can then move whatever muscles need to be activated to keep us on an even keel.

This system is still trying to work when a pilot is flying instruments, but, unfortunately, the semicircular canals don't do the entire job of maintaining balance. The brain also needs another input to augment the information it gets from the canals, and this secondary input is sight. The brain crosschecks the information that it receives from the canals with information from the eyes.

That's why you can be unsteady in a darkened room, with a blindfold on, or when you're otherwise depriving the brain of visual cues. When flying IFR, you can't see the natural horizon, so the brain isn't getting the normal visual information about the body's orientation that it needs to properly sense balance. So, your normal sense of balance isn't working when you fly without visual reference to the outside world. Unless you know this and are ready to deal with it, you'll never fly instruments for very long before you get so out of kilter that you won't keep the airplane under control.

You will on occasion feel as though the airplane is turning when it isn't, or your senses might fool you into thinking that all is fine, when the airplane is turning, diving, or climbing. This false sense of balance and the confusion that it creates is called *vertigo*. It's somewhat similar to the dizziness that is felt when you are spun around rapidly on your feet and you have to wait a few seconds for the world to settle down. The spinning motion caused the fluid in the semicircular canals to keep moving for a few seconds after your rotation ended, and the brain started to receive conflicting signals; the canals still sensed movement and the eyes saw no movement. It takes a short while for the brain to sort this out, and during that time a person is suffering what we all know as dizziness.

When you're flying on the gauges, you have to *ignore* your sense of balance and believe and follow what the instruments are indicating to your eyes. If you don't, you'll be out of control in a short period of time that might vary from several seconds to a few minutes, but it will eventually happen. No person can sense what the airplane is doing. You absolutely must believe what the instruments indicate. This point cannot be overemphasized.

Let's get on with covering some of the techniques and skills that might save your life someday.

THE BASIC FLIGHT INSTRUMENTS

The flight instruments that you'll use in emergency conditions are the attitude indicator, DG (or heading indicator), turn coordinator, altimeter, and airspeed indicator (Fig. 3-1). Some instruments will have more immediate importance than will others, but all are needed to some extent. In addition to the flight instruments, you'll need to refer to the instruments that measure the power output of the engine, which in most typical lightplanes means the tachometer. If an airplane has a constant-speed propeller, the manifold pressure gauge will be actually more important than the tach.

Fig. 3-1. *The basic gyro instrument panel of a lightplane.*

The purpose here is to learn to keep the airplane under control, to not allow gross deviations from the intended flight path, and to be able to get someplace you need to go. That "someplace" might be directly behind you, straight ahead, or off to one side. The precision that would be expected of a pilot training for an instrument rating is not a concern. Managed deviations are okay because the threat of overcontrolling can lead to as much of an ill result as not controlling at all.

Most primary students are taught to use the attitude indicator as the primary point of reference during emergency instrument flying. An IFR pilot uses the attitude indicator as the primary reference only while making changes in the airplane's attitude.

The VFR pilot is most concerned with basic control and keeping the airplane out of a spiral, dive, or stall. Many instructors, including myself at one time, taught that the turn needle or turn coordinator was the best instrument to consider as primary in order to keep the wings level. As experience is the greatest teacher of all, I've now come to the conclusion that perhaps this isn't so.

Turn needles and turn coordinators bounce around quite a bit and are extremely sensitive to the slightest rate of turn; hence, using one of them as the primary instrument to keep the wings level can easily lead to overcontrolling and will lead a VFR pilot into churning the yoke back and forth in response to every burble in the turn coordinator.

Go ahead and consider the attitude indicator as the primary instrument. It generally is quite a bit more stable and, especially in rough air, it won't bounce around nearly as much.

STAYING LEVEL

Fly the attitude indicator with the ailerons and the elevator. Don't use much, if any, rudder control unless a deviation from straight-and-level flight gets severe. Remember that the objective is not finesse; the objective is trying to keep the airplane upright and under rudimentary control. Using the rudder can easily lead to crosscontrolling, which you recall is trying to keep the wings level with the ailerons while accidently applying rudder in the opposite direction.

A pointer is at the top of almost all modern attitude indicators. This pointer and the indications of the instrument can be confusing to the pilot who is not used to interpreting them. In the real world, the airplane banks and the Earth's horizon remains stationary. But due to the mechanical limitations of the instrument, the "horizon" in the attitude indicator moves back and forth, and the little airplane symbol stays still. The reversal of these cues has fooled more than one pilot. The rule for most attitude indicators is *bank toward the pointer at the top of the instrument to level the wings*. Study movements of the instrument when flying, and learn to interpret the attitude indicator installed in your airplane (Fig. 3-2).

The horizon bar appears behind the center of the airplane symbol in the instrument when the nose is level. An adjustment knob moves the airplane symbol up and down because all gyro instruments precess to some extent. You should fly straight and level in VFR conditions and adjust the knob so that the instrument shows the correct nose position in relation to the actual horizon.

The second most important instrument is the DG, which is also called a heading indicator. A VFR pilot caught in the clouds will find the magnetic compass virtually useless for control of the airplane's heading. A magnetic compass is the most unstable of all instruments and will bounce around so much that the situation will only become more confusing. The purpose of using the DG is to verify straight-ahead flight; the attitude indicator has shown if the wings and nose are level.

If the DG indicates a turn, scan the attitude indicator to see if the wings are level. Unless you're applying rudder pressure and holding the wings relatively level with the

Fig. 3-2. *An attitude indicator and directional gyro in level flight.*

wheel (skidding through a turn), the only way that the airplane will turn more than a few degrees is if the wings aren't level. That's why we advise basically to stay off the rudder, even though the subsequent turns will be a little sloppy.

Some DGs rotate in reverse to the normal direction of a turn, but most up-to-date airplanes have a DG that looks like a compass rose displaying the entire 360° circle. An airplane symbol in the center of the instrument has its nose pointed at the heading in which the airplane is flying. Older airplanes have a rotating drum type of DG, and the pilot sees only the current heading and about 30° to either side of it. Old drum DGs appear to rotate backward.

Whichever type of DG you fly, there is a simple rule for making turns to a heading:

To add degrees, turn right; to subtract degrees, turn left.

Another way to put it is:

Less degrees, left turn. (Even though the use of "less" isn't grammatically correct, you get the idea.)

Next, even though the attitude indicator will show you if the nose is level, scan the altimeter to see what's happening in terms of climb or descent. Don't chase minor excursions above or below your desired altitude. It doesn't matter if you're a few hundred feet from the intended altitude (unless you got into this fix while flying very low beforehand). What does matter is the *rate* of change in altitude. If the altimeter is winding in any direction like a cheap watch, then you've got a problem. In all likelihood, you've lost control of pitch, and the attitude indicator will depict whether the deviation is nose up or nose down.

If that happens, you have to do two things quickly. First and foremost, make sure that the wings are level. If you're in a bank and also descending, you're well on the way to losing it entirely and ending up in a graveyard spiral. Correct the nose attitude only after the wings are level. Remember, do not try to pull the nose up first because that control input will only tighten the turn if the bank is at all steep. Relax a few moments before worrying about doing anything more than just keeping the airplane motoring on, straight and level.

Your most important task, always, is to keep the wings level and the pitch attitude under control. If you are descending and turning at the same time, it's imperative that the wings be brought back to level first. If the bank is allowed to continue, pulling back on the wheel in an attempt to raise the nose will only result in the turn getting tighter. The vicious circle has begun. The turn keeps getting tighter, the angle of bank continues to steepen, and the pilot keeps pulling back. We call that a "graveyard spiral" because that is precisely where it will lead you.

Once you've mastered the ability to keep the airplane level and the heading constant, you next need to be able to turn, climb, and descend. Getting out of the clouds could require any of these skills or, more commonly, some combination of them.

TURNING

Turning while on instruments is difficult for a pilot who hasn't been adequately trained. Because the airplane is undergoing a transition from straight-and-level flight into something different, the beginning of the process of turning is where you need to be especially vigilant and calm. You also have to be aware of the high probability that vertigo will creep into the scenario. You've got to follow the instrument's indications, not your senses.

Make turns by using very moderate angles of bank. You don't want your banks too shallow because the turns proceed very slowly (unless you add to the problem by "pushing" the turn around with excess rudder pressure) if the bank is abnormally shallow. By the same token, if you get the bank too steep, the airplane has a distinct tendency to drop the nose because more of the lift produced by the wings is being directed toward turning and less lift is overcoming gravity. Remember that the graveyard spiral—a steep-bank and nose-low attitude—has killed VFR pilots who are in IFR conditions more than anything else. Avoid this progressive scenario like your life depends on it because it does.

Do some turns in VFR conditions, and determine what angle of bank produces a standard-rate turn at cruise airspeed. The aircraft heading changes 3° per second during a standard-rate turn. A turn-and-bank indicator has a little doghouse-shaped symbol to the left and right side of the needle-centered position. These symbols indicate that the airplane is in a standard-rate turn when the turn needle is directly underneath the doghouse. If the panel has a turn coordinator, there will be a mark on each side of it, slightly below the horizontal; that mark indicates a standard-rate turn when the wing of the airplane symbol is lined up with it.

One word of caution is in order at this point. Turn coordinators give absolutely no pitch information; they display *only rate of turn*. The physical similarity in the appearance of a turn coordinator to an attitude indicator has fooled many a pilot. You can be in an absolutely vertical dive, and you can't tell it from looking at the turn coordinator unless the airplane is also turning.

If I were redoing a panel in an airplane that had a turn coordinator, I'd toss the coordinator out and get the older but, in my mind, better turn-and-bank indicator. At least the old "needle and ball" won't confuse a pilot into thinking the nose attitude is level when it isn't.

The angle of bank needed to produce a standard-rate turn varies with airspeed; the faster the speed, the more steeply you have to bank to turn at a rate of 3° per second. At the airspeeds normally seen in fixed-gear lightplanes, you'll need somewhere in the neighborhood of 20° of bank to get a standard-rate turn. If you fly a fast retractable-gear airplane, you might want to limit turns to one-half of standard rate, or 1½° per second, in order to avoid steep banks. But if you fly this kind of aircraft, chances are you already have an instrument rating; if you don't, you ought to.

To enter the turn from straight-and-level flight, use the attitude indicator to establish the angle of bank that you've previously discovered it takes to turn at standard rate. While you roll into the bank, do so positively, but neither too quickly nor too slowly. Overdoing it to either extreme just makes the job that much tougher. While rolling into the bank, and afterward, watch the attitude indicator to make sure that you keep the nose level. When you get to the desired bank angle, neutralize the controls.

Anytime that you enter a bank, you divert a portion of the wing's total quantity of lift to the task of pulling the airplane around in the turn. In order to maintain a constant altitude, the totality of lift must be increased. We do that by slightly raising the nose, which increases the angle of attack, adding the necessary additional lift. Be ready to add a little aft pressure on the control wheel. It's vitally important to avoid letting the nose drop because a spiral could only be a few moments away if you do.

Scanning

Every instrument-rated pilot is required to learn the skill of instrument scanning. Fixating eyes on any single instrument will never get the job done because no instrument in a lightplane provides all necessary information. Keep including the attitude indicator in your instrument scan. In some airplanes, it might be necessary to add a little aileron pressure against the direction of bank to keep the bank from becoming too steep. The first fatal step when flying on instruments in an emergency leads toward a bank angle that gets out of control and starts to steepen.

You perform a turn to achieve a specific heading; therefore, you have to scan the DG to monitor the progress of the turn. You need to also scan the altimeter to make sure that the nose attitude, as shown on the attitude indicator, is correct for keeping the airplane level. But the attitude indicator is still primary because your first task is to keep the bank angle and nose attitude under control.

As your view of the DG indicates that the airplane is nearing the target heading to which you're turning, it's best to think ahead and begin the recovery from the turn back to straight-and-level flight before you reach the specified heading. Try starting the roll-out about 10° before the desired heading. You don't have to hurry it, and you can make the rollout smoothly and consistently. If you end up a degree or two off the heading, nobody cares because the goal is positive control, not finesse.

It's also very possible that you might have to navigate some while you're flying on instruments. But be aware that the very first thing you should do after you have the airplane under control and yourself calmed down—as much as you can—is to let an air traffic control (ATC) facility or a flight service station (FSS) know about your predicament. Emergency instrument flying is an emergency that should be declared, and you should gratefully accept whatever assistance is available.

If you're flying in a radar-coverage area at an altitude where your target will be displayed on a radar controller's scope, you need that controller as much as you've ever needed anyone. Controllers are trained in the art of dealing with VFR pilots who get into IFR conditions. Calm and helpful controllers have assisted more than one pilot to find safety in the form of an airport runway and VFR conditions.

A controller can do several things. First, she can clear the area around you of IFR traffic that she or other controllers are handling to reduce the threat of a midair collision that you present to the people who are properly flying in the clouds. Next, a controller often knows the weather around his area, and can guide you to the nearest VFR conditions. If he doesn't know that information immediately, he can find out by asking for pilot reports from IFR traffic nearby or obtaining current weather sequence reports from reporting airports near your area.

The controller's scope displays all of the airports in the coverage area. As soon as she can identify your aircraft, she's in a position to offer you navigational guidance in the form of headings and altitudes to point you in the right direction. With this help, your level of required onboard navigation lessens quite a bit, so you can concentrate on keeping the airplane upright. Let the controller give you directions, or headings to fly, and offer you altitude suggestions that should keep you above the rocks.

Don't hesitate to declare an emergency and get help. If you don't know whom to call, just make a MAYDAY call on 121.5 MHz, and you'll get a response as long as you're in radio range of any ATC facility or FSS. Forget the hassles that you might have heard about declaring an emergency. There will be some paperwork later and maybe even an FAA regulatory enforcement case to deal with. But those very small problems shrink into insignificance compared with the major problem with which you are confronted—keeping yourself and any passengers alive.

For the day when you might not be able to talk to anyone on the radio, navigating by VOR while flying instruments can be a daunting task indeed. It is very easy to get confused and disoriented while trying simply to track or intercept a VOR radial if you're not instrument rated. There is no good way out of that problem, except for having a very thorough working knowledge of how VOR works and how to interpret and follow the indications on the VOR display in your airplane. During normal VFR flights, practice and practice until you know how to track VOR courses and intercept them. At least if you do have to navigate on your own while flying in the soup, make the job as easy as possible by not adding unfamiliarity with the VOR system to your list of woes.

CLIMBING

Practice straight-and-level flight under the hood and then turning. When you can do those two tasks, it's time to begin learning to climb. Climbing is a valuable emergency-instrument flying skill because there are many times when you might be able to climb out of a localized area of clouds and get into the sunshine. This is particularly true in a fog bank where the tops might be only a few hundred feet above your altitude. If the conditions are truly local, you can then overfly the cloud layer VFR until reaching an area where the undercast breaks up, permitting a normal, visual descent and continuation in VFR conditions thereafter.

Don't assume that a climb through the cloud layer will reach clear air unless the tops are known to be close by; also know where the cloud deck breaks up to allow for a VFR descent before fuel reserves and exhaustion become a concern.

Sometimes it is also possible to climb slightly and be high enough to establish radio contact with an ATC facility for assistance. This is a tough judgment call because you don't want to randomly start climbing in the clouds if it only means flying much deeper into a thick layer. There is no black-and-white answer to this situation. Pilot judgment will have to be used to make the final analysis.

Climbing is more difficult than maintaining straight-and-level or turning because almost all lightplanes require a power increase to be able to climb from previously established cruising flight. If you fly a higher-powered airplane, and if the load is below maximum gross weight, the airplane might be able to climb without adding power. But you have to add power in almost all fixed-gear airplanes, even if equipped with a constant-speed prop. So, you have more to do.

The easiest way to climb is add the power first, then raise the nose to climb attitude for a relatively fast cruise climb. Because you don't want to exaggerate any of the attitudes of the airplane, forget about using best-rate-of-climb airspeed during emergency instrument flying. You want what is often referred to as "cruise-climb speed." Look at the attitude indicator the next time you fly to determine what pitch attitude produces a steady 500-foot-per-minute (fpm) rate of climb with climb power applied. Knowing in advance what attitudes produce what results is the key, not only to emergency-instrument flying, but it also is the way an instrument-rated pilot does it.

When climb power is established, raise the nose attitude to a position that will produce the desired climb rate and airspeed (Fig. 3-3). Hold that attitude for a few seconds while monitoring the airspeed indicator to see what it's doing. You should see a steady decrease in the airspeed as it changes from cruise to climbing speed. Watch both attitude and airspeed indicators to make sure that you're holding the necessary pitch attitude and not raising the nose excessively to the point that the airspeed gets too slow. Make any minor adjustments in attitude slowly. Stay as relaxed as you can.

Fig. 3-3. *An attitude indicator and directional gyro in a straight-ahead climb.*

Begin the transition from a climb back to level flight when the airplane is about 100 feet below the target altitude. First, lower the nose to the level attitude on the attitude indicator, then wait a few seconds for the airspeed to build to the cruise value, and finally reduce the power to the cruise setting. If you end up 50 or so feet above or below the desired altitude, nobody cares; even 100 feet is OK.

If your airplane has a rate-of-climb (ROC), or vertical speed, indicator, you probably know that it has a noticeable time lag. This means that the ROC is really depicting history. The time lag might be several seconds. Don't try to chase the ROC's indications; the only result will be increased porpoising. The only thing that the ROC is good for in emergency instrument flying is to monitor the rate of an already well-established climb or descent.

Making turns during a straight-ahead climb isn't much different from turning during level flight. Use the attitude indicator to establish the turn, and monitor the turn-and-bank indicator or turn coordinator for rate of turn (Fig. 3-4). After the turn is in a steady state, watch the DG (heading indicator) to see how the turn is progressing and determine when it's time to begin the recovery. Just be sure that a climbing turn doesn't get out of control because you divert too much attention away from proper nose attitude to the task of turning. Keep scanning the attitude indicator, and watch the nose attitude.

DESCENTS

Descending is obviously the opposite of climbing, and during emergency instrument flying, the same thing goes, except the steps to establish a descent are the same as for starting a climb. Change the power setting first, and then alter the nose attitude. Practice during normal VFR weather to determine both the depiction on the attitude indicator and the power setting that produce a normal descent of around 500 fpm with the

Fig. 3-4. *An attitude indicator and directional gyro in a climbing right turn.*

airspeed remaining at cruise values. If the day ever comes that you're stuck on the gauges, there is no time for experimentation; know the values in advance so you can concentrate on controlling the airplane without having to figure out what attitude and power you want in order to descend at a reasonable and stable rate (Fig. 3-5).

Begin the descent by reducing the power to the predetermined setting; in most lightplanes with fixed-pitch propellers, you'll find that it will be around 1,800–2,200 RPM. Then, before the airspeed deteriorates, lower the nose to the attitude that will result in the desired 500-fpm rate of descent. When the power and nose attitude have changed, the exercise of descending straight and level is no more difficult than level cruising flight, except for the fact that you need to monitor the airspeed, rate of descent, and the altimeter.

Fig. 3-5. *An attitude indicator and directional gyro in a straight-ahead descent.*

Start the recovery from the descent when the airplane is around 100 feet above the target altitude. Simultaneously raise the nose the few degrees necessary to reattain a level attitude and restore cruise power. You can make whatever finite adjustments that might be necessary in the altitude by very small changes in nose attitude. Throughout the descent, monitor the nose attitude and bank angle. Don't let a spiral get started.

Primary training for the private pilot certificate probably taught you that altitude is controlled with power and airspeed is controlled with pitch attitude. Sure, that's true, but there is more to the complete story. Both altitude and airspeed are really a product of the relationship between attitude and power setting. When you're trying to make small corrections to altitude when flying on instruments, it's much easier to do it by just raising or lowering the nose a little bit, rather than by changing the power, assuming that the power is already at a cruise setting. Remember that during emergency instrument flying, we're only interested in keeping the airplane under basic control and the occupants safe until returning to VFR conditions. This is not an effort to achieve the proficiency necessary for passing an instrument-rating checkride.

If you need to change altitude by only 100 feet, or maybe 200 in a higher-powered lightplane, do it by raising or lowering the nose attitude. By reducing the number of tasks that you have to do, you're lessening the job of keeping things under control, which is the ultimate goal.

Turns during a descent are no different from turns during level flight or climbs. Use the attitude indicator as your primary reference, and continue to monitor the descent (Fig. 3-6). The only major complication occurs if you try to turn at the same time that the descent is nearing the target altitude. If that happens, you have to worry about simultaneously stopping the turn on or near the desired heading and recovering from the descent into level flight. While you might be able to do both of those jobs at the same time, I wouldn't recommend it. Plan your situation so that you are either turning or descending, but not doing both if recovery will be at or near the same time. Again,

Fig. 3-6. *An attitude indicator and directional gyro in a descending left turn.*

watch for any signs of an incipient spiral. Don't let the bank angle or nose attitude get away from you.

When you are inadvertently caught in the clouds, the fewer the demands, the better, in terms of tasks to be performed. You'll have your hands full anyhow, so don't add to the workload by attempting to do more than one thing at a time if at all possible.

At the risk of overrepetition, realize that no noninstrument-rated pilot can ever be sure of a successful outcome to an encounter with real IFR conditions. Get some dual instruction from an instrument instructor on a frequent basis to rehone the very basic skills that you acquired during your primary training. And then practice, and then take some more dual to get your skill level beyond the bare essentials, and practice some more.

Certain conditions require instrument-flying ability other than exiting a layer of clouds. Summer haze can cut flight visibility to near nothing, especially at higher altitudes. Flying at night over remote areas without lights on the ground to give you the normal visual cues can be just as disturbing.

Flying over water often requires instrument flying for at least a portion of the trip. The worst part of that adventure can occur immediately after takeoff when departing over the water adjacent to a shoreline airport. Airports like Meigs in Chicago, Burke Lakefront in Cleveland, and others similarly situated on the shore of a large body of water can present such a challenge. A hazy day over the water can be as murky as flying in the clouds or as confusing to the senses as overwater flying at night. The island nations of the Caribbean don't allow any night VFR flying, regardless of how beautiful and serene the weather might be. Night flying over water should only be undertaken by instrument-rated pilots.

Recognize the situations that might require instrument flying skills, and avoid them until you acquire an instrument rating. If you aren't IFR rated, make that the next step in your flying career. Don't wait to start instrument training until you meet all of the logged-time requirements to get the IFR ticket. It takes the average pilot several months to complete all of the ground and flight instruction to receive an instrument rating.

Start training as early as feasible for two reasons. The first is that any amount of instrument instruction adds to your ability to fly instruments and might save your life, and those of your passengers, if things go south in a big way during a planned VFR trip and you end up in the clouds.

The second reason to start your IFR training early is that you'll learn more in the process than just how to control an airplane without being able to see outside. The increased comfort that you acquire in dealing with ATC, the better your weather wisdom improves as you study the ground-school materials, the more precise your navigation becomes, and the general level of professionalism that accompanies learning to fly in the IFR world will coalesce to heighten your level of enjoyment of VFR trips as well.

Unlike some IFR-rated pilots, I don't file an IFR flight plan and fly on an IFR clearance on every flight. I enjoy flying where I want at the altitude I want and navigating directly from one place to another. That is not a condemnation of those who want to always be on an IFR clearance on a bright and beautiful day; it's just my preference. But once you have real instrument-flying skills and the rating to legally use them, you're a much more confident and able pilot in all weather conditions.

4
Electrical system failure

LITTLE FLIGHT ACTIVITY TAKES PLACE TODAY THAT DOES NOT INVOLVE the use of an aircraft electrical system. Some pilots fly ultralight vehicles, while others do their aviating in antiques, classic aircraft, gliders, and hot-air balloons; the majority of these aircraft do not have onboard electrical systems. But these forms of flight are generally within the realms of hobby flying and don't represent the majority of the hours or miles flown in general aviation aircraft in this day and age.

Most of us have either grown to depend upon the electrical components and accessories in modern airplanes or have never really known any other way to fly. The great majority of general aviation pilots active today have never taken wing in an airplane that is not equipped with an electrical system. To some degree, this evolution is unfortunate because so many pilots have missed the simpler joys of flight. But there is no way that the aviation industry could have evolved to anywhere near its present state without electrically equipped airplanes.

Yet, all pilots have to be ready, trained, and prepared for the day when the electrical system fails in any airplane, from the simplest fixed-gear lightplane all the way to transport-category airliners. Whatever machinery and accessory systems that man invents, something will eventually fail to operate normally; that's just the nature of the beast. The modes of failure will be different as the airplane type increases in complexity, but someday they will fail.

Managing the failure of the electrical system in a lightplane should not be a life-threatening emergency. If you understand the system in an airplane and take time to plan for the day when it lets you down, an electrical failure should be nothing more than a nuisance.

ELECTRICAL SYSTEM COMPONENTS

Recall that the focus of this book is upon typical emergencies faced by pilots of lightplanes and learning how to react to the situations. For this reason, it is assumed that you're flying a piston-powered single-engine airplane. The components of the electrical system on this type of aircraft aren't as numerous or as complicated to fathom as are the various pieces of hardware that comprise the total system on a more complex aircraft. Nevertheless, the idea is the same; it's just amplified when you start flying multiengine or turbine equipment.

The easiest way to think of your airplane's electrical system is to grasp the idea that electricity is a consumable item that you need for flight, just like fuel. A "tank" that holds electricity is the battery. The battery is the source of power for the electrical components in your airplane. Just the same as fuel, there must be enough electricity in the tank to serve your purposes.

Because electricity is consumed at a very high rate while in flight, pilots can't simply fill the "tank" before taking off as with fuel and oil. The science of designing and making batteries hasn't progressed to the stage where a battery can hold enough juice to last through a cross-country flight if it's asked to power very much equipment. Look at the long time that engineers have been trying to design a practical electrically powered car without much success. A method of constantly feeding a supply of electricity into the battery is needed so the airplane's system can draw upon that supply. There were days when pilots did fly with only a freshly charged battery and hoped that they wouldn't completely discharge it before the flight was ended. That is still done in antique airplanes, gliders, and balloons, and it works satisfactorily because most flights in those aircraft still tend to be short, and the batteries will last long enough to get the job done. A freshly charged battery can power a single communications radio for a few hours. But cross-country flights in airplanes equipped with several radios, a transponder, lights, and energy-hungry items such as electrical landing-gear extension systems and electric flaps can't depend upon a battery lasting until a several-hour flight is completed.

For those reasons, the battery is refilled by having either an alternator or generator installed in the airplane. Either device is driven by the engine, and the battery is being continually recharged anytime that the engine is running.

Older airplanes might be equipped with wind-driven generators. These gizmos have a little fan or propellerlike device that rotates the generator after the airplane gets enough forward speed to create enough airflow past the generator. They usually work fairly well, but due to the inherent drag of a rotating generator, they can't be large enough to generate enough power for today's needs. They're okay for powering a single radio and maybe the navigation lights on a classic airplane, but they won't put out enough juice to meet a modern airplane's requirements.

In the 1960s, most manufacturers went away from using direct-current generators and started making alternators the norm on lightplanes. Alternators have two advantages over generators. First, they are lighter, especially when built to put out large amounts of power, compared to a generator of the same capability. Second, they put out useful quantities of electricity at a lower operating RPM than will generators; thus, even when the engine is idling or at low RPM during taxi, the alternator is charging the battery. During these times, most generators can't keep up with the drain on the battery, so the battery is not being constantly recharged.

Alternators have a downside. In order to start producing electricity, there is a solenoid that must close, and to close it, there must be a little residual current coming out of the battery. If the battery is completely dead, you won't get the alternator into a charging mode by only starting the engine. That small amount of current has to be flowing from the battery to close the alternator's solenoid. That's why you can't hand-prop the engine, get it running, and then start charging the battery; if the airplane has an alternator, and if the battery is completely discharged, the solenoid in the alternator will never close to start the power output from the alternator to the battery. An external power source must be used in this situation to start the engine *and* make the alternator come "online."

Generators don't have this requirement. If you fly an older airplane that has a generator instead of an alternator, and if the battery is completely dead, you can get things underway by handpropping the engine; when the engine starts running, the generator starts recharging the battery.

(Before you try this technique, be certain that you know how to safely handprop an engine. Most pilots of my generation grew up on Champs and Cubs that had to be propped for starting because they had no electrical system. Few pilots who have learned to fly since the early 1960s have a clue how to do it safely. Don't chance disaster if you fit into the latter category. It's especially dangerous to handprop a tricycle-gear airplane because the propeller sits low to the ground, compared to a tailwheel airplane. I've propped tricycles before, and I would do it again, but I grew up propping airplanes and think I know how to do it safely. Never handprop any airplane without competent instruction, and then don't try it on a tricycle-gear airplane unless you have plenty of experience. You must feel totally comfortable with the starting technique and all measures that are necessary to maintain control of the airplane when the engine does start.)

The next component of an electrical system is a voltage regulator. Think of it as a valve that controls how much electricity is flowing from the alternator to the battery. When the battery is fully charged, or very nearly so, the input of current from the charging source to the battery needs to be slowed down. If the alternator were allowed to always put its full output into the battery, the battery would be ruined in short order. The electrolyte solution would overheat and likely boil from the excessive temperatures. In the more exotic aircraft types, a battery temperature indicator warns of this problem; however, most lightplanes don't have a battery temperature indicator.

ELECTRICAL SYSTEM FAILURE

The voltage regulator's function is to vary the output from the charging source (alternator or generator) so that the battery is being fed only the amount of current needed to keep it charged, or "full" if you think of the battery as a tank of electricity, without allowing it to be overcharged, or "overfilled." The regulator senses the power demands that are being put upon the system and keeps the charging rate at the proper level to keep the battery full without overcharging.

In order for the airplane's electrical system to function properly, the battery, charging source, and voltage regulator have to be up to par and working. A failure of any one is a failure of the system, and sooner or later your flight will run out of juice.

There is more to a functioning battery than many pilots realize. Most of us assume that if the battery has enough residual power in it to start the engine, everything is OK. But that's not the case. An aircraft battery can be low on electrolyte, just the same as a car battery, and still start the engine if the weather is warm and the engine starts easily. If the fluid level is low, the battery won't be able to accept a proper charge, or the electrolyte might be further depleted by the heat inherent in charging, which would lead to a complete failure of the battery.

Batteries might crack with age or abuse, leaking the corrosive electrolytic fluid into the engine compartment or wherever the battery is positioned in the airplane. The metal plates inside the battery can become shorted if they develop a path of current flow between them that results from age or contamination inside the battery. If this happens, the capacity of the battery will be woefully reduced, and it will only accept a very minor "surface" charge at best or no charge at all. A conscientious mechanic pays as much attention to the condition of the battery as any other item in the airplane.

The art of aviating involves risk management, and one risk to be minimized concerns the after-effects of an electrical-system failure. It's tempting to try to stretch the life of a battery, but if you do so, you're increasing the risk level if the alternator or regulator fails. Batteries aren't particularly cheap, especially 24-volt units that are installed in many of the newer airplanes. A 24-volt system has some advantages, primarily increased cranking power for starting a large engine or starting a cold engine in winter. Due to some of the physical laws related to the properties of electricity, the wires in a 24-volt system can be smaller and therefore lighter than wires in a 12-volt airplane.

You'll be less inclined to make a battery last beyond its useful life if you recall and keep in mind that the battery is a "tankful" of power. Because the lifespan of a battery is several years when maintained properly, and even though 24-volt batteries can cost about $200, what do you actually gain by attempting to get another flying season out of one? Maybe you save $25 to as much as $50. That's not worth the increased risk.

Few symptoms of incipient failure of an alternator, generator, or voltage regulator can be detected by a pilot from inside the cockpit. We pilots certainly can tell when one of them gives up the ghost, but we can't easily tell when it's about to happen. Because we pilots are unable to predict when one of these devices is about to fail, we have to be prepared to act quickly and preserve the juice left in the battery, which will be all that remains to complete the flight.

ALTERNATOR FAILURE

Alternator failure can sometimes be discovered before a flight begins. (Because most modern airplanes have alternators instead of generators, references to alternator failures will be synonymous with generator failures.) When you start the engine, look at the ammeter or voltmeter (as equipped on that airplane) to see if the alternator is charging. Because the battery is the only source of power to start the engine, it'll discharge enough in the starting process to need a good rate of charge for a short while to bring it back up to snuff.

The appropriate gauge will indicate if current is being put back into the battery. Look for a fairly healthy rate of charge for a minute or two. If the battery is in good condition, and if it was a normal engine start, that ought to be enough time for the recharge to occur. Then the charging rate will fall back to a "trickle," and the meter will show it. To make this point, it's time for a war story.

Many years ago, a few other fellows and I owned a Bonanza and an Aztec; therefore, we could use either a single-engine or multiengine airplane as the flight needs required. One fellow was a former military pilot who had previously picked up a quirk that caused me a few minutes of confusion and befuddlement.

I took off one morning on an IFR flight plan, headed to an airport about an hour's flying time away from our home base. All was proceeding normally until I noticed that the VOR needles were beginning to wander a bit. I called the center controller to see if there was a NOTAM out concerning any outage at the VOR station that I was using for navigation. The controller said no NOTAMs were out and then told me that the quality of the transmission from the Aztec's transceiver was not good.

In another few moments, I noticed that the red warning flags were intermittently popping up on the VOR heads. Finally, I got the picture and looked at the ammeter. It was showing a full discharge rate. Our Aztec had the optional factory installation of dual generators, so I starting noodling over the odds that both generators would fail at the same time.

Buried down deep at the bottom of the power quadrant on that model Aztec were two switches that were totally ignored by most of us except one, as it turned out. They were on-off switches for the generators. The military pilot had flown the airplane just before my flight, and I finally woke up to the fact that these generator switches had been turned off. A quick flick of two fingers promptly restored power throughout the system, and the radios instantly came alive. Their lifeblood of electricity was flowing, and they were happy again.

Why our partner chose to turn off the generator switches as a part of his postflight shutdown checklist remains a mystery to this day. My problem was that checking them wasn't included in my engine-start or pretakeoff checklists. That item has since been rectified, and I haven't missed checking the position of a generator or alternator switch in more than 20 years. If your airplane has a switch to turn off the charging source, make sure that the switch is turned on before every flight, and consult the POH for the correct stage in the pretakeoff steps to do so. Scan the ammeter, too; if I had scanned the meter properly, I would have detected the problem before taxi to takeoff.

Make the ammeter or voltmeter a regular item in your instrument scan. Even if it's way off to the right side of the panel, as it was in that old Aztec, look at it every few minutes to see what's going on. For if the alternator has failed, quick diagnosis of that sickness allows you far more options than you'll have if you don't know that a failure has occurred until radios and other electrical equipment stop working. At that point, the battery is just about out of juice, and nothing you can do will put any more juice in it.

SHEDDING LOAD

When the alternator or voltage regulator does fail, the very first thing to check—after you've assured yourself that the on-off switch hasn't been accidently knocked into the off position—is the alternator circuit breaker. This breaker will be large and will be labeled with a very large number on the breaker itself. The breaker will be rated for the maximum output capacity of the alternator. Some of the older alternators are rated around 50 to 60 amps, while modern installations will have alternators capable of as much as 125 amps of output.

If your airplane has a generator, it still needs a breaker to protect the circuit from overload. Most light aircraft generators have capacities from 25 to 50 amps. If you don't know the panel location of the circuit breaker that protects the charging device (alternator or generator), find out before further flight.

If you notice a discharge on the ammeter or voltmeter, check the alternator circuit breaker to see if it's popped out. If it has popped, wait a minute or two for the device to cool, then push the breaker back in. If it pops again, *leave it out* unless you absolutely have to have power to land; complete the flight as though the alternator had failed. Something is wrong. A short in the system might be creating the extraneous current draw that is causing the breaker to pop. Because in-flight fires are caused only by fuel or oil leaks and electrical problems, treat a recurrently popping breaker as you would any other ignition source in the airplane. Don't stubbornly continue to reset the breaker and risk starting a fire.

After you've checked the alternator switch and circuit breaker and confirmed that neither was the source of the charging failure, you now have to start a logical train of thought and action to preserve the "fuel left in the tank," which is the amount of power still in the battery. Power is consumed at a very high rate, especially if you're flying at night with all of the lights, strobes, and radios turned on.

Every component in an airplane is designed to be as lightweight as possible, consistent with its function and safety. Airplane batteries are similar to automobile batteries, except that they are generally smaller and therefore lighter and, as a consequence, have a lesser reserve capacity. This desire to save weight leads to the fact that an airplane battery doesn't have the same ability to put out power for as long as a similarly charged auto battery will because the airplane battery is smaller.

Because we've thought of the battery as a tank of electricity, conceptualize that now you need to manage the consumption of electrical power to make it last until the flight can end at an airport. Study the POH and the other manuals that accompany each item of avionics installed in the airplane. Learn how much current is demanded by each electrical accessory, component, and radio. When you need to get rid of electrical load, it's imperative to know how much current these devices consume.

The numbers printed on the circuit breakers tell part of the story, but not all of it. These numbers indicate how many amps (current) can be drawn through the various *circuits* protected by each breaker until the breaker pops. But this information doesn't reveal how much current is flowing through *each item* on that circuit. Except for the large power consumers like the engine starter and maybe a landing-gear motor, it's probable that more than one electrical device is wired into a single circuit. You need to know the power consumption of each piece of electrical equipment, not just the total capacity of a circuit to which it is wired.

Once the alternator has quit, your job is to start reducing the amount of power that is being consumed, which is called "shedding load." The procedure is just the same as reducing the fuel flow out of the fuel tanks. You're trying to lessen the amount of electrical drain from the battery in order to make the finite supply of electricity last as long as possible.

An alternator failure during the daytime should not be any real problem, unless you're IFR and flying in weather that doesn't allow you to get into VFR conditions in short order. Regardless of the flight conditions, start shedding the load at once to preserve as much reserve power in the battery as possible.

Assume that you're in day VFR conditions because most lightplane flying occurs in this scenario. Start turning off all of the avionics that you don't absolutely need. Get rid of the transponder unless you're in airspace where it's required to be on; tell the controller about your predicament before shutting it off. Transmitting equipment consumes far more power than items that passively receive. Because the transponder is both receiving inquiries from the ground based radar units *and* transmitting a reply, it can be quite a current hog.

Next, turn off the DME if it is on. A DME operates by transmitting a signal to the TACAN station on the ground, receiving a TACAN signal, and internally timing the period that it takes for the round-trip to occur. It then knows distance, groundspeed, time to station, and the other information that it calculates from successive timings of the transmissions and reception of them. DMEs take a lot of power to operate, so shed this luxury item.

Now deal with receivers. You don't need an ADF under these circumstances, so turn it off as well. If you have one of the older models with an antenna that incorporates an electric motor to turn the loop and hunt the null, that motor is drinking electrical power at a high rate. Even if it is a newer model that hunts the null solely by electronic means, get rid of this drain on the available power.

Shut off any loran or GPS unit that has become a luxury item for the short-term. (Perhaps you were able to use a receiver's internal database to electronically locate the nearest airport prior to turning it off. Beware of any power drain to do so.) Now you're down to the normal navcoms.

Immediately shut off one navcom. You need to apply a little more judgment regarding the last remaining piece of avionics, which is the sole navcom in use. Every pilot worth his or her salt can navigate without any electronic aids to navigation. The units are called electronic "aids" because they are "supporters," not the sole means of navigation when flying VFR. If you can't look through the windshield and windows and navigate with a chart and clock, you need to learn that talent, too (covered in chapter 5). Unless you're terrified at the thought of navigating without the VOR, shut off the last navcom, too.

Turn off anticollision lights, strobes, and the like. Now you have shed about as much load as you can during daytime operations. A fixed-gear airplane pilot has the situation in hand because there is no concern about gear extension with any remaining power. If a navcom is necessary to receive for a little while, that shouldn't consume much power at all. But be wary of transmitting over the radio. Remember that transmitting takes many times more electrical power than does passively receiving.

Save transmitting time until closer to the destination or alternate if that airport wasn't too far away when the alternator failed. If a long flight has just started, think long and hard about scrubbing the mission and landing at the nearest airport where you're likely to find a maintenance shop. Perhaps the nearest airport is home base. Sometimes an alternator can fail due to something as simple as a broken wire, which can be troubleshot and repaired quickly. Even if an alternator has to be replaced, that might be a fairly short job on some airplanes, but it might be very labor intensive on others. Some lightplanes with front-mounted alternators require that the propeller be removed to get the drive belt off and back on again.

Don't transmit needlessly until you have to talk to ATC. If you land a fixed gear airplane at an uncontrolled airport, there is no harm to be done by turning on the transmitter and making normal unicom calls approaching the airport and in the traffic pattern. If you deplete the battery at this last stage of a day VFR flight, who cares?

If an alternator quits at night, the problem is exacerbated a little, but not much, as long as you stay VFR. But because you need position lights during the airborne segments of the flight and very few pilots are really comfortable landing at night without a landing light, consider this event an emergency that requires immediate diversion to the nearest airport where a safe landing can be made. It's much harder to navigate at night without some electronic aids, and the last thing that you want to do is get lost at night with the possibility that you won't have enough reserve power to use the avionics to get found again. So, shed all possible electrical load at once.

When the battery runs down at night, you've got a potentially life-threatening situation on your hands because your cockpit lights will go out, too. It's been too long to remember since I've landed at night with no cockpit lights to be able to see any of the flight instruments, and I don't want to do it again. If you can turn down the brightness of the cockpit lights, do so; it'll save a little power. Always carry a flashlight for night flights, and make sure that its batteries are fresh. An extra flashlight, spare bulbs, and spare batteries expand the safety margin.

If I were to suffer an alternator failure at night in a retractable-gear airplane, I'd put the gear down as soon as I was near the airport where I was going to land. Don't put it down ridiculously early because that will only extend the time of the flight because the airspeed will drop, which will extend the time that you need precious battery power. I'd want the gear down as soon as it makes sense to do so and assure myself of having enough power remaining to get it all the way down and locked. An early extension allows for the time that might be needed to execute the emergency gear extension procedure if the gear does not fully extend and lock.

When the gear is down, or if it is a fixed-gear airplane, don't turn on the landing light until you're well into the final approach and within a few hundred feet of the ground. Landing lights are among the most power-hungry items on an airplane, and the extended use of them will make short order of the battery's remaining life. You'll likely need some sort of illumination to taxi safely after landing, so think of the large power waste that results from prematurely turning on the landing light.

Three tasks must be accomplished if an alternator fails while in IFR conditions:

1. Tell the controller what has happened and declare an emergency.
2. Immediately shed load.
3. Fly to VFR conditions as soon as possible.

Even when flying IFR, a lot of excess load can be shed. Immediately tell the controller about the emergency. It is an emergency because you need electricity to continue IFR flight. Tell her or him what avionics you're shutting down, and report that you want to transmit as little as possible to save electrical energy.

You should be able to fly IFR with only one navcom on, especially if in radar contact and you can be aided by the controller. Ask, in one of your very few transmissions, if you may turn off the transponder. If you can't get permission, you have to decide whether to avail yourself of the pilot's emergency authority to disregard the controller's instructions, and start telling, rather than asking, what you're going to do. (Chapter 12 has more about pilot's prerogative.)

Head for either a very close airport where it's highly likely that you can get down with only one shot at the instrument approach or head for VFR weather if it is closer. If the weather is low-IFR for a large area, the only viable option is to request vectors to the nearest airport with weather above approach minimums.

Never try to stretch an IFR flight after electrical failure. Your job is to get down as soon as possible if you can't get into VFR conditions very soon. Aggressively shed as much load as possible, then shoot an approach and land. Blundering around in the clouds after the battery has gone dead will ruin your whole day. You can't navigate or talk to anyone. The only remaining course of action is to take up a compass heading that you think will reach VFR weather before either hitting another airplane or running out of fuel.

Night IFR is especially crucial in more ways than one, and the general aviation safety record for night IFR is horrible. A pilot has to be even more aware of the electrical system's health at night because he or she is depending on it for your survival almost as much as the engine. I don't fly single-engine airplanes much at night anyhow, and never in night-IFR conditions because electrical failure during night-IFR operations is life-threatening. Once the battery goes dead, you're reduced to floundering about in the clouds with no way to navigate or obtain vectors. All you can do is fly a compass heading hoping that it takes you into VFR weather. Unless that flashlight is working well, you won't be able to see the instruments or the charts because the cockpit will be as dark as a cave. Not a pretty thought. That's why I want the two alternators that come with a twin-engine airplane, and I want the second-engine redundancy if I'm going to be flying IFR at night.

Think about getting a portable hand-held radio, ideally a navcom with either GPS or VOR navigation. The devices are another benefit of the electronic age that can be extremely helpful in the event of an electrical system outage. If you have one, or when you buy one, there are two things to accomplish.

First, no hand-held is any good unless it has good batteries installed. Just like the flashlight, it won't work if ignored until needed. Either recharge or change the batteries often. Second, ask your avionics shop to install the necessary wiring so that the hand-held can be attached to the airplane's external antenna. The effective range of a hand-held is increased severalfold if it is hooked up to the external antenna. The small "rubber ducky" antenna that comes with the radio is better than nothing at all, but effective coverage of the smaller antenna pales in comparison to the performance of an outside antenna.

The best way to keep fresh batteries in the flashlight and hand-held radio is to pick a certain day every year to change them: birthday, anniversary, or the like. (This would be a very effective technique to remember to put new batteries in home smoke alarms.) Carry spare batteries for both devices within easy reach of the pilot's seat.

By knowing how your airplane's electrical system works, and how much current every electrical device consumes, you're personally equipped with the knowledge that it takes to shed load and cope with an electrical system failure.

5
Getting found

THERE IS AN OLD SAYING THAT IS PRETTY ACCURATE: "THE ONLY PEOPLE who haven't been lost in an airplane are nonpilots and liars."

Pilots often kid about being "lost" as being "temporarily unsure" of their positions. But under the right set of circumstances, getting lost can be as real an emergency as many others. If a planned flight will stretch the fuel range of an airplane to the limit, if the route is over very sparsely populated terrain, or if it's night, disorientation becomes a real problem if your navigational techniques have inadvertently failed and you suddenly realize that you're really lost.

While this chapter will review how to get found after becoming lost, the actual problem occurred before you became lost. Pilots who get lost attempt flights in areas or in conditions beyond their personal limitations, or they were inattentive, lazy, complacent, or all of the above. Getting lost is a pilot problem, not an aircraft malfunction. Even if the radios fail or the electrical system fails, the well-trained pilot with the proper mental attitude about flying won't get lost without a personal malfunction.

This doesn't serve as an indictment of general aviation; rather, it means that certain problems in aviation are caused only by the pilot. Pilots with the proper attitude and training can minimize these occurrences but probably will never eliminate them. The most common reason that pilots get lost is that they attempt flights beyond their limitations, as you'll see from the following examples.

I've been lost twice. The first time was as a newly certificated private pilot and the second happened right after I got my commercial license.

I bought a Taylorcraft BC-12D in 1965 for my first airplane. I built up most of my solo time in it to qualify for the private pilot checkride. I received the license and subsequently flew it for about a year to build time to qualify as a commercial pilot. The Taylorcraft was about the cheapest form of powered flight in a certified airplane that was available at the time, and it's probably true now. It was inexpensive enough to venture forth on a long trip on a student's budget.

During the spring break in my freshman year of college, I decided to fly the Taylorcraft to Florida to see two friends who had moved down there from Ohio after we all got out of high school. When I left our small airport in Ohio to start this trip, I had about 100 hours in my logbook and hadn't flown any farther from home than the 100-mile cross-country then required to get a private license. The Florida trip was quite an ambitious undertaking, as I was to discover.

Because the Taylorcraft had absolutely no radio equipment of any kind, nor any electrical system to power one anyhow, the trip was planned to use pure dead reckoning and pilotage as the only available means of navigation. Because I was going to be flying over the mountains of West Virginia and North Carolina, and then later in the flight over the swamps of southern Georgia and northern Florida, the better part of valor told me to follow as many rivers, roads, and railroads as I could. I did just that, and the trip down there was totally uneventful.

I visited one friend in the Lakeland area for a couple of days and then flew down to Ft. Lauderdale to see my other high school buddy. After spending a few days with him, he decided to come back to Ohio with me, to see some of his family. He was another airplane nut who had progressed further in his training than I; he had at least 150 hours of pilot time under his belt.

When we got the charts out to plan the trip back to Ohio, he chuckled at my plan to retrace my route of following roads, rivers, and the like back home. He opined as how "real" pilots fly direct courses between places and don't wander all over following the bends in highways and rivers. I knuckled under to the pressure to do it "right," and off we went. Certainly, at his level of experience, he must have known better than I.

Everything went fine as we chugged up through Florida at all of 95 mph. (Wouldn't it be nice if airplanes built 50 years later cruised at 1.5 mph per horsepower like the T-Craft did on its little 65-hp engine?) It was nice and flat down there, the visibility was excellent, and there were lots of little towns to guide one's way. I even sneaked a glance at a highway or railroad now and then, and we made it to somewhere near Augusta, Georgia, the first day. The next morning we got an early start because we were less than halfway home; we had a lot of flying ahead of us to reach Ohio by the early nightfall that occurs at that time of year.

Again, there was no problem through Georgia and the Piedmont Region of the Carolinas: lots of little villages and towns, several big freeways, and good visibility. Then we got into the southern foothills of the Appalachian Mountains. Remember that in 1966 the national interstate highway system was far from complete. No major freeways cut through the mountains. Even the West Virginia Turnpike was mostly a two-lane road with several tunnels through the high mountain ridges. And because real pilots didn't follow roads, we launched on a leg directly over the most sparsely populated part of the mountains flying a compass heading as our only guide.

Within 45 minutes we didn't know what state we were over. In that part of eastern Kentucky, West Virginia, or wherever we were, there weren't any features on the ground for checkpoints. One large expanse of forested mountain ridges looks like any other. I woke my buddy up from his nap and proclaimed to him that we were lost. He examined the chart and the view out front, then agreed. We had no idea where we were.

We continued to fly in a straight line, a technique that is subsequently better described in this chapter. In what seemed like an eternity but was probably no more than 15 or 20 minutes, we spotted a freeway that had been built but wasn't yet open to traffic. Now we had a way to get found. We flew along at the lowest safe and legal altitude and soon came to one of those big green exit signs that had just been installed: CHARLESTON. Because we figured that we were closer to Charleston, West Virginia, than the city of the same name in South Carolina, we had it knocked at this point.

I flew down the road leading from the freeway, and as we came to the outskirts of the city, we got reoriented. By now, fuel was a problem because the old T-Craft only held 12 gallons in a nose tank and another 6 in a leaky wing tank that was seldom used. Even though the airport at Charleston was controlled and the airplane had no radio, I opted to land there. We entered downwind in the normal fashion and saw a steady green light from the tower. As I taxied into the FBO, the line attendant said that the tower wanted me to call on the telephone. It didn't take a very long call for the controller to agree that landing at a controlled airport without benefit of a radio was preferable to running out of gas over the mountains.

Today, the FAA would probably file a violation against a pilot so dumb as to get in that fix, but things were a little bit more laid back 30 years ago.

I've made several trips over the same route since. Some of the subsequent trips have been in classic airplanes, and a few had no radios. Without a radio or other electronic aid to navigation, I swallow my pride and let the highways be my guide. I've never been lost in that part of the country since.

The second time that I was "unsure of my position" revolved around a scenario that can happen to any pilot as he or she upgrades to faster airplanes. I learned to fly and got my commercial and flight instructor certificates before an instrument rating or time in complex airplanes were necessary to qualify for the advanced ratings and certificates. Before this incident, the fastest airplane I had flown was a Stinson 108-3, which cruised at about 120 mph.

I was instructing at a small airport to put myself through college. My employer at the airport needed a part picked up in a city that was about 200 miles away. Because he needed the part quickly, he offered to let me take his Cessna 205 on the flight. The checkout consisted of two trips around the pattern; I didn't crash on either landing, so off I went. Thankfully I had at least read some material on how to operate a constant-speed propeller.

After about 20 minutes of flying time, in gorgeous weather, I was about 15 minutes behind the airplane, which was screaming along at about 160 mph, 30 percent faster than I'd ever gone before. But because this airplane was IFR equipped with two navcoms, I "found" myself by crosschecking two VOR radials from different stations. All the way to the destination and most of the way home, I was still behind the 205's progress over the ground.

This type of problem will present itself to every pilot the first time that he or she flies a fast airplane. Hopefully most people today have enough sense to get a thorough checkout in a different airplane type. If the new airplane is appreciably faster than you're used to, the checkout should include cross-country work with VOR intercepts and tracking. There's more to flying a new type than simply assuring yourself that you can land it without bending it.

These stories are funny now but weren't that way when the events unfolded. One of the many advances in general aviation since the 1960s has been the evolution of more proper and professional pilot attitudes. An "around the pattern" checkout was common, even when the new type of airplane was significantly different from whatever the pilot had been flying previously. Today, only the renegades of our industry would introduce a pilot to a new airplane with such a cavalier attitude toward transition training.

GETTING FOUND WITHOUT RADIOS

If you're undertaking a flight in a no-radio (nordo) airplane, it's much easier to get lost compared to flying an airplane that is fully equipped with the latest bells and whistles. Every pilot gets some introduction to basic nordo navigation in primary flight training. But just like most of the basic skills that aren't really used much anymore, few instructors stress the importance of navigating long distances without electronic aids. The key to avoiding the unpleasantries associated with trying to get found is to do a good job of basic dead reckoning and pilotage and not getting lost in the first place.

The two terms "pilotage" and "dead reckoning" are often used interchangeably, and this discussion will do so, too. But the techniques are technically different types of navigation. Dead reckoning is a misnomer. The term comes from "deduced" reckoning, which is the art of navigating by a compass, clock, and with knowledge of the winds and distance to be flown. To be totally accurate, dead reckoning doesn't involve the use of checkpoints to visually keep track of one's progress along a flight.

The "dead" in dead reckoning comes from the word deduced, and you'll rarely see someone refer to the practice as "ded" reckoning. Somewhere in aviation's antiquity, ded came to be spelled as dead. Some of the old-timers will tell you that the latter spelling is better because it serves as a reminder that "if you don't reckon right, you're dead." This name implies the fact that the practitioner deduces headings and times to fly from figuring, or reckoning, certain mathematical formulae and procedures to determine headings and estimated times from the known facts of the course line, magnetic variation, and wind direction and velocity. An old-time sailor would navigate this way on a cloudy day or night when an octant or sextant could not be used to navigate by the sun or the stars. Dead reckoning was also used to fly over oceans, deserts, great forests, and other terrain where visual checkpoints were nil prior to the advent of electronic aids to navigation.

Pilotage is navigation by looking out of the windshield to see where you are and where you're going and adjusting the compass heading accordingly. Even if you use pure pilotage, you'd be expected to do some elementary dead reckoning to at least get an idea of the suitable heading to fly and how long it ought to take to go from one checkpoint to another. In aerial navigation over normal terrain, the two techniques are mixed together, so it's not really important which term you use to describe how you navigate in a nordo airplane.

What is important is to navigate and at all times keep a much closer track of your present position than you normally do when using electronic aids. The focus of this book isn't about cross-country navigation, but it must be stressed that it's important to retain the ability to get where you're going without depending upon the latest black box.

Training and preparation are the ways that a pilot effectively deals with all of the in-flight emergencies that might occur. Far too many pilots have either forgotten their basic dead-reckoning skills or never developed them in the first place. Dead reckoning is needed not only for flights in basic or classic aircraft that aren't equipped with avionics, but also for the day when either the radios or the electrical system fails.

Calculate actual groundspeed during a cross-country flight. Keep track of the visual checkpoints that pass by. Estimate the time it should take to reach the next checkpoint. Verify that the previously computed compass heading is doing the job; if not, the winds might be different from forecast and a heading adjustment needs to be made before you get lost.

Do these three basic tasks of navigation, regardless of the means, and it's less likely that you'll ever wander very far off course. When you do get a little fuzzy about exactly where you are, if you've kept track of things up to that point, getting found will come much more quickly, and you'll discover that you weren't that far off to begin with. If you haven't really navigated, you might be surprised by just how far off course you can be before you realize that something isn't going properly.

When you first start sensing that things aren't right, the first thing to remember is not to lose self confidence in what you've done up to that point. The wind has not suddenly shifted measurably—especially if you've been watching the compass heading and making small corrections between checkpoints as necessary—unless you're flying within or very close to a front. Most of the process of getting lost is mental, and so is getting found. The biggest mistake that most pilots make when they first start feeling the panic pangs in their bellies is disregarding all that made the flight plan work up to that point. Don't fall into this trap.

Instead, keep going in a straight line following the compass heading that you previously determined to be appropriate to fly the courseline over the ground. If you do this, at worst you'll be a little off course to start, and then you'll parallel the desired course. If the wind has shifted dramatically, you'll diverge slightly from the planned course. If you start aimlessly turning, all bets are off, and who knows where you'll end up.

Many pilots get lost because they select unusable checkpoints while planning a flight without realizing how difficult the selections will be to spot or discern while aloft. Small rivers are okay to follow, but trying to pinpoint the spot where a route of flight crosses a river doesn't do much, unless the spot is accompanied by a recognizable town or some other feature that distinguishes this part of the river from any other. The same goes for places where a course intersects a power line or highway. Crossing these landmarks doesn't indicate much about the airplane's location in relation to that power line's or highway's course across the countryside. Another distinguishable land feature must accompany the power line or highway to provide a precise pinpoint position.

Small towns can be confusing unless you're in sparsely populated areas where they're few and far between. Some small towns have particular features alongside them: a track, a major freeway, or a river. But if you're looking for a town that isn't discernible from any other town, you might see the wrong one, thinking it to be your checkpoint.

After you've lost confidence in where you are, and if you have returned to your predetermined compass heading, start looking for the checkpoint that should be next. You'll often be surprised to find it, albeit maybe in a slightly different place than you expect. Look where you think it should be, but also scan the area all around the airplane. When you do find the next checkpoint, you've got two alternative courses of action.

You can fly directly over the checkpoint and resume the compass heading that should get you to the next checkpoint. While this process is inefficient and wastes time, use it if you're very far from the checkpoint when you find it or if you're a new pilot who doesn't have much cross-country experience. Depending upon how far you are from the checkpoint when you see it, you could simply go on from there and make a heading change that you compute to reach the next checkpoint. This method saves a little time, but because you got off course to start with, don't try it if the next checkpoint is a long distance away.

A large part of getting found is to make sure that you always have current sectional charts prefolded so the route of flight is fully displayed. The tight quarters of a lightplane's cockpit are not a very handy place to try to unfold a chart to its full extent and then refold it into a usable panel or two. I know far too many pilots who, after they get an instrument rating, think that sectional charts are no longer needed by "the pros." Before the flight, use a pencil to draw the course line on the chart. Some pilots like to circle checkpoints with the pencil; others don't. If you're inexperienced at this type of navigation, I'd recommend positively identifying the checkpoints by circling them with a light pencil line.

When the radios fail or the alternator quits and you need to turn them off, it's time to revert to dead reckoning, and you need that sectional chart to do it. IFR charts are great for what they're intended to do, which is provide data needed for IFR flight. They aren't worth a hoot when you have to get your head out of the cockpit and start looking around in order to navigate. World aeronautical charts (WACs) are not used by many pilots these days and eventually might be dropped from publication. If you do carry these old-fashioned charts, they are better than instrument charts for unexpected dead reckoning navigation, but not much better. Carry current sectionals.

The best way to hone your skills at dead reckoning is to practice the art. Try flying your next good weather cross-country without turning on any navigation avionics. The sky won't fall, and you'll find that it's fun when you get back into the swing of it. Watch out for areas of airspace where you're required to talk to ATC, such as Class B or C. Don't inadvertently stumble into one.

If you think that you're hopelessly lost, still fly in a straight line. Unless fuel is very low or the flight is over a desert or some other sparsely settled area, eventually you'll come to a river, highway, or railroad. All of them go somewhere. By then following the highway, or whatever, maybe you'll get to Charleston just as I did. Seriously, a highway will take you someplace where you can see the ground features; crosscheck them with the chart, and you will probably reorient yourself. Don't push the fuel when flying nordo navigation. Keep all planning conservative.

There are two last resorts when you're really lost and reasonable attempts to solve the problem haven't worked. First, don't be ashamed to get on the radio and ask for help. If you're flying a typical lightplane that cruises around 110 knots, and if the weather is good enough that you are high enough to be in range of an ATC facility, look on the sectional to find a tower frequency near where you either think you are or near your last known position. By calling a tower, the controller can provide the frequency of a terminal radar facility or air route traffic control center from whom you can get the needed help. If you see an area of Class B or C airspace near your hopeful location, try calling directly into the radar facility frequency that is shown on the chart.

Flying as high as possible helps, unless haze restricts visibility that decreases with altitude. Being high not only improves radio range, but helps a pilot get his or her bearings better because he or she can see more of the terrain and find a checkpoint or other landmark.

The absolute last resort is to make a forced landing off an airport while fuel is available and the engine is running. If the situation deteriorates to the point that fuel is critically low, don't keep on wandering until it runs out. Brain lock can also be a killer. Take advantage of the options while they are still available. Running out of gas leaves only one remaining choice, and that's not a very good one.

Review chapter 2's material regarding progressive engine failures. Running out of gas is the last thing that you ever want to have happen. If truly lost and running into the last half hour or so of the fuel supply, it's time to think about landing as soon as possible while the engine is still running normally and there is time to select a good place to land. Don't give up on finding an airport because you might do so before it's too late. But use good judgment and don't drone on denying the inevitable when the fuel level drops critically low.

Practice finding small grass airports during normal flights. Many private and commercial pilots have never landed on a sod field; hence, few can find them with ease. It can be a haven to stop, sort out where you are, and get things back on track after becoming lost. Be careful about the condition of the runway; winter snows and spring rains can turn many sod fields into quagmires.

Flying cross-country at night with or without radios has its own special sets of problems. Any night flying depends more upon instruments than the same operation in the daytime. Because many features that make excellent checkpoints in daylight are virtually invisible at night, you will have to depend more upon electronic aids to navigation.

At night, it can be hard to recognize what you do see. Almost every little town looks like every other, unless there is an airport very nearby and it has a rotating beacon to distinguish its village. You won't be able to see the tracks, factories, rivers, and all of the other landmarks that are easily seen in the day. Also, visibility on a clear night will be far better than you might expect. You might see the glow of a major city from as far away as 75 miles or more. Until accustomed to the difference, astoundingly good conditions can be as confusing as poor visibility.

GETTING FOUND WITH RADIOS

Because most cross-country flying takes place in airplanes with at least some avionics equipment, getting lost isn't as prevalent as it used to be, as long as everything is working properly. Even with avionics, it's still possible to get confused. This confusion will be lessened and probably close to totally eliminated when a pilot learns how to properly operate the black boxes. If you don't have an instrument rating, you probably have more to learn about VOR navigation. Even if you have a loran or a GPS unit, you might only know the rudiments of how to operate it.

With VOR equipment, the first key to its use is to realize whether you're within reception range of a station. Because VOR uses the VHF frequency spectrum, the signals are broadcast by the transmitting station in what is known as "line of sight." This means that the signals emanate outward from the station in a straight line. When viewed from a hypothetical profile, or side view, the signals are covering an area from the top of the station to the surface of the ground at the station's transmitting antenna. When you're more than a very few miles from the station, you can't receive the signal at ground level.

The radio waves don't bend (meaningfully) or bounce off of the upper layers of the atmosphere, and they don't follow the curvature of the earth. When the beam projects outward from the station, the line of those signals is getting higher in altitude as distance from the station increases. This is called the line-of-sight range because a person would have to be high enough to "see" the station on the horizon (if he or she could see that far) before the signal can be received. If the station is behind the curvature of the Earth from your location, the signal cannot be received.

If you're lost and the VOR receiver is working, climb as high as is practical to increase the reception range for the selected station and to be in range of more stations. Look on the sectional chart. Find a VOR station somewhere near where you might be. Try to choose one that is off either the nose or tail of the airplane.

Tune in the appropriate frequency, and then turn the omni bearing selector (OBS) control until the course deviation indicator (CDI), often referred to as the needle, centers. Look at the TO-FROM indicator; if it's showing a TO indication, rotate the OBS 180° to center the CDI and display a FROM indication. Look at the radial number, in degrees, that is shown on the OBS (Fig. 5-1). You're somewhere along this radial. Take your pencil and plotter (You *do* fly with these items, don't you?), and draw a straight line, *outbound* from the station for about 50–75 miles along that radial. You've drawn what navigators call a *line of position*. You're somewhere on this line, but the task is not completed.

Fig. 5-1. *A course deviation indication on an outbound radial.*

Knowing a line of position doesn't get you found because you need to know a *point of position*. Recall from high school geometry that a point is located at the intersection of two lines. To get a point of position, another line of position must be determined to intersect the first one. To do that, repeat the process of tuning in a VOR station, except it must be a different station.

Find a station off either side of the line of position that you've drawn. The best station will be close to a right angle from the first line; the angle of the intersection between the first and second lines of position should be as close to 90° as is practical. If the second station is only 45° or less to one side, the plotted point won't be as accurate as if determined from a station at a more angular position to the first line of position.

Redo the steps: Tune in the second station, rotate the OBS until the CDI is centered with a FROM indication, notice what radial is shown on the OBS, and then draw that line outbound from the station along the indicated radial. That is the second line of position. The two lines of position cross at your location, or more correctly called the *point of position*. You're found.

This process is easy if two VOR receivers are installed in the airplane, but it can be done with a single VOR receiver. If you have only one VOR, it stands to reason that the airplane will move a little bit in the time it takes to draw the first line and retune to the second station and determine the second line of position. But at typical lightplane speeds, this small inaccuracy is imperceptible if you chose stations that are far enough away.

Try to pick out stations that are at least 30–40 miles away—the farther, the better, if reception is strong. Radials are crossed very quickly when the airplane is near a station that is perpendicular to the flightpath. The second line of position might change dramatically in only a few moments and produce a very deceiving intersection with the first line.

THE DF STEER

Pilots get lost for many reasons, and poor weather is one of the major reasons. The day might come flying cross-country that the weather starts going down unexpectedly. If the ceiling lowers too much, you might have to fly too low to receive a VOR station; however, you might be able to raise a flight service station (FSS) or some other ATC facility by using the communications radio.

Many FSSs are equipped with a direction finder (DF) device. DFs have found more than a few wayward aviators. The DF console in the FSS will have a display that looks like a very large compass rose; it will be very similar to, though larger than, the display head of an airplane's ADF. A needle centered within the compass rose of the DF swings to point toward the source of an incoming radio transmission.

If contact is established with an FSS, ask for a DF steer toward that location if no other problem, such as a low fuel state, is an issue. The specialist at the FSS might request a frequency change for the steer; otherwise, the first frequency will be used. You'll be asked to make a rather long transmission while the specialist watches the needle on the DF console. The FSS specialist will determine the position of the airplane (the transmitting radio) relative to the DF's antenna, which is usually on the roof of the FSS building or very nearby. By knowing where you are in relation to the location of the FSS, the specialist can give you a heading to fly toward the DF antenna, or more aptly put, toward the FSS.

Since most FSSs are on airports, an FSS makes a fine place to head toward. The specialist will likely amend the heading instructions with minor corrections from time to time to factor in any wind that is blowing the airplane off the first direct course. Depending upon the airplane's altitude and therefore the radio communications range from the FSS, the DF steer might last for up to an hour depending upon the distance to be flown.

It's quite possible that during the steer you might get reoriented and be able to request that the FSS discontinue the steer. Keep in mind that the DF equipment can only indicate the airplane's line of position relative to the DF antenna. This device does not determine distance from the antenna site. So as the steer goes on, don't be surprised if the specialist asks questions about the terrain or manmade features underneath you. That is one of the few ways he or she can determine how far you are from the DF receiver.

Before the FAA's consolidation efforts to create large automated facilities, many more smaller FSSs were around. About eight FSSs used to be within a range of 150 miles of Columbus, Ohio. Now it's three. If the specialist talking to you gets on the telephone with other stations that might be within range of your transmissions, your location can be pinpointed quickly. If another FSS with DF equipment can hear you, a specialist there can also take a DF bearing. Then the two stations can quickly calculate the intersecting point of the two lines of position that are known by using their respective DFs. When that is done, they know your point of position, which can then be relayed to you. Unfortunately, with the demise of so many FSSs, you might be within range of only one at a time, unless your altitude is fairly high.

The DF steer has been around for decades and predates transponders and primary radar. It can be a tremendous aid for a lost pilot. The only negative is the fact that the airplane must be within line-of-sight radio-range of the station because a DF steer depends upon the ability of the ground station to receive the transceiver's transmissions, and the steer also depends upon the ability of ground personnel and a pilot to talk to each other.

USING LORAN OR GPS

The advent of GPS has caused some writers to predict the demise of the VOR-based airway systems in use since the 1950s. The newer forms of electronic navigation, embodied in loran and especially GPS, do things that weren't possible or were available only at a very high cost by using VOR alone.

I predict that loran will become an outdated mammoth in a short time. The cost of maintaining the ground transmitter stations is high, and the U.S. Coast Guard is presently considering shutting down the entire system. About 10 years ago, everyone was praising the capabilities and the information derived from loran, which had been around for decades as a system of marine navigation, for which it was originally developed. GPS provides the cockpit with the same data and more.

GPS uses a system of 24 satellites for military navigation. It doesn't cost a penny more to make the GPS network available for civilian use, so there isn't much point in spending the money to maintain the expensive loran stations. Ships, aircraft, tanks, and even hikers can navigate with GPS. Perhaps the pundits are visionary, and the government will seek additional cost savings by eliminating the VOR system as GPS becomes more popular, and everyone in aviation gets accustomed to it.

If you have a Loran or GPS receiver, you should never get lost if the unit is working or, in the case of loran, if the signal transmission system is functional. Both receivers operate very similarly from a pilot's perspective, but technically the units are very different. Each has the ability to determine present position at the push of a button. The position will be displayed in latitude and longitude coordinates. A pilot reads a sectional chart and plots the aircraft position by determining the location of the coordinates on the chart.

GETTING FOUND

The foible of these modern electronics will come as pilots become too dependent upon them, and further lose their skills at basic, dead reckoning navigation. No matter how many gizmos are in a cockpit, be a complete professional. Learn how to use them, and use them for all that they are worth, but also be prepared for the day when either a gadget or an electrical system that powers them fails and you have to revert to the time-honored way of flying a path from point A to point B—dead reckoning and pilotage.

6
Control systems emergencies

WHEN WE LEARNED TO FLY, WE WERE TAUGHT TO CONTROL THE AIRPLANE by means of manipulating flight controls and engine controls. The flight controls are the ailerons, elevator, rudder, trim, and, on most airplanes, flaps. Engine controls in primary trainers are generally limited to the throttle and mixture; more complex aircraft have a propeller control, too. Complex piston-powered single-engine aircraft have retractable landing gear.

If any control device fails, the pilot is faced with an emergency of varying degrees of severity. Given his or her wishes, any pilot would rather have the flaps on a light-plane fail to come down rather than lose control of the elevator. But whichever luck you happen to draw, you need to be prepared to deal with it. Some of these failures can have dire consequences for the ill-trained or unprepared. With proper training, virtually all of the malfunctions are manageable, and the odds favor the airplane being landed without devastating injury to it or its occupants.

Don't hesitate to declare an emergency if any part of the control system fails. If you're working an ATC facility at the time, immediately tell the controller what is going on, but recall that control of the airplane is the first priority. If you are flying VFR and not under any ATC control, you might want to consider getting in touch with a controller as soon as feasible. Landings with any measurable lack of control are risky, and, very candidly, an accident of some severity is likely.

I'd rather have an accident at a large, controlled airport for several reasons. (It isn't pleasant to muddle over these options and consequences, but they have to enter into whatever decision you make.) First, controlled airports probably have more than one runway, and crosswind landings should be avoided with most flight-control failures, which is subsequently detailed in this chapter. Second, controlled airports, particularly the large ones, are more likely to have fire and rescue personnel and equipment stationed right on the airport. The tower will know about the problem, and the rescue people will be ready to react immediately, probably following the airplane down the runway.

Lastly, large airports are usually associated with large cities, which have larger, better-equipped hospitals and perhaps specialized trauma centers close by. Studies have concluded that the chances of surviving serious injuries go up dramatically if a victim receives prompt treatment at a trauma center with medical staff trained and equipped to handle a life-threatening situation. This infamous "golden first hour" is more easily attained in a large metropolitan area rather than in a sparsely populated area. Allow yourself this edge if you can.

AILERONS

The ailerons serve to change the effective angle of attack of a portion of the wing, thereby either increasing or decreasing the lift produced by each wing. This change in lift causes the airplane to bank in one direction or the other. When we turn the control wheel to the left, or push the stick to the left, the aileron on the left wing is deflected upward, which decreases the angle of attack on the outer portion of the left wing, ahead of where that aileron is mounted. Simultaneously, the right aileron is deflected downward, which increases the angle of attack of the portion of the right wing ahead of that aileron; hence, the right wing produces more lift, and the left wing produces less lift. The right wing goes up, the left wing goes down, and the airplane is in a bank to the left.

When a bank is established, the airplane starts to turn, assuming that the pilot is not crosscontrolling by applying rudder pressure opposite to the direction of bank. This turn is a product of lift acting perpendicular to the wings and "pulling" the airplane around in a turn in the direction of the bank. When we lower the left wing, we're also raising the right wing.

The right aileron, deflected downward into the relative wind, produces drag as it sticks down into the oncoming stream of air. Because the right aileron is producing a lift increase, the induced drag that is a by-product of lift increases with the increase in lift. Conversely, the aileron on the left side is deflected upward, which reduces the angle of attack, and therefore the lift, acting upon the left wing. Because leftside lift is being reduced, leftside induced drag is also being reduced.

All of these factors combine to result in "adverse yaw," which is the effect of the increased drag on the upward wing when the airplane is in a bank. When we want to turn left, we raise the right wing, and the drag acting on that wing wants to yaw the airplane to the right. But we want to turn left. To counteract the adverse yaw, we apply a little left rudder pressure, and the yaw inputs equalize, allowing the airplane to smoothly enter a left bank and left turn. Primary training covered this "coordinated-turn entry," but many pilots did not learn the real reason for using rudder to enter and recover from turns.

The control wheel is attached to cables in most lightplanes which in turn run out through the wings. These cables then attach to bellcranks, which are attached to the ailerons, raising or lowering an aileron in response to the input from the wheel in the cockpit. There are lots of opportunities for failure in this mechanical system, but, thankfully, such problems are rare. During each 100-hour or annual inspection, all cables and connections are thoroughly examined, and components are replaced or repaired as needed. Almost all pilots fly for an entire career without thinking about a failure in this system because manufacturers and mechanics routinely do a very good job of designing, manufacturing, and maintaining aircraft.

Aileron control failures are very rare because the amount of physical force put on the system is fairly light. You don't deflect an aileron very much to get the job of banking done, so there isn't much load put on the system, unless you're flying aerobatics.

If I had to lose control of a primary flight control—rudder, elevator, or aileron—I'd choose the elevator. But failure of the aileron system is not that much more difficult to deal with and be able to manage nearly normal flight; however, adaptations in how you approach flying the airplane have to be made. If an aileron jams in a deflected position, that's another story.

If the failure is a breakage or disconnection of the cables, or in a very few airplanes, the pushrods that connect the control wheel to each aileron, the ailerons will simply trim themselves in line with the trailing edge of the wing. You won't be able to use them to bank, but you can still turn the airplane, and in turning, you'll get some angle of bank.

When you can't deflect an aileron, turns must be made with the rudder. Try it sometime at a safe altitude, and you'll see that it's weird at first, but it does work. The turn entry will be uncoordinated and sloppy, accompanied by less than precise yawing. As the turn progresses, you'll have to constantly work your feet on the rudder pedals to keep the turn and the ensuing bank angle under control.

Make such turns gingerly to allow for the delayed action of rudder-pressure-producing bank to take effect. You don't want to overcontrol and allow precipitous bank angles to develop. Make the turns shallow and take your time, and you'll be able to turn all right. The rudder is the only means that you have to keep the wings level in between turns. Again, slight control pressures are the answer. Accept the fact that control will be imprecise, and concentrate on being as smooth and gentle as possible.

The rudder will be used for several things. It's your only control for entering, maintaining, and recovering from turns. Allow plenty of time for recovery from a turn;

therefore, keep the pedal pressures light. During a turn, especially if you need to change heading more than about 45° or so, be ready to use opposite rudder to keep the angle of bank from becoming too steep. Naturally, use rudder into the direction of the turn if the bank shallows out to the point where there's little turning action.

Landing presents a new set of considerations. The "control power" that is produced by any control surface is, in part, a function of airspeed. The faster the air is flowing over the control surface, the more power and leverage that surface has to act upon the airplane. So, when you reduce airspeed, every control surface loses some of its control authority. That is why the controls get sloppy in slow flight and you sometimes have to deflect them to the full extent of the mechanical stops to produce a desired result when flying very slowly. The control harmony designed into every airplane is a compromise. If the controls were crisp in slow flight, they'd be so twitchy at cruise and faster airspeeds that the airplane couldn't be flown by the average pilot, and it wouldn't meet the certification standards.

So, when you slow down to approach and land, be ready for the decreased control power available from the rudder and the resulting decline in your ability to quickly respond to any banking of the wings. If you see a problem developing during the approach, you shouldn't try to slow down anymore; in fact, you might have to actually increase the airspeed to keep things on an even keel.

It's far better to approach, and even land fast, than it would be to get so slow that you can't control the attitude of the wings and a wing dips that can't be raised with opposite rudder. Cartwheeling accidents are always very serious and most often fatal. You don't want to get a wing down, close to the ground, when your airspeed is so slow that you can't get it back up in time to prevent ground contact. If you have to land fast, you might have a smaller problem after you're on the ground, but at least you're on the ground in a level attitude. If you land near the approach end of the runway, there should be ample runway available to slow down enough and prevent any life-threatening accident.

A crosswind landing cannot be accepted when aileron deflection is uncontrollable because a wing cannot be lowered to maintain runway alignment: no crabbing. You have to land into the wind. That fact as much as any other will determine the airport that you select for landing—where the runway is nearly perfectly aligned with the surface wind. If there aren't any, use pilot judgment again to analyze the situation. Is there an airport where you can land across a runway, with sufficient room not to run into anything? Depending upon the strength of the wind, you might have to consider an off-airport landing into that strong wind. This dilemma has no black-and-white answers; what is the windspeed and availability of runways or other landing sites?

The failure might occur in a fashion that allows the pilot to have normal aileron control in one direction but not in the other: able to bank normally to the left but unable to use the ailerons to recover from that bank or bank to the right. If this situation presents itself, I'd prefer to not use the ailerons because in the excitement of the moment, it's quite possible to bank excessively in the direction where control is maintained. The bank might become too steep for a recovery by normal means; a whale of an opposite rudder input would be necessary to level the wings again. The airplane would be slithering all over the sky in an exaggerated slip while the pilot was trying to get the wings level. It would be better to forget using the ailerons and control the wing attitude with gentle rudder pressures as previously described.

About the only time that the ability to bank in one direction but not the other might be beneficial is if you absolutely had to accept a crosswind landing and the wind direction is from the side toward which you have aileron control.

Landing in a gusting crosswind with complete control capability requires constant adjustment of bank angle and rudder to remain aligned with the runway centerline on final approach, flare, and touchdown. I'll take a landing into the wind if the ailerons are ailing.

If the cable break affects only one aileron, things aren't so bad. You can still bank and recover from banks by using the good aileron. Control-wheel deflections will be made in the normal direction. Because only one of the ailerons is deflecting, expect some loss of control precision and a lag time before a control input has a desired result.

If an aileron jams in a deflected position, problems increase severalfold over losing the ability to deflect it. Because ailerons are mechanically interconnected, seldom will one jam without also deflecting the other in the opposite direction. You may try to cure the problem, but when you exert extraordinary amounts of force on the wheel, don't turn it in the direction of the preexisting bank. Sometimes a mechanical connection can be forced further into the direction in which it's jammed, but not the reverse. Only try to force the control wheel or stick *away* from the bank, not into it. It's not very likely that you can put enough force into the system to break a cable connecting the cockpit control to the jammed components.

Since you can't tell if the jamming is caused by the control cables, or the bellcrank, or even the hinge that attaches the aileron to the wing, this emergency is one of the few where there isn't much that can be done to cure it. Certain failures in airplanes aren't curable from inside the cockpit, and this is one of them. We all know that there is a level of risk associated with everything we do, even getting out of bed in the morning. Flying has a few of these perils, such as catastrophic structural failure of the airplane. A jammed aileron also comes close to this level of severity.

Depending upon how much the aileron is deflected when it jams, you might be able to control the airplane by using opposite rudder pressure. The airplane will be in a slip with the wings level and opposite rudder applied, but at least everything will be upright. Remember that control authority of the various control surfaces increases with airspeed. If the offending wing cannot be held level or close to level at cruise airspeed, perhaps slowing down would help. Slowing down will decrease the amount of leverage that the aileron can exert upon the wing, lessening the rolling moment. You might then be able to apply enough opposite rudder to maintain some semblance of control.

Landing with a jammed aileron will be a dicey affair at best. But unlike the situation just covered concerning total loss of aileron control, without jamming, a crosswind might help in this latter situation. It would simplify the procedure if a pilot can select a runway where the crosswind is blowing from the direction in which the wings want to bank. Because you would normally bank into the wind, the jammed aileron might help. Your application of opposite rudder and flying the final approach in a slip would be closer to normal than otherwise. Your feet will be busy as you use the rudder to control both bank and yaw to keep the airplane over the runway and properly aligned for touchdown.

Airplanes aren't tested with these failures. You'll be an experimental test pilot doing something for the first time without an army of engineers to offer suggestions and predictions. The most help available will be from yourself. Keep your cool. If you can get the airplane on the ground in a wings-level attitude, your chances of survival go way up. Impact with a ground object is a natural concern, especially immediately after touchdown at high speed. The airplane might be damaged, but you'll probably be okay. Impact forces increase and decrease with corresponding changes in speed at the time of impact. The key is to touch down with the wings as level as possible and have time to slow down before hitting anything.

RUDDER FAILURE

The rudder pedals in the cockpit are connected to the rudder in the same manner as the ailerons, generally by means of cables that run under the cockpit floor, through the fuselage, and then either out each side of the rear of the fuselage to each side of the rudder or to a bellcrank located inside the tail assembly. A very few lightplanes use push-pull tubes to accomplish the mechanical connection. Regardless of the connection method, the rudder rarely suffers the same failure modes as the ailerons. A cable can break, denying the pilot any control over rudder deflection; the rudder can jam, either in trim with the vertical stabilizer or deflected to either side.

The most likely failure, and it is very rare, is that a cable will break and the pilot can't deflect the rudder in the direction of the side where the break occurred. You could still apply normal rudder pressure and move the rudder toward the side where the cable is intact, but you couldn't use normal control to correct. This isn't as bad as the case where you can only input aileron control to just one side. The entire fuselage serves as a vertical stabilizer in addition to the fin on the tail. Airplanes tend to recover from a yaw much more quickly, and to a better degree, than coming out of a bank on their own.

If you lose total rudder control, you'll need to handle that problem in a manner very much like the loss of aileron control. Turns can be made only by using the ailerons, and you'll have to accept the decrease in precision that comes with the inability to coordinate turn entries and exits. Adverse yaw will cause some slipping that can't be avoided. Banks ought to be kept from shallow to medium, so the adverse yaw's effect is minimized, both entering and recovering from the turns.

Be extra careful about airspeed control. Hopefully all pilots have been taught that when a wing banks, or "falls off" during a stall, it should be brought back up again with opposite rudder, not aileron, or with coordinated inputs of aileron and rudder, depending upon the airplane. Because you don't have rudder control, you can't get a wing back up if the airplane stalls. Attempting to use the aileron can make the situation that much worse. Don't stall or even get close to it when you have any kind of control problem, especially a rudder failure.

Allow plenty of room to maneuver when close to the airport and in the traffic area. Widen the pattern segments so you don't need to make precise turns . . . because you can't. Fly a longer than normal final approach to have plenty of time to line up with the runway.

Landing won't be easy, and it needs to be done into the wind. Any crosswind landing depends upon the proper use of rudder and ailerons for effective crosswind correction. This is true during the final approach and while flaring and touching down. Make the landing into the wind to reduce the severity of the emergency with which you're confronted.

You should know whether the airplane that you fly, assuming that it has tricycle landing gear, has a nosewheel steering arrangement that disengages when the nosewheel extends after takeoff. Some airplanes, predominantly Cessnas, are designed this way. Others, notably Pipers, have a system that is a hard connection between the rudder pedals and the nosewheel. In this latter type, the nosewheel is steering in response to rudder pedal pressures even while the airplane is in flight.

With that in mind, you realize the possibility of jamming the rudder control if the nosewheel steering is damaged. That can happen during a poorly executed crosswind landing where the airplane is allowed to contact the runway with the nosewheel cocked to one side. Hitting a chuck hole or other obstruction during takeoff can also damage the nosewheel mechanism and, in turn, jam the rudder control. If you have an airplane with the direct connection type of nosewheel steering, be especially careful and vigilant for damage to it.

You have to deal with a jammed rudder much the same as a jammed aileron. Depending upon the degree of deflection, you might be "in a vise that can't be loosened" if the rudder is so far over to one side that you can't overcome its effects by banking the wings. This risk is so small that it's almost statistically insignificant, and we accept the risk as a part of flying.

A close friend spent most of his career as an experimental test pilot for a major manufacturer of military aircraft. During a flight in a Navy jet trainer, a major structural failure in the tail jammed the rudder and negated almost all rudder-control authority. He could keep control of the airplane only above about 200 knots, and when he tried to slow below that figure, the airplane went out of control. He thought for a few moments and had several conversations with company engineers about what to do. He was advised to find unpopulated terrain and eject, but he was the pilot in command and rejected that option.

The situation improved markedly when he lowered the landing gear. He surmised that the extra vertical stabilizing effect of the landing gear extended into the wind made the difference that enabled him to get the airplane slowed a little bit more. He landed at a nearby air force base, touching down at over 200 knots; the tires blew and the brakes were turned to scrap. The best part is nobody was hurt, and he's still around to tell me these stories and a few more just as hair raising. I pass this along for what you might make of it, if you fly a retractable. Lowering the gear might help to partially off-set the effects of a jammed rudder.

My friend's controllability problems weren't limited to rudder alone. He also had severe problems with the elevator, and a major portion of all tail surfaces was lost. But if you have normal elevator control, remember the leverage that a jammed rudder is putting on the fuselage, and remember that the tendency to enter a roll or turn might be reduced if you can slow down. Control authority is a function of many variables, and airspeed is important among them. If you can reduce the airspeed, the power of a de-flected control surface declines.

THE ELEVATOR

The elevator of an airplane is used to control pitch attitude, which most pilots equate with raising and lowering the nose attitude. The elevator is also connected to the con-trol wheel or stick by cables or push-pull tubes. Cables or tubes are connected to a bell-crank that moves the elevator up and down. Elevator failure modes can be the same as aileron and rudder failures. You might lose total control, where movement of the wheel produces no effect because of broken cables; you might have control movement in one direction and not the other; or the control surface might become jammed.

You can deal with almost all of these. The one event that might not be recoverable would entail an elevator jammed in a downward deflection, which could produce a dive that can't be overcome. Because large downward elevator movements are almost never used outside of aerobatic flight, this risk is very small in normal operations.

If you have an elevator failure, you have an ace in your pocket that you don't have with rudder and aileron failures in most lightplanes. That ace is the presence of a trim tab (Fig. 6-1), or on planes with a stabilator, an antiservo tab (Fig. 6-2). Both work in the same manner, as far as the pilot is concerned, from the viewpoint of con-trolling the airplane in normal flight. Regardless of which mode of failure besets the elevator, the trim can be used as a very small control surface, and it can restore some measure of pitch control. The trim tab (from here on we won't restate that some air-planes have antiservo tabs because you'll use them in nearly the same manner in these emergencies) has separate cables operating it. So if your problem is associated with a failure in the cables connecting the wheel or stick to the elevator, you'll still have full trim control.

A few airplanes gain trimming control by moving the entire horizontal stabilizer, not by altering the position of the elevator. Notable among these designs are the Mooney and Piper Cub series and the Cessna 180. Even in these airplanes, you can still probably trim after an elevator control failure.

Most elevator control problems are a product of one of two things. First, the cables can break or get jammed in their routing from the cockpit to the tail. Second, some-thing behind the instrument panel can get out of place and jam the tube that goes into the panel from the wheel, blocking movement of the wheel in and out. From the acci-dent reports that I've read, the second cause is more common.

Fig. 6-1. *The elevator trim tab on a conventional tail.*

Fig. 6-2. *An antiservo tab on a stabilator, or flying tail.*

Using the trim to control pitch is tricky because you might have to reverse the normal inputs that you're used to. To understand this, you have to get a grip on how the trim works. The trim tab is a control surface that exerts force to move the elevator, which acts upon the airplane as a whole. If you need nose-up trim during normal flight, the elevator needs to move slightly upward, which will raise the nose a little. To do that, the trim tab moves *downward*, which in turn forces the elevator *upward*, producing the desired trim (Fig. 6-3).

The next time that you go to the airport, look at the tail of your airplane. Visualize what we're saying by running the trim to its extremes in both directions. Imagine the airflow over the trim tab, and see what effect that flow over a deflected trim tab will have upon the elevator. From that, you can then see what the effect will be upon the elevator, which in normal flight alters the pitch attitude of the airplane.

Fig. 6-3. *A conventional trim tab in the full nose-up position.*

Most elevator failures that don't result from a jammed control wheel come from a broken control cable. Seldom do both cables break; so you will probably have normal control of the elevator in one direction and no control at all in the other. Again, the trim system saves the day.

You'll quickly figure out which direction of elevator travel is affected by the cable break. You can restore the ability to pitch the nose in both directions by aggressively trimming in the direction in which the control wheel has no effect and then overcoming that trim force with the control wheel. Let's assume that the up-elevator cable broke. You can apply normal down force with the wheel, but you can't raise the nose.

Trim nose-up very aggressively, and counteract the control force with nose-down pressure on the wheel. When you need to lower the nose, just push harder on the wheel. If your need is to raise the nose, release some of the back pressure that you've been holding, and the trim will get the nose up. Obviously, the reverse is in order if the break occurs in the cable that normally gives down-elevator movement.

Trim hard, maybe even to the stop. Your arms will ache from overcoming the high trim forces, but you need these forces to be able to get the nose to pitch in the direction in which you've lost control. If you need to get the nose up or down in a hurry, you don't want to fool with the trim. Releasing pressure on the wheel will "pop" the nose in the direction you need it to pitch, but only if you have a lot of trim established.

If both elevator connections have broken and the wheel is a wet noodle in your hands, you can regain quite a bit of elevator authority by aggressively using the trim tab in the *NORMAL* manner. Trim up to get the nose up; trim down to get the nose down. This type of elevator failure is maybe the least serious of the three primary control surfaces: ailerons, rudder, and elevator. You have the ability to move the elevator, but the ability is by abnormal means. To get the changes in pitch attitude that you need, you'll have to roll the trim wheel or turn the trim crank quite a bit, but you've still got the means to move the elevator. Airplanes have been landed successfully using trim alone with no resulting accident.

I don't advise it for everyone, but you might want to fly with an instructor and try a landing using trim by itself. Be careful, and don't do it unless you and the instructor are very current in the airplane and the instructor is ready to take over normal control in an instant. Obviously use extra caution, use a long runway, and avoid windy days. I'd probably not practice the maneuver in a tailwheel airplane, even though I have well over 1,000 hours in the type and have logged hundreds of landings on conventional gear. Tailwheel planes are less tolerant of sloppy landings, and any landing with trim alone won't be pretty, but it'll more than likely be successful in a tricycle-gear airplane.

If the elevator jams in a deflected position, naturally your problem is different and potentially worse than breaking a cable, which allows the elevator to respond normally to trim inputs. When the elevator jams, you still have one big advantage that you don't generally have with the other primary control surfaces in lightplanes, and that is the presence of the trim tab. Few lightplanes have a rudder trim, and some that do use a bungee arrangement to relieve the pressure of holding rudder-pedal pressure without actually having a trim tab attached to the rudder. But all airplanes have a method of actually trimming either the elevator or the horizontal stabilizer, and that makes all the difference in the world.

Before you can use a trim tab as a miniature primary control surface, you have to revisualize how it normally works. Remember that it moves opposite to the direction that you want the elevator to move to produce the desired trimming effect. If you need nose-up trim in normal flight, the elevator needs to go up too. To do that, the trim tab goes *down* and pushes the elevator up, which results in the nose-up pitch attitude. When you need nose-down trim, everything works in reverse, and the trim tab goes *up* (Fig. 6-4).

Fig. 6-4. *A conventional trim tab in the full nose-down position.*

Unfortunately in the circumstance of a jammed elevator, you have to deal with a trim control in the cockpit that indicates either nose-up trim or nose-down trim. When the elevator is no longer movable, you have to resort to using the trim tab as the primary control surface. Doing so will resolve some of the lack of pitch control, but might not allow you to fly in a somewhat-normal fashion. It all depends on the position of the jammed elevator. If it's deflected near its limits of travel, you might not be able to regain control with the trim tab; but if it's jammed in the neutral position, or nearly so, you can fly with the trim tab.

Since the cockpit control displays the direction to move the trim control to achieve either nose-up or nose-down trim in normal flight, you have to *REVERSE* the direction of trim tab movement when you're using the trim tab as a primary control surface. When the elevator is jammed, it simply becomes an extension of the horizontal stabilizer, and the trim tab is the only control surface you're left with. Then if you want nose up, you need to move the actual trim tab up. Remember that moving it up in normal flight would produce nose-down trim.

Flying with reversed controls is seldom successful, and is the cause, now and then, of an accident when an airplane comes out of maintenance. When this happens, mechanics generally hook up the aileron controls backwards, and the unsuspecting pilot is in for a wild ride. But if you are trying to use trim as a "backward" elevator, at least you know what to expect in terms of control input. That might not prevent the occasional mental lapse, which might cause you to put in the wrong trim movement, but as soon as you see what's happening, you should realize the mistake and be able to deal with it.

Again, you have to recall that control authority is, to some measure, a function of airspeed. The trim tab is minuscule in area compared to the elevator, so if you're controlling primary pitch using the trim tab alone when it can't move the elevator because the elevator is jammed, you'll have very little control authority. Maybe an increase in airspeed can help this deficiency in control power from the trim tab if the elevator is jammed in the neutral position, and then maybe you won't be able to get enough increase in speed to matter. If the jam happened with the elevator deflected, an increase in airspeed will be counterproductive because the elevator is exerting force upon the airplane, and the jammed elevator's leverage only increases as airspeed does.

In all of these areas, the pilot who is suffering from the effects of these failures is an experimental test pilot, perhaps trying techniques for the very first time for that particular aircraft type. There are no guarantees of what will or won't work.

If you fly the type of airplane in which normal trim effect is generated by moving the entire horizontal stabilizer, you would control the pitch attitude with a jammed elevator by *NORMAL* trim inputs. In these airplanes, there is no trim tab, so there is no reversal of its final effect on the control force put upon the whole airplane. Nose-up trim produces a downward movement of the leading edge of the stabilizer, which "cocks" the entire stabilizer upward. If you have a jammed elevator in this type of airplane, the horizontal stabilizer becomes the primary method of pitch control. You still want it to move in the same direction as in normal flight to accomplish the same control effect.

That is only one of many reasons why every pilot needs to know the airplane. The pilot with the professional attitude knows more about the airplane than just how to fly it without bending it. When a pilot flies airplanes that require a type rating, which comprise all jets and all airplanes with a maximum gross weight over 12,500 pounds, the training for the rating and the oral and flight tests cover and require in-depth knowledge of the aircraft systems in addition to acquiring and demonstrating the ability to fly. Unfortunately, lightplane pilots aren't tested to see if they know anything about a different airplane.

If you've flown a Cessna 172 and then get into a Mooney, you should know of the difference in how the two are trimmed. Obviously, you know that the Mooney has a retractable landing gear and the 172 doesn't, but that is far from the end of the disparities between them. Study the POH for any airplane you fly, and follow its dictates and suggestions. But more than that, study the airplane; talk to your mechanic about it. Learn its systems and idiosyncrasies if you want to be really safe in it.

There is one last way to control pitch without a functioning elevator. Your primary instructor probably showed you the relationship between power settings and pitch attitude, given no change in trim. If the elevator is stuck in the neutral position, or close to it, you might want to try power changes as a way to modulate pitch attitude. Primarily, increasing power will raise the nose, while decreasing it will allow the nose to drop.

This effect of power settings on pitch attitude is a product of the fact that airplanes seek to remain at their trimmed airspeeds. When you reduce power, the only way for the airplane to remain at the same airspeed is for the nose to drop and for the plane to descend. Conversely, when the power is increased, airspeed will also increase, unless the nose is raised. If nothing else works well to control the airplane without elevator function, remember these effects that power changes will have on the nose attitude.

Flaps also affect pitch attitude. Extended flaps increase the downwash off the wing and alter the airflow over the tail. Particularly in Cessna singles, flap application will pitch the nose quite a bit. In Piper's Cherokee series, once the airplane is in trim, the nose drops successively farther with increasing flap application.

When you're flying an airplane with an elevator failure, avoid the use of flaps except in rare circumstances. Adding flaps will change the pitch attitude, and if your elevator is useless, that might be fatal. If the failure is such that the pitch change is beneficial, then add flaps very slowly, maybe only a degree or two at a time, and see what the effect is. If it's positive, great. If not, you've got time to reverse the flap input before you totally lose control.

This is just one more reason to know your airplane, how it flies, and to experiment with it under normal control for the time when this knowledge might save your life. Know what flap application does, how much the effect is, and how rapidly the pitch change builds in the airplane that you fly.

TRIM FAILURE

Since the trim tab isn't a primary control surface, it wasn't included in the hierarchy of control system failures that ranked elevator failure as perhaps the easiest to cope with. Certainly, if any control surface has to suffer a problem, then a trim-system problem is the least severe of all. Unless the trim tab jams in an extremely deflected position, controlling the airplane should not be a herculean event.

When I was an active flight instructor teaching primary students, I did not stress the use of trim to the extent that most flight instructors do nowadays. I learned to fly in an Aeronca Champ, and I can't remember ever being taught to trim the airplane, except when we started dual cross-countries. My first instructor was of the opinion that a student learned the feel of the airplane and the various control pressures necessary to produce a given result throughout the flight envelope of the airplane much better if the trim remained at the setting for normal cruise.

That worked well in the Champ because its loading envelope and airspeed range were both quite narrow. Even in a Cessna 150, control pressures for climb, descent, and glide don't build to excessive levels if the trim is left at the cruise setting. Because I learned this way, old habits are hard to break. But having been trained to accept reasonable control pressures as a part of everyday flying, I don't miss trim as much as a pilot who was taught to constantly trim away control pressures for every regime of flight.

When you fly faster airplanes, and particularly aircraft with wide loading envelopes, like a Cessna 210, A36 Bonanza, Piper Saratoga, and other heavier aircraft, trim becomes more important. The control pressures associated with an out-of-trim condition can get fairly heavy, especially if the airplane's center of gravity (CG) is near either the forward or aft limit. Some of the six-place lightplanes, like the Cessna 210 or 206, can be a real handful to properly flare for landing if they are flown with only the front seat(s) occupied and there is no baggage or other weight farther aft; a lot of trim will be necessary in those instances.

If a trim-tab cable breaks and disconnects the cockpit controller from the tab, the tab will just trail itself in line with the trailing edge of the elevator. This shouldn't be much of a real problem for a competent pilot, although your arm might ache some from the force you have to apply to flare and land. If the failure is a jammed tab, the forces to control the airplane will be very high because those forces will be working against the trim setting established by the jammed tab. The forces should still be within the capability of the average pilot, but you might huff and puff a little.

If you have to fly an airplane with a jammed trim tab, be ready for the angle of pitch attitude to change much faster when you release the pressure that you're holding against the trim setting than it would from normal control inputs. This is probably the biggest danger associated with flying an airplane under these conditions. The nose will pop up or down, depending on how the trim is jammed, when you release the opposite pressure. Because you eventually have to land the crippled aircraft, prepare yourself for this effect and release any opposite pressure carefully, and be ready to counteract any undesired pitch change immediately.

For this scenario, there isn't any difference in what the pilot must do if the airplane has a trim tab, antiservo tab, or if it's of the variety where movement of the horizontal stabilizer accomplishes normal trim. The airplane will still be out of trim for some flight regime or another, and the pilot just has to be ready for increased control pressures and rapid pitch changes when pressure is released.

WING FLAPS

We started to see the general use of wing flaps on lightplanes right after World War II. Piper put them on the Pacer and all subsequent designs. Cessna began equipping its airplanes with flaps starting with the Cessna 140 and 170. By 1950, virtually all of the new designs coming out of airplane factories had flaps.

Flaps serve two purposes. They increase the angle of attack of the wing, and in some installations, they move rearward on rollers as they extend, which increases the gross area of the wing as well as adding to the angle of attack; hence, the wing produces more lift. Recall your basic knowledge of aerodynamics, and remember that the process of producing lift also generates induced drag. As the pilot extends flaps, the totality of the drag acting upon the airplane also goes up, so flaps produce both lift and drag.

Most general aviation airplanes have flaps attached to only the trailing edge of the wing. There is no conventional, factory-built lightplane of which I'm aware that has leading-edge flaps similar to those used on heavy aircraft to increase the area and camber of the wings, allowing a wing to grossly change its shape. Thereby, the same wing can be designed to function at slow airspeeds during takeoff and landing and also function at fast airspeeds. Some lightplanes, such as the Stinson, Helio, and some European machines, have either leading-edge slots or slats.

Slots in the leading edge allow the airflow over the outer portion of the wing to remain below the critical angle of attack after the inner portion is stalled. If there is a Stinson 108 series aircraft on your airport, look at its leading edge ahead of the ailerons. By letting the airflow continue unstalled over that section of the wing, aileron control is improved during stalls, and the stall characteristics of the wing are far more benign than would be the case with the same wing if the slots weren't there.

Slats are movable panels that slide forward and sometimes down as airspeed decreases. In lightplane installations, most slats are automatic, having been installed with springs that exert a constant pressure to extend them out from the leading edge. They are extended until there is sufficient airflow pushing them back in, working against the springs. When the airplane is slowed for approach and landing, the springs overpower the lessened airflow and extend the slats again. Slats can accomplish two results:

- Increase the wing's shape and area, producing more lift.
- A slotting effect that keeps airflow over some portion of the wing after other portions are stalled.

By far the more popular and numerous lightplanes in the general aviation fleet have only trailing-edge wing flaps, neither slots nor slats. In typical installations, wing flaps can be extended anywhere from 30 to 40° downward from the chordline of the wing. As designed by the engineers, lightplane flaps usually produce most of their extra lift in the first 20° or so of extension; putting them out farther than 20° adds lots more drag but little if any additional lift.

Flaps can be extended for takeoff if the pilot needs to lift off the ground at a slower-than-normal airspeed. Circumstances when this is desirable include soft-field takeoffs and departures from short runways where there is no immediate obstacle at the end of the runway to clear during a climbout. If you use them for takeoff, pay attention to the POH's instructions because they will tell you how much flap extension will produce more lift without adding any punitive amounts of drag. Go beyond the recommended amount of flap extension, and you'll get counterproductive results because the added drag will prolong the takeoff run and dramatically reduce the airplane's ability to climb.

If you're faced with a short runway that has obstacles at the departure end, pay particular attention to the POH's instructions. Using any amount of flap extension will add to the airplane's total drag. There are many types of airplanes where using some small flap extension will enable you to break ground sooner on takeoff, but the drag penalty will lessen the angle of climb to the degree that the entire distance from the beginning of the takeoff run to clearing the obstacle will be longer using any flap extension than it would be if the flaps were left retracted. Even though the takeoff-run portion will be a little longer without any flap deflection, the better angle of climb will more than make up for the slight increase in ground run. Know your airplane and its POH.

When approaching to land, any amount of flap extension from none to full can be used in almost all lightplanes. Full-flap extension usually allows the airplane to be landed at the slowest possible speed, which is always desirable. But the added drag of full flaps steepens the approach angle and in some airplanes results in a very low nose attitude on final approach. When the nose is low, the pilot has to achieve more degrees of angular rotation of the "deck angle" of the airplane to flare properly and land in a tail-low attitude.

If you use full flaps during windy and gusty conditions, you are likely adding to control problems. When the air is moving rapidly and unsmoothly, you'll probably have some wind shear present, and you'll need to be able to increase the airspeed with power as you fly through the shear layers. The added drag of full-flap extension makes it more difficult for the engine power to quickly accelerate the airplane. When the wind is blowing, use full flaps with care, and perhaps don't use full extension unless you absolutely need to for a short runway or to clear obstacles on the approach.

Full-flap deflection can cause another problem if a meaningful crosswind is present. By using full flaps, you are adding to the surface area upon which the crosswind will react. Sometimes you can get into a condition where the use of full flaps will make the effects of a crosswind exceed the controllability of the airplane, when landing with little or no flap would be possible and probably much easier. In strong crosswinds, use as little flap extension as is consistent with the runway's length and the approach's freedom from obstacles.

Wing flaps can fail in three modes:

- Failure to extend
- Failure to retract
- Failure of a single flap to extend, which is called a split-flap condition

These possible failures are ranked in the order of the severity of the problem for the pilot.

If the flaps don't come down, that should be of no real consequence to any able pilot. All of us should have been trained in no-flap landings during primary training, and the procedure should be frequently practiced by all lightplane pilots. The only by-products of landing without flaps are the need for a slightly increased airspeed on final approach and recognizing that the approach angle will be shallower than with flaps. Also, the airplane will probably float more between the initial flare and touchdown. The landing rollout will be a little longer because the landing speed has increased slightly and the airplane is deprived of the aerodynamic drag that extended flaps normally provide during the landing roll. For those reasons, about the only operational consideration in a no-flap landing is to avoid short runways where the extra room for float and the longer landing roll isn't there.

It's also not very difficult to deal with extended flaps that won't retract unless you prematurely extended them and are flying an airplane with marginal engine power to overcome the increased drag. When Cessna changed the model 150 to the 152, the maximum flap extension was reduced from 40° on the 150 to only 30° on the 152. There had been some accidents where inexperienced or sloppy pilots encountered difficulty trying to outpower the drag effects of 40° of flap extension with the meager 100 horsepower that is optimally available from the 150's engine. In this day of litigation, Cessna probably did the wise thing for its interests in making this change. Too bad that we just didn't train pilots to control what they had because the 150 is an excellent short-field airplane with its 40° of flaps hanging out.

Apply the last half of your airplane's flap extension only when you need it and when you have the runway made. For one, I think it is poor practice to put the flaps all of the way down while still a long way out on the final. If the engine quits or if you need to make a go-around for any reason, you have to worry about getting the flaps retracted to either glide to the runway or climb normally. If they won't come up, then you've painted yourself into an unnecessary corner. Flaps should always be used to produce a desired result, not by rote or just because they are there. In most lightplanes, don't ever count on being able to make a go-around with full flaps extended; many airplanes simply can't do it. They don't have enough power to overcome the drag and either won't climb at all or the climb angle and rate are both meager.

The worst problem associated with flaps is the possibility of a split-flap condition. This will occur as you lower them and one flap goes down without its companion on the other side. Of course, try to retract the offending flap immediately; if it won't come up, then you have a problem—one very big rolling moment as the extended flap acts as an aileron, rolling the airplane in the direction of the clean wing and away from the wing with the extended flap. If you're sharp, you can handle this. Landing with a full split flap is a certification requirement for airplanes with flaps, so at least the factory's test pilots have done it successfully.

One of the ways to minimize a split flap is to extend flaps slowly. Then if a split condition develops, you can recognize it and stop any further flap extension and attempt a retraction. Obviously, the farther down, the greater the rolling moment and the harder it becomes to control the airplane. Because the flaps are always inboard of the ailerons, the outboard ailerons can exert more leverage on the wing and overpower the rolling moment of the single deployed flap.

If you're ever faced with this emergency, and *it is an emergency that should be formally declared*, don't attempt a crosswind landing unless there's absolutely no other choice. If you can land into the wind, you won't be too concerned with crosswind correction. Anytime you have any emergency, think what you can do to lessen the severity of the problem, and make it as easy on yourself as possible. Keep your speed up on final, so that the ailerons have plenty of control authority. In some airplanes, the extended flap might overpower the ailerons if you get too slow because the area of the flap is much larger than the counteracting ailerons.

LANDING GEAR FAILURE

Two types of problems are associated with landing gear:

- Miseries that can beset a fixed-gear system
- Problems that only affect a retractable-gear system

Fixed-gear concerns

Too little attention is paid by most pilots to the fixed landing gear underneath their airplanes. In primary training, we are all taught to examine the tires for damage and proper inflation during the preflight inspection. Good instructors show their students how to look at the brake lines to check for brake-fluid leaks. The best instructors teach students to look at the entire system: tires, lines, calipers, pads, and wheels plus the gear legs to which everything is mounted. Any of these components can break or otherwise fail and cause a real problem.

Today's modern lightplanes are normally equipped with wheel fairings, which in the old days we called wheel pants. These fairings enhance the appearance of the airplane as compared to its appearance with exposed bare tires. Fairings often help to streamline the airflow over the gear, reducing the drag that fixed wheels engender and therefore increasing cruise speeds a little. Exotic fairings for the gear legs, shock absorbers, and tires are approved for certain airplanes and measurably increase speeds. But the installation of wheel fairings has a dark side, too.

First, they hide most of the tire, often they cover up the brake caliper and pads, and usually you can't see much of the wheel. So preflighting the gear components gets much more difficult with wheel fairings installed. Only you can decide how thorough you want to be in inspecting your airplane before you put your life at stake. If you want to do it right, you have to preflight the fairing-equipped landing gear in steps, slightly pushing or pulling the airplane some so that you can look at all of the tire as it rotates and see other components when exposed.

Consider removing fairings in the winter if you are based in a cold climate or you'll be flying in a colder climate than usual. The clearance between the inside of the fairing and the tire is rather tight. An accumulation of snow or mud might build up inside the fairing during taxi and takeoff then freeze solid as you climb into air temperatures aloft that are below freezing. Chances are very high that this ice block won't melt during your descent, and you'll land with it. If the ice buildup is enough to seize the tire so that it can't rotate freely, that's the same as landing with the brakes fully applied and locked. Sometimes only one tire will freeze up if only that side of the airplane taxied through puddles or snow. Then you get the pleasure of landing with just one side frozen; you'll explore the weeds as soon as you land if that happens.

Other than a careful preflight inspection and repair or replacement of any suspect parts, there isn't much more that a pilot can do to protect a fixed-gear system from failure. The things that do go wrong are blown tires and locked brakes during takeoff and landing. When one of these occurs, it'll most probably happen to one side of the main gear but not both. The occurrence will result in a violent jerk toward the side with the problem because the friction on that side will increase tremendously. You can do two things to be prepared.

First, expect trouble at all turns in a flight. Don't get complacent as you flare to land. Most of the nonserious accidents in small airplanes happen during landing, including but certainly not limited to ground loops. Second, land in the center of the runway to take advantage of the most room available to deal with an airplane that wants to depart the pavement.

If you fly a low-wing airplane, pay attention during the preflight to the scissor joint that is a part of the main gear on almost every low-wing design. These are installed on the Piper Cherokee series and others. If the scissor joint fails in flight and separates, the lower part of the air-oil strut will probably fall out, away from the upper half into which it slides, taking the wheel and tire with it. That would leave you with no tire or wheel on that side; just the stub of the upper half of the strut will remain. Because the gear in a low-wing plane cannot be seen from the cockpit, you won't have any idea that the failure has happened until you touch down. Then you'd better hang on because the world will be going around in a big way during the ground loop.

Don't forget the nose gear in your preflight. It doesn't have a brake to lock up, but its tire can fail or the strut can break. Always check for proper strut inflation (as well as the tire), and have a mechanic bring the strut up to snuff if it's low. The nose gear installation is geometrically unstable, and that is why they're so easy to damage in poorly executed landings. Also check to be sure that the strut appears to be vertically going down from its mountings. If not, the strut or the mounting system might be bent.

The nose gear is all that's protecting the propeller, cowling, and engine from contacting the ground. Any prop strike should be justification for a complete engine teardown and inspection in accordance with the engine manufacturer's recommendations. Obviously, the propeller will need an expensive overhaul or a more costly replacement.

If you learn to land properly, you can lessen the wear and tear on the nose gear and also reduce the damage to the airplane if it fails. Learn to land a lightplane slowly with the tail down and preferably at or just above a stall. Too many pilots today fly onto the runway at a near-level attitude and then release back pressure on the wheel. The nose gear slams onto the runway and suffers the imposition of loads upon it that might exceed its design capability. Small airplanes are meant to be landed as slow as is consistent with the existing wind conditions. One of the many benefits of learning to fly a tailwheel airplane surrounds that lesson; if you land too fast in a tailwheel airplane only once, you'll bounce enough to get the message.

Retractable landing-gear concerns

Retractable landing gear has all the same potential for problems as fixed gear, except for the concerns surrounding fairings. Other possibilities have to be on the mind of any pilot who flies an airplane with retractable landing gear, such as partially or completely failing to retract or extend. A properly trained pilot knows how to inspect "retracs" and deals with whatever they dish out.

Allow me another couple of stories to bring out some points. A couple of years after I bought a Piper Comanche in 1984, I was on an extended final approach to Runway 9 Right at the Ohio State University Airport, where I kept the airplane. Traffic was heavy that day, and the controller was running a long pattern. The university's Agriculture College has a long pasture field off the west end of the runway. And west of the pastureland is a heavily traveled road; farther west is a major river that is about a mile or so from the approach end of Runway 9.

When I was about 3 or 4 miles out on final with the gear down, I heard a loud BANG, and the engine sounded like it was in a battleship. The noise was deafening. I perked up and started wondering if the engine was about to quit. The thought raced through my mind to retract the gear so that I could glide farther if the engine did call it a day, probably gliding over the river and road and, at worst, landing in the pasture if I didn't make it to the runway.

Then I remembered an old axiom. If the engine is running, the wings are still on the airplane, and if you're not on fire, leave good enough alone, and land. So I left the gear extended, the engine ran fine but loudly, and I landed without incident.

When I taxied off of the runway, sounding like a car with no muffler, I went over to the maintenance hangar, shut down, got out, and opened the cowling. I saw that the exhaust crossover pipe from one bank of cylinders to the muffler had broken, and the piece was lying in the bottom of the cowling. No wonder it sounded like there wasn't any muffler because there wasn't for one side of the engine.

When I looked at the piece of pipe in the bottom of the engine compartment, I realized that if I had raised the gear during the approach, the nosegear would probably have become jammed by the pipe lying over the retraction mechanism. I am certainly glad I left good enough alone.

The next misstep happened about four years later in the same airplane. I was going to fly to a city about 120 miles away to attend a court hearing, so I was dressed in a business suit and overcoat. The Comanche sits very low to the ground, and to get under the wings to properly preflight the gear, it takes a crawl or squat-step to get into a position where you can see the wheelwell. Naturally, I omitted that step to stay clean.

Everything went normally through the takeoff until I raised the gear. It went up partially, then the circuit breaker for the gear-motor circuit popped, and the retraction cycle stopped. I lowered the gear after waiting a moment for the breaker to cool and resetting it. The gear went down normally, and I had three green lights. By this time, I was about 15 or 20 miles out from the airport. Federal judges don't take kindly to lawyers being late for court, especially if the cause is something perceived to be so ridiculous as problems with flying your personal airplane.

So I decided to fly the last 100 miles with the gear down because the relatively fast gear-extended speed limit on a Comanche permits a reasonable cruise speed. The flight was uneventful after that, as was the landing. I taxied over to the FBO at the destination and got out. It only took a few seconds to see the bird droppings on the left main gear tire. When I was finished in town and back to the airport, I asked one of the line personnel at the FBO to look under the wing, into the wheel well. The attendant pulled out a bird's nest that had jammed the gear as it tried to retract. That was the last time I didn't preflight the wheel wells, regardless of how I was dressed.

Let's deal with the time when the gear doesn't retract. A failure to fully retract is different from the problem that might cause the gear to not even begin the folding cycle. If you select gear up and nothing happens, you have to come to a decision of whether you think the process ever began. Sometimes, as with the bird's nest, the gear will begin the retraction cycle and for some reason or another fail to complete it. Other times, the sequence won't get started.

If the retraction of the wheels never gets started, the problem might lie in either the electrical wiring from the gear switch, or in the hydraulics if the gear system is either hydraulic or hydromechanical. The indicator lights in the cockpit will have some sort of "gear unsafe" indication. Gear status is usually displayed on the cockpit panel by means of the normal green light or lights that indicate the gear is down and locked. Under normal conditions, the light or lights go blank while the gear is coming up, and then a light illuminates to indicate that the wheels are up and stowed.

If the green lights never go out, you might make a calculated judgment that the retraction process never began, depending upon exactly how the system works and the information in the airplane's POH. If you come to that conclusion, fly the pattern. If you're operating at a controlled field, ask the tower for permission to do a fly-by, and ask them to put the binoculars on your airplane and see if the gear is still hanging out. If it is, land, but use the technique described below for the time when you aren't sure whether the gear is extended or fully or partially retracted.

The next possibility is when the green lights go out when you pull the gear switch up, but the "up and locked" indication never comes on. Several possibilities can cause this. Maybe the gear started to retract and jammed somewhere in the cycle. Or the gear could be up but not locked and the sensor in the system failed to display the correct cockpit indication. Or the bulb in the "gear up" indicator is burned out.

If the gear is still hanging out of the wells, you should be able to sense this condition by the fact that the airplane won't reach normal cruise speed at the usual cruise power settings. You'll have to level off, set cruise power, and see. Of course, depending upon the cruise speeds of the airplane, the gear system might have almost finished its retraction sequence before the failure occurred and the amount of drag being produced by the almost-retracted gear isn't enough to affect the airspeed discernibly. Again, do a fly-by and ask for what the controllers or other people on the ground can see. Fly a low approach over the runway or near the tower if it's a controlled field. The airplane should be close enough to the person to whom you're talking so that he or she can properly examine the underside of the airplane. (Remember that safety and flying the airplane come first; for any observation maneuver, don't fly too slow, too low, or too close to anything.)

If you can't get this assistance, treat the problem as a gear-up situation and proceed as described below for gear-up landings. Or course, if you're flying a Cessna 210, Cardinal RG, 172RG, or 182RG, look out of the cabin side windows. You should be able to see what's going on.

Similar problems can arise when you try to lower the gear for landing at the end of a flight. Whenever you get a "lights out" indication, especially if your airplane has only one gear-down light, like a Comanche, check for a burned-out bulb. Spare panel indicator bulbs should be carried aboard any retractable-gear airplane. You will breathe a great sigh of relief if you're prepared with spare bulbs and find out that a dead bulb is the cause of your concern. Whether the uncertainty about the gear's position occurs during retraction or extension, a fly-by is still called for.

If there is any doubt about the gear's position, revert to the emergency extension procedure spelled out in the airplane's POH. This is no time to be reading the instructions for the first time. If you fly a retractable, you should know the emergency procedure by rote. Use it. If the gear does come down, in most airplanes you will see the normal indication on the panel for "gear down and locked." Even then, prepare for a gear collapse upon landing because some indicators will falsely show that the gear is locked when it isn't.

I handled a legal case a few years ago where a high-time pilot type-rated in a corporate jet was making one of his first flights in a retractable-gear airplane. He landed with the wheels up. He knew he had a problem but didn't know how to use the emergency gear-extension mechanism. Except for the genuine fright in his voice, it was very educational to listen to the tower tape. He flew around for about an hour while the controller made telephone contact with a mechanic who knew the airplane. The mechanic was telling the controller what instructions to relate to the pilot about using the emergency system. No matter how experienced you are in different airplanes, it's knowledge of the airplane that you're flying on any particular day that counts.

After this pilot's gear-up landing, the airplane was jacked up off its belly, and the mechanic who was on the telephone proceeded to extend the gear on the first try, using the emergency method. The airplane was towed in the normal manner on its wheels to the maintenance shop where it took tens of thousands of dollars to overhaul two engines and propellers and make the needed airframe repairs.

Once it's been determined or it's strongly suspected that the gear is not down and locked, you've got to prepare for a gear-up landing. There are some old tales about how to do it, and most don't make good sense to me. Some pilots are pathologically worried about damage to the airplane, and in so being, they advocate taking chances that involve a great degree of risk. One of these tales is to fly at a high altitude over the airport, kill the engine, and do a deadstick landing after using the starter motor to "tickle" the propeller horizontal. If the technique is successful, the prop or engine won't be damaged during the landing. If unsuccessful, you'll land short of the runway or beyond it and do far more damage to the airplane and risk injury to people in the process.

If I had to do a gear-up landing, I'd plan for a few things. I'd find a large airport where there are fire and rescue facilities available for the same reasons mentioned for a landing after a control-system failure. Gear-up landings seldom result in much damage to the airframe and even less often result in injury to the occupants. But if you have a choice of airports, why increase your risk anymore than is absolutely necessary?

I wouldn't worry about the propeller or the engine. If you have to do a gear-up landing, the damage will be covered by your aircraft hull insurance, unless there is some reason that the insurance isn't in force for that flight. Insurance protects our investment in the airplane and our personal liability exposure. If you have the proper amounts, limits, and kinds of insurance, and if you aren't violating the provisions and exclusions in your policy, let the insurance company worry about damage to the airplane. I'd rather land with the ability to use power normally and accept some damage to the engine and prop. You're going to be nervous and on edge about a gear-up landing anyhow, and there is no reason to add to the anxiety by trying to do a deadstick landing.

You have to decide whether to use flaps or leave them retracted. Unless the runway is very short, the answer to this question depends mostly on the type of airplane you're flying. It it's a low-wing plane, I'd leave the flaps up. By leaving them retracted, you do increase your touchdown speed by a small extent, and that increase in speed might cause some additional damage to the airframe. But in a gear-up landing, the flaps will most likely contact the runway. If they do, one might break off the trailing edge of the wing while the other remains attached. The airplane might skew, and you might lose directional control sliding down the runway, further increasing the potential for a more serious accident.

If you're flying a high-wing retractable, most probably a Cessna, go ahead and use the flaps as you would for a normal landing. They won't hit the ground and will allow you to land with as little forward speed as possible. Depending on the characteristics of the particular plane, you might use less than full flaps. In some airplanes, especially if they are heavily loaded, full flap extension can cause a very fast sink rate if you get the airspeed too slow on approach. That can, in turn, cause a high-impact landing if you don't add some power, fly out of the sink, and flare just right.

As you flare for the landing, reach down and turn off both the electrical system's master switch and the engine's magneto switches. You want to eliminate all electrical power as a possible source of ignition to reduce the chances of a fire if the landing ruptures a fuel tank or line.

When you land in either a low-wing or a high-wing plane, plan to touch down at the minimum possible forward speed. So doing will lessen damage to the airframe and the chances of any physical injury to the occupants because the forces of impact decrease exponentially with decreases in speed at the time of impact. Try also to accomplish a smooth touchdown, and don't bang the airplane onto the runway. Lastly, remember that without the support of the landing gear, the airplane will sit lower on the ground. Plan for this different visual perspective as you begin your flare and touchdown.

As soon as the airplane comes to a stop, get out fast. There is always the possibility, especially in a low-wing aircraft, that you could have ruptured a fuel tank, and a fire could be starting even if all of the switches were turned off before ground contact. There will be quite a sparkler show from the metal of the underside of the airplane sliding along the runway, and that is plenty to get a fire going. Treat the after-landing evacuation seriously, and don't dillydally. Get far enough away from the airplane that you are away from any hazard if the airplane does burn or if the fuel tanks explode. Then wait. The wait won't be long because gear-up landings tend to draw attention pretty quickly.

ENGINE CONTROL FAILURES

This section examines situations when either the throttle, mixture, or propeller controls let you down.

In typical single-engine lightplanes, each of these controls works by means of a simple cable that runs from the cockpit knob or lever, through the firewall, into the engine compartment, and finally attaching to some type of actuating arm at the rear or bottom of the engine. Sometimes the cables can break, and other failures involve a jam of the cable.

The throttle control

The cockpit throttle and its associated cable and hardware inside of the cowling can fail in two modes. A break in the connection can happen, or the cable can become jammed, prohibiting any further travel of the throttle. Both of these are serious.

If the cable breaks, it's probably due to the fact that the pilot was jockeying it with too much force and broke the terminal connection either at the cockpit end or at the carburetor or fuel injection system. There's no excuse for that. Even though the engineers design airplanes to take some abuse, why test their mettle? Cables corrode with age, and connections work loose. If you ever note any play in the throttle connections, have it looked at by a mechanic before further flight.

There is no way in these pages to predict the power setting of the engine at the time that the cable breaks. If it happens, the engine might roll back to idle or remain at whatever throttle setting it had at the time of the break. There is some chance that it could go to full power, but that's not as likely. If the break occurs as you advance power for takeoff, do whatever you have to do to shut down the engine and abort the takeoff. Turn off the mags, pull the mixture to idle cut off, maybe even turn off the fuel supply. You don't want to become airborne.

If a cable break occurs in flight, you're stuck with whatever the engine is going to do, and you can't control the power setting anymore, except to shut the engine down at the right time. If there isn't enough power left to maintain altitude, you've got a forced landing coming. If the engine is producing some power, your options increase as to where to land because your glide will be extended by the amount of power being produced. If I were caught in this jam, I wouldn't count on the engine continuing to run for any protracted time. I'd find a place to land as soon as possible.

Because you can't control the throttle, the only way you might have to accomplish a landing is to intentionally shut off the mags, pull the mixture, and shut off the fuel while still high above the landing site. Refer to chapter 2 concerning engine failure, because that's precisely what you have here. It's nearly impossible to land with the engine producing any meaningful amount of power, so you eventually have to shut it down.

There is a technique that might allow you some degree of control over the engine's power output. You could pull out the mixture control toward idle cut-off and bring the mixture so lean that the engine starts to quit running. But don't kill the engine; just get the mixture leaned to the point where it begins to quit. Then you could increase the mixture when you need to restore power, and lean it back again to reduce power. I would not recommend this for the faint of heart or the inexperienced pilot. It might result in work overload and cause more problems than it solves.

If the cable breaks while the engine is at full power, continue the climb, but increase your climb airspeed. In case the engine reverses output or quits altogether, you don't want the nose attitude excessively high. Fly at a cruise-climb attitude so you won't inadvertently stall if things go silent quickly. Fly to a landing site, which is probably the airport from which you just took off, and get ready for a forced landing. If you can't reduce the power, again your only option is to shut down the engine, or modulate its output with the mixture control as previously described, and make a power-off approach and landing.

The same techniques apply to dealing with a jammed cable. Except the engine will probably continue to run at whatever power it's producing at the time of the jam because the connections are still likely to be intact. Throttle cables are usually made of a two-piece cable. An outer cable is firmly affixed to the back of the throttle control and to the engine. This outer layer doesn't move but gives the system rigidity and provides a channel in which the inner cable moves back and forth.

A mechanic can clearly see the outer layer of the cable assembly during inspections but can't tell very much about the inner one, which actually does the movement and, hence, the control of the power setting. When you preflight your airplane before every trip, look at the cable connection at the engine. If you don't know what it looks like, have a mechanic show it to you. Be sure that it's attached. If you ever feel any binding or play in the throttle, don't fly again until the entire system is competently inspected.

When a throttle cable jams, you're stuck with the power then being produced. Don't try to make the airplane do something that it can't at that power setting, like climbing at reduced power. I've seen at least one accident resulting in the death of the pilot when it was strongly suspected that he had a throttle cable failure at low altitude and tried to climb with reduced power. From the crash kinetics, it looked like he stalled and did about a half-turn spin before impact. Had he pulled the mixture and shut off the mags and dealt with the situation as a power failure, he could have at least made ground contact in a level attitude when the chances of survival increase by a dramatic margin.

MIXTURE CONTROL FAILURES

An interruption in the pilot's ability to control the mixture is not nearly so disturbing in normal operations as is loss of throttle control. Mixture control failures are relatively rare because the mixture isn't changed as often as the throttle setting and because many pilots never lean the mixture during low-level flights.

The mixture control knob or lever in the cockpit is connected to the carburetor or fuel injection system via a two-piece cable, much the same as the throttle connection; therefore, the cable can become separated at either the cockpit or engine end, or it can jam and prevent further movement.

About the only time that a cable break or jam produces critical results is when the mixture is very lean or the control knob is pulled back to idle cutoff. Years ago there was a pilot examiner who, according to local folklore, made an applicant do the spot-landing portion of the flight test in a unique way. On the downwind leg, this examiner would tell the candidate to bring the power to idle, execute a power-off approach, and land near a predetermined spot on the runway. That's a good idea, and every certificated pilot should be able to do it.

What wasn't a good idea was that after the candidate reduced the throttle to idle, the examiner would then ceremoniously jerk the mixture to idle cutoff to try to simulate a failed engine. The objective was to let the applicant see, maybe for the first time, how much differently an airplane glides with no power versus an idling engine. One particular day the examiner might have been a little extra demonstrative in his jerk of the mixture control because he soon had about 3 feet of cable in the cockpit. He had broken it off at the engine end after the mixture control arm on the carburetor hit the idle cutoff. The student apparently passed the checkride because the only unusual ending to the flight was their having to call for a tow tug to get them off the runway. When you intentionally want to make your first approach and landing in a real glider, do it in a Schweizer, not a Cessna.

If the mixture control breaks or jams, you're probably going to have to finish the flight and land at whatever setting there was before the failure. Many pilots think that an engine is going to self-destruct if the mixture is reduced below full rich at less than 5,000 feet of altitude. Who knows where this myth originated, perhaps with old round engines before World War II. In modern engines, almost all POHs allow leaning at any altitude as long as the power is below 75 percent. Never assume this is the case for all airplanes. Always check the POH for the airplane that you are flying.

The reason for this power limitation has to do with engine cooling. When you apply full power to the modern lightplane engine, the mixture goes to extra rich. This setting sprays extra fuel into the cylinders, above that amount of fuel that can be burned during the power stroke, which therefore helps control temperatures in the combustion chamber. Once you reduce power below 75 percent, the need for this extra cooling disappears.

When the mixture control freezes at a given position, you need to use your judgment about how lean the mixture is. If you have an exhaust gas temperature (EGT) gauge, there's no mystery; you can read the temperatures. You goal is to keep the power, through slight reductions if necessary, to a point where maximum permissible EGT is not exceeded. If you don't have the instrument, you probably do your leaning by the old-time method of leaning until the engine gets a little rough, then enriching it a little until the roughness smooths out.

If you've got a broken or jammed mixture control, do the same thing as if you had an EGT. Keep the power to the place that the engine runs smoothly. I would declare an emergency if I were making the landing at a controlled field, or I'd at the least let the controller know that I had an engine control problem. If the mixture is leaned at all, you don't want to be faced with any requirement for full power or close to full power. You don't want the controller to unsuspectingly put you in a situation that might demand a go-around. Let her know your problem so she doesn't do that.

If the failure occurs at altitude, you might need to reduce power as you descend but probably not nearly as much as you might imagine. If you're cruising at an EGT close to peak and attempts to enrichen the mixture fail, usually a small power reduction gets things back on an even keel. Plan your approach conservatively and remember to avoid a situation that might require full power during the landing.

PROPELLER PROBLEMS

A failure of the propeller control will naturally be possible only in an airplane equipped with a constant-speed propeller. If you fly a 172, Warrior, or a similar airplane with a fixed-pitch prop, simplicity gives you an extra margin of comfort. Every time we increase the complexity of an airplane that we fly, going from a fixed-pitch to constant-speed propeller, and from fixed-gear to retractable landing gear, we gain a little in performance and capability. Whether that gain justifies the extra expense in initial purchase and then maintenance of these goodies is a decision for everyone to make who is contemplating the acquisition of an airplane. Unless your routine trip is several hundreds of miles, you might come to the same conclusion as I have after nearly 25 years of owning airplanes—bells and whistles are very costly luxuries.

Constant-speed propellers

The prop control is also a two-piece cable, just like the throttle and mixture. It can break or jam the same as they can. Often the break or jam occurs when the pilot exercises the propeller during the runup before takeoff. That's the best time to have any problem, when you can either shut down right there, or taxi back to the barn and find your mechanic.

If the cable breaks in flight, the propeller might go to full RPM, or it might stay where it is, depending upon its design. Either way, it's not a life-threatening situation. You need to land as soon as practical; don't bore on for the remainder of a long flight. If the prop stays at cruise RPM, you don't want to have to use full power unless absolutely necessary, and this depends upon how slowly the engine is turning when the failure occurred.

In the average direct-drive engine with cruise RPM set around 2,350 or 2,400, you could apply full throttle if you needed to, and it would be very unlikely that you'd damage the engine. If the same engine had a fixed-pitch prop installed, it probably wouldn't pull much more RPM than that at full power, static or in a climb. If you cruise at lower RPMs like I do, down around 2,200 in order to economize fuel consumption, then you might damage the engine with any prolonged application of full throttle.

Fly the descent and pattern entry normally, and let the controller know of the problem if you're at a controlled field. You don't want to have to do a go-around. Reduce power to idle only when you're sure that you have the runway made. The perfect pattern for this situation is a series of ever-increasing power reductions, going down to idle as you cross the threshold and just before you begin the landing flare.

Another failure can cause propeller problems, and that is loss of engine oil. Most constant-speed propellers work by having engine oil plumbed to the prop hub, where the oil pressure works against either springs or centrifugal force to keep the selected RPM. If you lose the engine oil through a fracture in the prop oil line or from any other cause, the propeller will likely go to full RPM.

Depending on what breaks and whether oil streams over the airplane in a position where you can see it, a runaway prop going to full RPM without warning or command might be your first indication that the engine has lost its oil. Naturally, if you frequently scan the oil-pressure gauge, you'll see it drop off, too. If this happens, the engine is about to seize, and you have a for-real forced landing on your hands. Other than making sure your airplane receives timely and thorough maintenance, there isn't much you can do about this one.

If a runaway propeller shoots up to an extremely high RPM that is way above the engine's redline, that RPM might soon ruin the engine and can cause failure in a very short time. If I were faced with this emergency, I'd shut the engine down before it blew. Maybe you help the engine a little, but you would probably save a catastrophic failure of it. If an engine really lets go, it can spray oil all over the windshield, reducing your ability to see outside. That never helps the situation.

BROKEN PROPELLER BLADES

When you first learned to preflight an airplane, the instructor taught you to check the propeller blades for cracks and nicks. A broken propeller blade is a dire emergency, as shall be explained in a few moments. The best prevention is a thorough preflight inspection and overhauls of the prop at the manufacturer's recommended intervals, regardless of whether it's a fixed-pitch or constant-speed.

Nicks in the propeller can lead to cracks and blade failure in the course of one short flight. If you detect a nick, refer to the POH to determine if it's deep enough to ground the airplane until a mechanic can look at it. In years gone by, there was an informal standard of ¼ inch as the maximum depth of a nick. I don't go along with that.

The laws of metallurgy are too variable to set any depth standard. It all depends on the depth, size, shape, and location of the nick. I'd ground an airplane for an inspection by a competent mechanic if I found any nick in the blade(s) more than ⅛ inch deep. Even with that slight nick, I'd get a mechanic to look at it if I could.

Constant-speed propeller blades move inside of a hub. The blades are retained inside the hub by a flange and some sort of clip, which varies from one design to another. Lots of things can happen to impugn the integrity of a constant-speed prop. Corrosion can develop inside the hub, which no amount of exterior inspection can detect, but which can weaken the system to the degree that a propeller blade is thrown in flight. The oil seals harden and crack with age and need to be routinely replaced. The blade flanges can develop cracks that can't be viewed externally.

These are all of the reasons that propeller manufacturers recommend overhaul of constant-speed propellers based upon a certain number of flight hours or calendar years in service, whichever comes first. Adhere to these times between overhaul (TBO) because your life could depend on it. Propellers are some of the most neglected components of general aviation lightplanes. Don't let yours be among them.

When a part of a blade breaks off or the blade entirely departs the airplane, the prop is instantly thrown out of balance, usually catastrophically. Because it's rotating in excess of 2,000 RPM, the amount of imbalanced centrifugal force that it's imposing upon the engine is immense. If only a tip breaks off, you might be able to get the engine stopped before it rips out of its mountings. If a major portion of a blade or the entire blade leaves, the engine will probably be wrenched from the mounts in a few seconds.

If you react very quickly and kill the mags, you might get the engine stopped before it gets torn out of the mounts, depending upon how much of the blade broke off. Regardless of the breakage, try to stop the engine. Even if the engine twists out of the mounts, you can still do a forced landing if you act quickly enough to keep the engine inside the cowling. The real disaster occurs if the engine gets so thrashed around that the mounts break completely, is thrown out of the cowling, and leaves the airplane altogether. Thankfully, that happens very rarely, but if it does, you've got a very real problem.

Without the weight of the engine near where it belongs, the airplane will be so out of balance and the CG will go so far aft of normal limits that the airplane will probably not be controllable at all. Then it's a falling leaf, and the pilot can't do anything but be along for the final descent. The thought of this outcome should be enough to motivate any pilot to properly maintain and preflight the propeller.

CONCLUSION

Some control-system failures are dire, while a good number of them are manageable. To live through such an experience takes a well-trained pilot who understands how the various systems work and how to make them function to get the airplane on the ground with little or no damage. But there is a better solution.

Almost all control-system failures are the products of either abuse or poor maintenance. Don't skimp on maintaining your airplane, and don't abuse it. If you follow those rules, this chapter will probably be of academic interest only.

7
Water landings

LANDING IN THE WATER IS A FRIGHTENING EXPERIENCE TO ALL WHO HAVE either endured it or thought much about it. Before we get into the nitty-gritty details of ditching, let's talk about overwater flying.

When you choose to fly over water, out of gliding range of land, you increase the risk associated with flying. This statement isn't meant to overly discourage overwater operations; it simply states a reality. Pilots who fly in the continental United States never have to fly over water for any great distances. Sometimes a direct routing between two places might be over one of the Great Lakes or out along the coastlines of either the East or West Coasts farther than you could glide back to shore. For sure, you'll be doing some real overwater flying if you tour the Bahamas or elsewhere in the Caribbean.

There is more to know about overwater flying than just how to ditch an airplane into the water. There are several additional precautions to take and more knowledge to gain. Get some good books on the subject, such as TAB/McGraw Hill's *Ocean Flying—2nd Edition* and other authoritative texts on the subject. Talk to experienced pilots who have "been there, done that."

Many pilots haven't filed a VFR flight plan since they were students. I'll confess that I seldom do for routine trips in good weather. But when you venture out over the

water, think again. Prompt rescue is your key to survival after you successfully nego-
tiate a ditching. One way to get the search process begun early is to file a flight plan.
If the route of any flight takes you into the coastal or domestic ADIZ/DEWIZ, filing a
defense VFR (DVFR) flight plan is legally required. If you neglect to follow the rules,
you'll be intercepted by either a military fighter, the Drug Enforcement Administra-
tion, or the U.S. Customs Service. Meeting these fellows is not a pleasant way to either
begin or end a vacation in the sun. They will lead you to a landing at a place where
you'd rather not be, and then you get to answer some really embarrassing questions.
You might also get to help retire a portion of the national debt with the monetary penal-
ties that are imposed for disobeying the rules.

Neither this book nor this chapter is dedicated to covering the U.S. Customs requirements for private aircraft leaving or reentering the United States. But if you do fly
an international trip, know what's expected and how to do it. Back in the early 1970s,
I owned a Piper Aztec that we occasionally took south. On one trip, we went over to
the Bahamas for a day. Coming back, we landed at West Palm Beach to clear customs.

Aztecs have a nose baggage compartment in addition to a compartment behind the
seats. In those days, radios weren't solid state, so the nose compartment was full of am-
plifiers, tuners, and other tubes and boxes. We never used it for baggage. But because
it was equipped with a door, the customs inspector wanted to see inside. I didn't even
have a key to it on my key ring.

The inspector gave me two options: produce the key or drill out the lock. Drilling
the lock would have grounded the airplane for at least a couple of days while we found
a mechanic and rounded up the parts to fix it. As usual, my wife saved the day because
she thought ahead and had a key with her. After he snooped till his heart was content,
he was satisfied that we weren't drug lords, and we were on our way home.

Even if a flight plan isn't required by the FARs or Customs regulations, always file
one for any overwater flight. Even in relatively warm water, your survival time is limited if you have to ditch, so give yourself a break by filing a VFR flight plan. The
search-and-rescue system (SAR) will be activated if you don't close a VFR flight plan
within 30 minutes of your ETA. Without a flight plan, someone has to start the SAR
process. That person is usually some business associate who gets worried because you
didn't make it to a meeting. Sometimes, a frightened family member gets to make the
call to the missing persons bureau of the police department when you don't get home
on time.

Regardless, if you don't file a flight plan, it will be several more hours for sure and
maybe even a day or two until SAR gets notified that you are missing, and the system
gets the search for you underway. Then searchers have no real idea of where you went
down along your route of flight. The search process must cover all of the area from
your point of departure all of the way to your intended destination. That prospect ought
to be enough to motivate anyone to file a flight plan for any overwater flight.

Always fly as high as practical on overwater flights, trying to stay within gliding
range of land. That might not be possible, depending on the weather and the performance of your airplane. Even when flying along the shoreline, there isn't any need

to fly so low that you can't make the beach if you lose the engine. Then consider the nature of the shore near you. If it's strewn with rocks or cliffs, it's not an acceptable forced-landing site anyhow. In that case, maybe flying a little higher would allow you to glide over the shore to a forced-landing site just inland. A decent field might be farther inland, necessitating an even higher altitude to remain within gliding distance of it.

The other option to ditching is to avoid overwater routing when possible and add a few minutes to your flight. Even if the distance adds 50 miles or so to a trip, that's less than 30 minutes in all but the slowest of airplanes. As we've repeatedly said, flying is an exercise in risk assessment and acceptance. Use your own judgment about flying over water, out of gliding range of a suitable shoreline or other place to land. I do my utmost to avoid it.

Flying overwater can have other risks, especially for the pilot who doesn't have an instrument rating. On some days, the horizon over water will be as distinct as it is over land. At other times, it can get very murky and disappear completely.

If I weren't instrument rated, I'd avoid flying over water if there is any appreciable haze. A hazy sky ranks right up at the top of the list for creating an indistinct horizon over water.

Cloudy days can also be confusing. When the color of the clouds matches or comes close to the color of the water, the horizon isn't very distinguishable. In the winter, if a large body of water, like one of the Great Lakes, has frozen over, it doesn't make much of a contrast with a cloud layer above it.

If you fly in the Caribbean, sun shadows produced by clouds can confound your thinking. A large cumulus cloud will produce a shadow on the surface of the water that looks, for all intents and purposes, just like a small island when you're very far away from it. If you're island hopping, navigation gets a little harder when you think that a cloud's shadow is the island you wanted to see.

Landing on islands or on airports located on the shore can also be tricky. If the runway is located on a small island, depending upon the direction of the wind (and it's usually windy in the islands), you might have to fly the entire traffic pattern, specifically the final approach, over the water. You won't have the normal visual cues available to judge your altitude during the final. The water looks the same from 300 feet as it does from 600. A final approach flown over water is to some degree an instrument approach regardless of how beautiful the weather might be. Because you're deprived of the visual cues that you normally use, you've got to rely more on what the altimeter, airspeed indicator, and rate of climb (descent) indicator are telling you.

Night VFR is prohibited in the Caribbean for good reason: There is no visual horizon at night over the ocean. Keep that in mind if you're tempted to cross any large body of water at night if you can't maintain perfect visual contact with the land across the lake. For many reasons and in many situations, night flight becomes IFR flight at least some of the time. This is particularly true during takeoff before the airplane is high enough to acquire the visual horizon. Taking off over a body of water can be disastrous if you can't fly instruments.

OVERWATER SURVIVAL EQUIPMENT

Before you launch on any overwater flight, learn something about the kinds of survival equipment available. As you'll soon see, the temperature of the water dictates how long you can survive in it after a successful ditching. For some reason known only to the FAA's rule writers, there is no requirement to carry any overwater survival equipment on single-engine airplanes operating under Part 91. Section 91.509 sets forth the rules for large and turbine-powered aircraft; if the flight is planned for more than 30 minutes or 100 nautical miles from shore, this regulation mandates a far more extensive list of equipment than for shorter flights.

This rule defies logic, except for the assumption that large airplanes and jets carry more people than singles. But the bigger airplanes and jets seldom have to ditch. Yet every year at least a few lightplanes will get their feet wet in the Caribbean alone. If you make an overwater flight, use FAR 91.509 as your own guide for the equipment you should carry. If you're going more than 50 nautical miles from shore, this reg requires the airplanes covered by it to have a life preserver on board for each occupant. That's the minimum equipment that you should consider for any flight that takes you out of gliding range of land.

Fifty miles is a long way to swim in a life preserver. When was the last time you swam 1 mile? If you did, it was probably in a pool, not in open ocean with swells and unfriendly critters about. A life preserver gives you some extra time to be rescued, but not much unless the water is extremely warm and nothing wants you for its next meal. Also think about the fact that the warmer the water, the more attractive it is to sharks. Add that together with the proposition that you will probably receive some slight injury in a ditching and evacuation of any airplane. If you're bleeding and in shark-infested water, you don't want to be dangling in a life vest. I won't fly over any body of water where I can't glide to land without both a life preserver and a life raft if the flight is over any ocean. If I'm flying over Lake Erie in the heat of the summer, I'll go with just a life vest.

Wear the life vest at all times while flying over water. Uninflated, it's not that uncomfortable. There won't be time to unpackage it, unfold it, and put it on after the need for it arises. Plus, you would have a monumental responsibility to your passengers to supervise and assist them in doing the same thing. When faced with the imminent possibility of ditching, that's no time for anyone to be fooling around trying to don a vest. *Never* inflate it inside the airplane, even after the ditching; you'll never get out of the airplane. The actual openings created by the doors in lightplanes are minimal. Think about the gymnastics you normally have to go through getting people in your plane who aren't accustomed to flying. Trying to get out of a sinking airplane with a life vest inflated is probably impossible while mental shock is trying to panic everyone.

A raft gets you out of the water, which keeps you from suffering hypothermia from exposure to the water and helps some with the worry about shark attacks in salt water. If the water temperature is anywhere below your 98.6°F body temperature, you start losing body heat as soon as you're immersed. The thermal conductivity of water is approximately 240 times greater than that of calm air. The colder the water, the faster you lose body warmth. Even if the water temperature is at a fairly warm 65°F, you'll have a 50-percent chance of death from hypothermia if you stay in it more than 4 hours (Fig. 7-1).

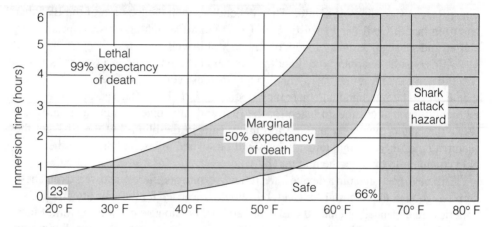

Fig. 7-1. *A chart of expected survival times in water at various temperatures.*

I absolutely won't fly a lightplane over water in the winter. The chances are too high that you'd die before you could get rescued. Even if you could get out of the water and into a raft, your clothing would still be wet, and you would be losing body heat until they dried out. More likely, wet clothing would not dry but just freeze. I don't even fly over the Great Lakes in the winter, except for Lake Erie, which is so shallow that in most winters it freezes from shore to shore; cars even drive out to ice-fishing huts. But if there is any open water, I go around it.

A life raft is much easier to see from a rescue aircraft or boat. One person swimming around in a life vest is almost invisible from the air and almost as hard to see from a boat. Particularly if there is any wave action, you'll never get rescued. Also, if there are any passengers in the airplane, you need a raft so you can stay together after the ditching. If passengers are spread out over the sea in life vests, somebody won't get found, even if others are. In high seas, you'll lose sight of each other in just a few minutes. Being together in a raft makes you much more visible and also enables you to huddle together to stay warm much longer. You've got to stay warm and dry to live. If any of the airplane's occupants get injured in the ditching or evacuation, they won't live for long if they're not in a raft.

The next item that should be required equipment is a signaling device. If you're in a life vest or a raft, you'll see an oncoming aircraft or boat long before its crew will see you. You increase your chances of rescue severalfold if you can signal to them and get their attention. The legends of the sea are filled with stories of search aircraft flying directly over a person afloat in the water without making a sighting.

By far, the best signaling devices are electronic. You can purchase portable emergency locator transmitters (ELTs) that you can put in your flight bag and get out before you ditch. Take one with you, and activate it as soon as you get into the raft. If the batteries are fresh, it'll operate for at least a day. The United States and Russia have satellites in Earth orbit that listen for ELT signals on the emergency frequency. When any of these satellites gets a "hit," it transmits the coordinates of that hit to the U.S. Air Force Rescue Coordinating Center. Then depending upon the location of the ELT that has been heard, Civil Air Patrol or U.S. Coast Guard search-and-rescue aircraft are alerted and sent out, and the process of saving you is well underway.

Also consider wrapping your hand-held communications radio in a waterproof covering so you can take it into the raft and greatly increase your odds of being rescued. Remember that the international emergency frequency is 121.5 MHz. Search aircraft will be monitoring that channel to listen for the ELT and any voice communication. Don't waste the battery power by making too many calls in the blind. Let the ELT get the search aircraft in your sight range, which will be several miles, and then use the hand-held comm radio to direct them to you by voice.

The next best signaling devices are reflective mirrors, flares, and sea dye. These aren't as good as the electronic devices, but should be carried for the time after the ELT's batteries are expended or either the ELT or hand-held radio gets too wet to work. Many life rafts come equipped with survival kits that include these items; if yours didn't, buy them separately. Remember that visual signaling devices only work when a SAR aircraft or a boat is close enough to see you. Obviously, electronic aids extend that range many times over.

The best signal mirrors are made of shiny metal. Glass mirrors are too fragile, but in a pinch, any piece of glass can be reflective enough to get a search aircraft's attention. Metal mirrors don't break or have batteries to wear out, and they can be used by almost anyone without any extensive training. If the sun is totally obscured by heavy cloud cover, they don't work. Fortunately, most of the time in the warmer ocean areas of the world, the weather is usually good with only scattered to broken clouds.

Take a look at Fig. 7-2 for the recommended way to use a signaling mirror. Doing it this way will reflect the sunlight toward the search aircraft and direct its attention toward the source of the reflection. You can do the same thing when signaling a boat that is within visual range.

Flares come in two applications, one for use during the day, the other for night. If necessary, either can be used anytime, but they're most effective if used in the light conditions for which they're designed. A day flare puts out dense smoke and some light. A night flare gives off an intense light. If you've expended your supply of one type, use the other if a rescue craft is close. Even a day flare puts out enough light that it can be seen at night from quite a distance.

You can select among hand-held or projectile flares. The hand-held variety is very similar to highway flares. Projectiles are fired from a device that looks very much like a pistol. These shoot up several hundred feet and can be seen for miles, especially at night. When rescue personnel have spotted the projectile flare, a hand-held flare can be lit as they approach to better pinpoint your position.

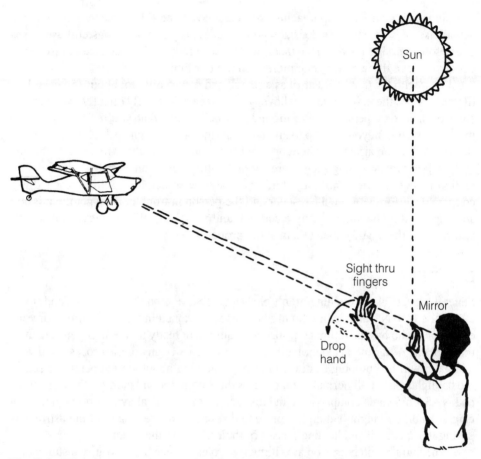

Fig. 7-2. *The proper way to use a signal mirror.* <small>Tacoma Mountain Rescue Unit</small>

A day flare, with all of its smoke, can be a great aid to a rescue helicopter in determining wind direction and velocity. If you see a helicopter coming to save you, fire off a hand-held day flare to help them. If it's one of the U.S. Coast Guard's amphibious choppers, it can then land very near you, enhancing the process of getting you aboard. Before you use a hand-held flare, read the instructions carefully; burn injuries from a flare can be horrific.

Sea dye is a chemical that does just what its name implies; it changes the color of the water around you. It makes a big spot in the water and is generally quite effective in enhancing your visual target for rescue aircraft or ships. Don't use it until you see an approaching aircraft or boat. You have to be constantly watchful for any possible approaching rescue because the odds are that you will see them in the area long before they will see you. Even a raft is a very small dot in the expanse of the ocean. Don't waste the dye by using it when the rescue craft is so far away that the crew doesn't have the slant-range visibility to clearly see the surface at your location. As with all visual signaling devices, the approaching rescuers have to be able to see the dye and then actually see it before the dye does any good at all. Hasty and other wasteful use of sea dye before there is a good chance that it will be seen reduces your chance of rescue because you have thrown away one more item in your limited inventory.

I flew with the Civil Air Patrol as a search and rescue pilot for about 15 years. Until you've been there, it's hard to believe how very easy it is to fly directly over a crash-sight on land or a person on the ground and never see what you're looking for no matter how vigilant you are. A person on the ground or water who is looking up toward the sky can see an airplane or helicopter without much difficulty. The crew of the aircraft is, however, scanning such a large area that they can't concentrate their visual attention to any one area until they think that they see something. Getting rescued is a cooperative effort between the rescuer and the person in trouble. Help get the mission accomplished by having as many electronic and visual signaling devices as possible. Learn to use them, and expend them at the proper times.

DITCHING

Several aspects about ditching aren't pleasant. First, it's tough under any conditions, even for a U.S. Naval aviator who has been as well trained in the procedure as anyone can be and who has the ultimate in survival equipment ready to use after getting out of the airplane. As a general aviation pilot, you can't practice any of the process, and your adrenalin will be pumping as never before. Something about water operations scares the daylights out of all normal people. After the Apollo moon landings, the U.S. Navy and NASA did some comparisons and discovered that a Naval aviator doing a normal carrier landing at night had higher pulse and respiration rates than did the astronauts during the approach and landing phases of their flights to the Moon.

When you're ditching, you are filling two roles at once. First, you're a student pilot teaching yourself to do a totally new procedure for the first time without the assistance of an old hand. Second, you're also an experimental test pilot because the airplane that you fly never had any ditching testing as a part of its certification, and who knows how it will perform on contact with the water. So, you're trying a maneuver for the first time. Mental preparation is vital. If you lose your composure and let panic set in, you probably won't make it. If you stay as cool as possible and keep the airplane under control at all times, you actually have a pretty good chance of survival if the water is reasonably warm.

A forced landing on water is different from one on land, and before you venture over any body of water where you'll be out of gliding distance of the shore, you need to be able to distinguish between the correct actions for water or land landings. Yet there are some similarities. If your engine quits cold, it's obvious that you're coming down. If you suffer a progressive engine failure, that's another story.

If things start going sour progressively, don't wait to announce your predicament. Get on 121.5 MHz and transmit in the blind. If you're relatively close to shore, you'll probably be heard by an ATC facility. If you're a long way from land, overflying airliners and ships at sea monitor 121.5, and you'll most likely get a response from one or more of them. If you're anywhere close to land, immediately turn and head for it.

No wise pilot ever pushes fuel reserves for any overwater trip. If you've somehow calculated incorrectly, gotten lost, or suffered some other malady that has caused your fuel situation to become critical, you've got a decision to make. Again, you can control the ditching far better if the engine is running and you don't wait until it quits. Is there a reasonable chance that you're improving your odds by flying on and not ditching while you're sure that there is enough fuel left for the approach? Can you get that much closer to land, a ship, or shipping lanes? Only the pilot can call this one. If you are really close to land or boats, maybe it's better to press on. If not, it might be better to ditch now, while you can do it better, pick the ditching spot better, and be able to make water contact where you need to. You decide based upon the unique circumstances of any such emergency.

Most general aviation overwater flying occurs in the Caribbean because it's natural for pilots and their passengers to visit the numerous islands by air. Unless you're really adventuresome and are flying to some of the more distant and remote out islands, you're probably already near some boats. Although on one trip, I don't think we saw more than two boats the entire flight. As you fly along normally, try to keep an eye out for the boat traffic. Especially in the summer, the shipping lanes between Florida and the Bahamas get a large amount of recreational use.

In a progressive failure situation, you've got to use some judgment that can only be dictated by the unique circumstances of your situation, how long to stay aloft, and when to accept the inevitable and set up for a ditching. If your problem is a massive oil line failure and oil is streaming all over the front of the airplane, you know that the engine's life is about finished. Just like on land, it's better to ditch while you still have the engine running than to wait for it to totally give up the ghost. If the problem is brought on by something like a swallowed valve, where the engine is running as rough as a washboard but not getting any worse, you might be able to fly indefinitely. Even if one entire cylinder quits producing power, you might be able to fly on the rest of the engine, albeit more slowly and not as comfortably.

This is another of the many reasons to know something about how your airplane works. The correct diagnosis of a progressive engine failure is crucial if it happens over water. Nobody with any sense wants to ditch if a crippled but still running engine has a good chance of lasting long enough to get to land. Yet in the appropriate circumstance, denying the inevitable and blindly flying on will result in ditching without power when the engine quits for good. Pilots with a professional attitude about their flying know more than how to fly; they know how things work.

As you're transmitting in the blind, send out your position. Hand-held GPS unit prices are low enough to justify the purchase if only for rescue "insurance." No one should do any overwater flying without one if the airplane doesn't have a panel-mounted loran or GPS receiver. Your position is expressed in geographical coordinates in the flash of an eye by pressing the button on a GPS for "present position." Whoever hears these radio calls needs to know where you are. When you can give a precise location, rather than just an idea of how far you are from some island or another, you're doing a great deal to assist in your own rescue.

Since you're flying over water in the first place, you should be cruising as high as practical. Altitude equals safety in most situations in aviation, but that axiom is particularly true when over water. All of the water beneath you is likely the same; therefore, you don't have to worry about *where* to land as if over a landmass, but you do want to delay for as long as possible *when* you have to land. You want time on your side. If you know the airplane's minimum sink speed and the cruise altitude is nice and high, you can glide for quite awhile. If you can attain a minimum sink of about 600 fpm, and if you're flying at 9,000 feet, you've got about 11–12 minutes of gliding time before you get down to 2,000 feet and need to shift all of your concentration and efforts toward the ditching. Use this time wisely to get on the radio and keep talking, stating your call sign, aircraft type, position, number of people on board, and the fact that you're about to ditch.

Naturally, if you do see a boat, you want to ditch near it but not directly beside it. Because the airplane engine is quiet and most powerboats are fairly noisy when underway, the folks on the boat might never know you're coming until very late in the process. Try to plan your approach to fly over the bow of the boat so you can be seen, but don't try to land directly in front of it where you might get run over if you're not seen until too late. When you're trying to get near to a boat, you might need to glide at the best glide (L/D) speed to increase the gliding range. Stay alert, and modify your procedures to suit the needs of the circumstances that confront you.

When you are about 2,000 feet above the water, it's time to concentrate on the landing. A successful ditching has two primary elements: contact the water correctly and do it at the slowest possible airspeed. Let's deal with airspeed first.

Recall that the forces of impact increase exponentially with any increases in the speed at which the impact occurs. This is no different for a ditching than it is for a landing on terra firma. When contacted at speed, water is every bit as hard as land and can be similar to running into a concrete wall if done incorrectly. It's vital that you touch down at the slowest possible speed, consistent with maintaining control of the airplane in the wind conditions present. It's best to contact the water with the airspeed just about at a stall speed. Only a few extra knots might be enough to do substantially more damage to the airplane and cause impact injuries to the occupants, neither of which bode well for a quick evacuation and ultimate survival.

When you make a forced landing on land, your first goal is to land into the wind, the same as you normally do on a runway, unless the ground conditions dictate against it. Furthermore, when flying over land, there are many visual cues to tell a pilot the direction of the wind. Unless you're an accomplished sailor, you can't get the same information from looking down at an unending expanse of water. Sections of the *Airman's Information Manual* (AIM) that cover ditching procedures go into a great deal of oceanographic terminology, most of which is meaningless to us landlubbers.

Waves are created by local winds, while swells are waves that have come a long way, usually left over from some distant storm or other disturbance to the sea. In the open sea, more than one swell pattern can exist in a given patch of water. There can be primary, secondary, and even tertiary swells. Waves created by the local wind conditions can then be going in different directions from any of the swells. And the ocean has riverlike currents flowing in it that add another term to the final equation. If the sea has much action to it, the complete situation on the surface might be extremely complex.

The goal of any ditching is to avoid landing into the face of a swell, which is the side of it toward the person seeing it. To put it in other words, don't land into a wall of water. This is all much easier read and contemplated from the comfort of a chair on dry land than it is to do in an airplane. When the surface wind is from one direction and the swells are coming from a different direction, the swells win out over the wind in your level of concern. Make a crosswind landing, but you will be doing it onto a surface that is simultaneously undulating and moving horizontally and vertically. Take a look at Fig. 7-3, which is an excerpt from the AIM. You can see that the best position for contact with the water is on the crest of a swell, and the next best is to touch down on the backside of one.

In order to do this, you will probably have to be able to fly the airplane in a sideslip because you won't be likely to be landing directly into the wind, and the swell's crest will be moving laterally away from you to one side or the other. Most pilots know how to do a forward slip, while many don't know the difference between the two. If your usual crosswind landings use the wing-down method, you are slipping down the final approach toward the runway. I prefer this technique because it eliminates the last-minute gyrations of getting the airplane ready for contact that are inherent when you crab down final and transition to a wing-down opposite-rudder condition just before you land. This is a forward slip, so-called because the path of the airplane over the ground is forward with no lateral movement.

A sideslip is different. The goal in a sideslip is to slip while simultaneously moving the airplane's path of travel sideways over the ground. Sideslips were commonly taught at one time but aren't anymore, and that's too bad. You should try a slideslip. Align the airplane with a road, fence row, or other such landmark. Enter a glide, and put a wing down. But instead of applying enough opposite rudder to totally overcome the turning tendency produced by the bank, add less opposite rudder pressure. The airplane will still be slipping, but will be going over the ground laterally. You should see the road or whatever else you're using slide underneath the nose and away from the direction of bank. When the time comes to ditch in the sea, you shouldn't complicate the ditching with trying to learn how to sideslip at the same time. You have to sideslip because the swell is moving laterally and you're trying to stay directly over its crest for the landing.

Another reason that it's best to land on the crest of the swell, down the long axis of the swell, has to do with the aftereffects of water contact. If you take the second-best shot and land on the backside of the swell, some bad things can happen if the conditions of the sea's surface are working against you. When you land across the swell and contact the water on the back side, your initial contact will be OK, but you're faced with the possibility of running headlong into the face of the next swell. If the aircraft

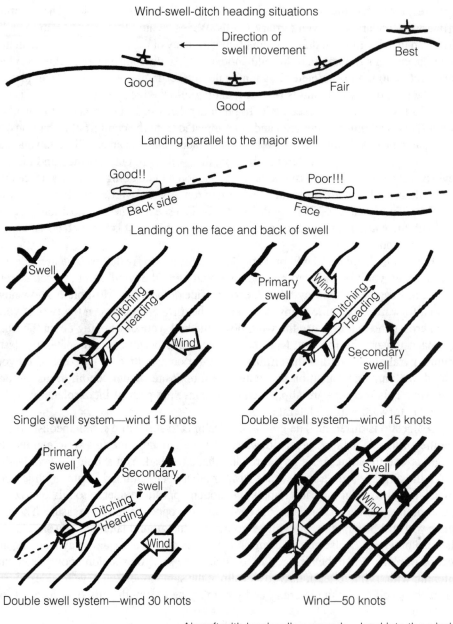

Wind-swell-ditch heading situations

Direction of
swell movement

Best

Good

Fair

Good

Landing parallel to the major swell

Good!!

Poor!!!

Back side

Face

Landing on the face and back of swell

Swell

Ditching Heading

Wind

Single swell system—wind 15 knots

Primary swell

Wind

Ditching Heading

Secondary swell

Double swell system—wind 15 knots

Primary swell

Secondary swell

Ditching Heading

Wind

Double swell system—wind 30 knots

Swell

Wind

Wind—50 knots

Aircraft with low landing speeds—land into the wind.
Aircraft with high landing speeds—choose
compromise heading between wind and swell.
Both—Land on back side of swell.

Fig. 7-3. *A drawing from the* Airman's Information Manual *depicting a situation of complex swells and good ditching techniques.*

120

skips upon first contact with the water, much the same as a stone skips over a pond when tossed out from shore, you could run into the face of the next swell at a fast speed, which would be an undesirable event.

Landing on the back side of a swell takes perfect timing. If the timing is off, the airplane will contact the water either too early, which means into the face of the swell, or too late, which puts you into the next swell coming toward you. The crest of a swell is indefinitely long and makes a much better "runway" to aim toward. Give yourself all of the breaks that the situation presents.

Even if the airplane does not skip (airplanes almost always skip some at first water contact), you might see the nosewheel or entire nose of the airplane plow into the next swell, causing a somersault. That's why it's best to do all that you can to land on the crest of the swell, landing down the long axis of the swell just as if it were a runway.

If you're flying a fixed-gear airplane, plan to go inverted at some point in the ditching because the nose gear digs into the water, pulling the nose down, which submerges farther. Fixed-gear airplanes have stayed upright in many ditchings, but be prepared to go upside down, and don't be frightened by the unexpected if it occurs. It's no fun, but at least you know that it might happen.

When flying a retractable-gear airplane, ditch with the wheels up to eliminate the gear's digging into the water. You will increase your chances of staying upright and allow the airplane to slow without high-impact forces. Leave the wing flaps up (even on a high-wing airplane) unless you really need them, and I can't see why you would need flaps because there aren't any obstacles to clear. Don't ditch with the flaps extended, particularly if you're flying a low-wing airplane. An extended wing flap will probably tear away during the water contact, which will skew the airplane. The skewing movement will increase the chances of upset and add quite a bit to the impact forces as occupants are jerked around in their seats from the "ground loop." Minimizing disorientation and impact forces will enhance the odds that everyone can get out of the airplane successfully after it comes to a stop.

If the surface of the sea, called the "sea state," is very calm, you've got a different problem. It's very difficult and sometimes impossible to judge height above calm water. If you've read anything about flying seaplanes, you've learned that seaplane pilots have a totally different technique for landing on glassy water compared to landing on water that has some action to its surface. Until you've experienced a calm-water landing, you have to take the word of those who have done so concerning the difficulty with visual perception on glassy water.

If you're confronted with a calm sea state, you won't be able to tell when the normal flare point is reached in the last stages of the final approach. You risk either flying into the water with no flare at all or stalling while still high enough that the airplane pitches over, rolls, or both. Neither is the way that you want to contact the water.

When confronted with with a glassy surface, set up a steady glide at a minimum-sink speed if the engine has failed. Or establish a speed that produces no more than about a 300-fpm descent if the engine is still running. Either technique should produce an attitude with the nose high enough to prevent you from flying into the water with the nose down. You just have to sit there and wait for water contact.

Regardless of how you make the approach, before you actually contact the water, pop a door open, or at least a window. There are two reasons for doing that. First, structural deformation of the airframe during the ditching impact is possible. How sad it would be to successfully ditch but be unable to open a door and get out. Second, as soon as the airplane starts to sink, a tremendous amount of water pressure will be exerted upon the outside skin of the airplane because the cabin will be filled with air. If there is no opening for water to get in to equalize that pressure, the airplane only has to sink a few feet before no human is strong enough to force some airplane doors open against the pressure of the water. The larger the doors, the more total water pressure will be pushing against them.

If you don't have a door open prior to impact, you're likely to become disoriented very quickly because the airplane might go inverted and start to sink. Terror sets in. You need to get that door open very quickly, before it becomes impossible to do so. How do you even find the door handle in such a panic? One suggestion is to intentionally try not to find it instantly, but use a different technique. Have you ever tried to find your way through a dark hall or room in your home, where you know the "lay of the land" extremely well? Most people put out a hand, feel for a wall, and then follow the wall to the door. Do the same thing in trying to find the door handle of the airplane. Put your hand in a place intentionally above the handle, like on the bottom of the side window, and follow the inside of the door down to the handle. That's a whole lot easier than stabbing for a very small point on the entire area of the door, hoping that you can hit the handle. At the risk of excessive repetition, you have no way to appreciate how disoriented you will likely be immediately after ditching.

Break a window to let water in and equalize the pressure if the door is still closed and the handle cannot be located. When the door is open, the next step is to get out. But don't be in such a hurry that you forget to take the life raft along. If you have an ELT, hand-held GPS, communications radio, and other signaling devices that were previously discussed in this chapter, they won't do you a bit of good at the bottom of the ocean. Store these lifesaving devices where you can get to them, and get them ready during the descent for the hectic egress. You cannot "prepare" after you're in the water. If the airplane's ELT is mounted in a bracket inside the cabin, take the transmitter out of the bracket during the glide. Then be sure that you take the ELT into the life raft. You can turn it on and use it once safely in the raft.

As you exit the aircraft, you might not be able to tell which way is up, especially if the airplane went inverted during the landing or if it sank below the surface before you got out. Get yourself and your passengers out of the airplane and into the water. If you're in a high-wing airplane, use some care not to injure yourself by hitting the wing or its edges as you evacuate. You will have two new goals: get away from the airplane and get to the surface.

You shouldn't be very deep in the water, if even below the surface at all. If submerged, swim away from the airplane before you inflate the life vest. It could be ripped by scraping against some part of the airplane's structure, and then the vest is useless. Worse yet, inflating it under water could jam your head or body up against the wing or tail, trapping you. If you don't know which way is up, let a little air out of your mouth or nose, and follow the bubbles, which always go up. Once safely outside and away from the airplane, inflate the life preserver, and continue to assist any passengers.

A good life raft will float of its own accord, even before being inflated. Check out yours in a swimming pool before you do any overwater flying. If it doesn't float in the uninflated state, take it back because you don't want a raft that has any sinking tendency when you're trying to get it out of the airplane and to the surface. If the cord from a raft is wrapped around an arm or any part of your body, the sinking raft would pull you down as you try to get away from the plane.

Never inflate the life raft anywhere in or near the airplane. Inflating it in the airplane will almost always block any avenue of evacuation and trap all of the occupants. Get far enough away before inflation that the raft is neither torn by rubbing against any aircraft structure nor jammed against a wing or part of the tail.

When you're on the surface, go ahead and pull the lanyard to inflate the raft, but hang onto the cord. Hold the cord very tightly. An inflated raft without anyone in it is extremely buoyant. If there is any surface wind or wave action, the raft can get away from you in the bat of an eyelash and will quickly blow across the surface faster than you can swim after it.

Climb into the raft and immediately check the condition of electronic signaling devices. They will probably work okay if they only got slightly damp through whatever wrapping you had over them. You will need to dry out any device that is soaked. Unwrap them, and dry them off as soon as possible. ELTs are supposed to work when soaked, but don't count on it. Hand-held transceivers and GPS receivers are not designed to get wet and still function.

So far, so good. Be thankful that all has gone as well as it has, and start expecting to get rescued. Getting this far unhurt and on top of the water has taken a good amount of luck or divine intervention. Be ready to use a signaling device when the opportunity for rescue arises. A low-flying search aircraft can pass overhead rather quickly. You wouldn't want to miss the chance to get found by fiddling around and taking too long to prepare or deploy a signaling device, resulting in never being seen.

If you do much overwater flying, strongly consider attending one of the relatively inexpensive schools that offer underwater egress training. All U.S. Navy aviators get their day in the "Delbert Dunker," which is a device that has a pilot's seat mounted on tracks at the edge of a pool. The seat slides down the track under the water and rapidly inverts with the pilot still strapped into the upside-down seat. That's about as close as anyone can come to a real ditching experience. A session in the dunker has been a life-saving training experience for many naval aviators, particularly during World War II.

No ditching will ever be easy or routine. Each ditching is done under different conditions by pilots of different skill levels. If you have the proper equipment, proper training, and a good attitude, you'll probably come out okay if you have to ditch into reasonably warm water.

WATER LANDINGS

If you routinely fly over water, think about the added safety of a multiengine airplane. I am loath to fly over water in a single. I'll do it for very short distances in warm climates. I'd never do it in the winter no matter how short the flight if I would be beyond a safe gliding distance to land. I would also not take long flights over water in a single even during the warm times of year. Maybe I'm too conservative, but I'm here.

There is also the continuing disagreement among many aviation professionals over whether twins are any safer than singles because so many twin-engine pilots fly on one engine, only to "get to the scene of the accident." But the only reason that problem exists is that some multiengine-rated pilots aren't basically proficient in handling their airplanes on one engine, especially during an approach and landing. Because you have a professional attitude about flying and maintaining proper pilot proficiency, you wouldn't let yourself be among them, right?

8
Icing

ICE DOES A LOT OF NICE THINGS FOR OUR DAILY LIVES. ICE CHILLS OUR beverages and gives us a surface upon which either to skate or watch others do so, and ice can make the world as gorgeous as an expensive Christmas card. But when we're flying, there's nothing pleasant about ice in any of the forms that it takes when associated with aviation. We'll talk about ice from three viewpoints: engine problems, airframe icing, and what special considerations attend the presence of ice on the surface of the ground. If you encounter any of these scenarios, an in-flight emergency might arise.

ENGINE PROBLEMS

Ice can affect an airplane's engine two ways. First, it can form in the carburetor of the engine, blocking the travel of the fuel-air mixture through the carb and possibly resulting in engine failure. Second, ice can also form over the air inlets through which the stream of air must flow on its way to the intake system of the powerplant.

To understand how ice develops in a carburetor, let's review a little physics. Deep inside of the carb, there is a little passageway through which the fuel-air mixture is forced on its way to the cylinders. This device is called a venturi, and it is shaped similar to an hourglass. As the mixture enters the venturi at one end, it is compressed slightly as it goes from the wide end into the narrow neck at the center of the venturi tube.

Because the mixture is primarily a gas, it can be compressed. Recall that liquids can't be compressed; we wouldn't have the ability to use hydraulic systems to transfer pressure via liquids. But also recall that gasses can be compressed. The fuel-air mixture is mostly air, so compression of the entire mixture does occur. After the mixture goes through the neck of the venturi, it leaves that narrow space and again enters a wide area of the tube at the opposite end (Fig. 8-1).

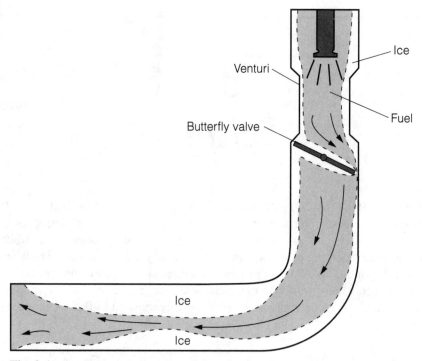

Fig. 8-1. *A carburetor's venturi and throttle plate.*

As the gaseous mixture of fuel and air goes out of the narrow neck, and into the wide end of the tube, there is no longer any compression occurring, but to the contrary, it expands. When the mixture is forced through the narrow neck of the venturi, its internal temperature is increased. Again recall that a by-product of compressing any gas is an increase in its temperature because the compression physically forces the molecules of the gas closer to each other. When the compressive force is removed, as it is when the fuel-air mixture travels back into a wide opening of the venturi, the temperature of the gas drops. Cooling occurs because the compressive force has been removed and the molecules spread out; hence, molecular activity (heat) declines.

A small flapper that controls how much fuel-air mixture is allowed to go into the cylinders is placed in or very near the venturi tube. This flapper device is called a "throttle plate." When you push in or pull out the throttle control in the cockpit, you're moving the throttle plate in the carburetor. In turn, the throttle plate is regulating the amount of the fuel-air mixture that is being fed to the intake system of the engine: more flow, more power; less flow, less power. It works the same way in a car engine, if you still have a car equipped with a carbureted engine.

In most installations, the throttle plate is downstream of the narrow neck of the venturi tube; hence, it's put in the area where the mixture moving past is dropping in temperature. This temperature decrease can be as much as a 90°F drop from the ambient temperature, even before the compression of the mixture occurred. So if there is any water vapor in the air portion of the fuel-air combination, that water vapor can come out of solution in the gaseous air and form ice on the throttle plate. When the air is colder than freezing, ice loves to form on the edges of hard objects that are placed in the stream of the air laden with water vapor.

So ice can form on the throttle plate, blocking the flow of the fuel-air mixture to the engine. Because the temperature drop in the carburetor can be as much as 90°F and the freezing point of water is 32°F, carburetor ice can be a possibility anytime, unless you're flying at lower altitudes over the Sahara Desert in the summer.

Some reciprocating engines are more prone to the formation of carburetor ice than are others, but the ice can be a problem in any of them. Certain engines have oil pans that contain the hot engine oil in a reservoir located beneath the engine itself. These engines often have their carburetors mounted at the bottom of the engine in close proximity to this reservoir full of hot oil. The heated oil tends to keep the temperatures of the carburetor elevated; therefore, the temperature of the fuel-air mixture is warmer than normal. That reduces but never eliminates the tendency of these engines to ice up.

Another style of engine has a separate oil tank, often mounted to the rear of the engine, that serves as the oil reservoir. While the oil in this tank is also hot during operation of the engine, the carburetor in this type of engine is mounted far enough away from the oil tank that the hot oil has little if any effect on the internal temperatures of the carburetor and the fuel-air mixture going through it. Regardless of which type of engine your airplane has, you need to know the circumstances under which carb ice might form, how to recognize it early, and what to do about it.

CIRCUMSTANCES WHERE ICE IS PROBABLE

Remember that carb ice is caused as the cooled mixture of fuel and air passes by the throttle plate and there is enough water vapor in the mixture that the water can come out of solution, adhere to the throttle plate, and freeze. Sometimes the ice will stick to the walls of the venturi too, adding pain to misery. When that happens, the throttle plate gets ice on it, and the opening of the venturi narrows because ice is on its walls. The result of this doubling effect is even more restriction to the flow of the fuel-air mixture through the carburetor. Since less flow means less power, the engine can't produce normal power when there is ice in its carb.

When the engine is operating at high power settings, the flow of fuel and air through the carburetor is traveling at very fast speeds. When the mixture is traveling that fast, there is less time available for a particular molecule of water to come out of solution, adhere to the throttle plate or venturi wall, and freeze. For that reason, most engines aren't very prone to carb ice formation when they're running at full power or at high cruise settings. But if the atmospheric conditions are right and the proper combination of air temperature and humidity is present, carb ice is possible at any power setting.

After power is reduced from full throttle, the likelihood of carb ice increases. When the power setting decreases, the speed of the fuel and air flowing downstream from the throttle plate in the carburetor also slows down; therefore, more time is available for the water molecules to go through the process of changing from harmless water vapor to hunks of ice inside the carb. The lower power setting and slower flow increase the possibility of ice formation.

If you're flying on a humid day, which means that there is already lots of water vapor in the air, be all that much more watchful for the signs of ice forming. If you've got a combination of high ambient humidity and air temperatures above freezing but below about 55°F or 60°F, really look out.

Carb ice is a real probability when you're operating at very low power settings, such as in a descent, or in the traffic pattern. Certain airplane POHs recommend applying carburetor heat before bringing the power back to idle, while other POHs modify those instructions. Know what the POH says and follow it.

When you're flying in the colder times of year and the ambient air temperature is already well below freezing, carburetor ice is less likely. The water molecules in the air are probably frozen, and they will pass through the carb intact. But never rely upon colder temperatures to totally negate the possibility of carburetor ice. Water can exist in the liquid form at temperatures below 32°F, which is called "super-cooled water." Also, the compressive heating of the fuel-air mixture passing through the carb can heat the mixture to the extent that already frozen water melts and is ready to re-form as ice on the throttle plate or the venturi's walls.

What all of this means is fairly simple. While the type of engine, ambient atmospheric conditions, and power setting all affect the probability of ice forming inside a carburetor, carb ice is possible anytime.

WARNING SIGNS

When carburetor ice forms, it restricts the flow of fuel and air through the carb. A loss of power ensues. The warning signs of carb ice are all of the symptoms normally associated with less power.

If your airplane is equipped with a fixed-pitch propeller, the primary indication of lower power is a decrease in RPM. In its early stages, carburetor ice doesn't affect the smoothness of the engine. You'll only notice a slight reduction in RPM in the beginning. As the ice blockage grows, the RPM will continue to decline. At some point, the engine will begin running rough, and after that stage of the process, the accumulated ice will soon be sufficient to cause a complete engine failure.

The keys to avoiding real trouble are straightforward. Know when to expect carb ice, anticipate it, and apply carburetor heat before the ice forms. If you don't do that, learn the incipient warnings that the engine provides. If you have to push the throttle in a little bit more every few minutes to keep the RPM where you want it, you're probably icing up. Apply the carb heat while the malady is still curable. If you wait until the engine is about to quit, you might not be able to get rid of the ice. When you do apply carburetor heat after any significant amount of ice has built up, expect a few seconds of rough running while the ice is melted and small chunks pass through the engine. Occasionally a pilot who doesn't know what's coming after the carb heat is turned on will incorrectly think that the heat is making matters worse and will then turn it off before it has done the job.

If you have a constant-speed prop, you won't see any RPM decrease in the early stages of carburetor icing, and probably not at all until it's too late. The constant-speed propeller is built to change the pitch of its blades to keep the RPM constant regardless of the throttle setting until the physical limits of the propeller's design are exceeded, when the RPM will respond to throttle inputs.

With a constant-speed prop, power changes are mainly noted through different readings of the manifold-pressure gauge. Manifold pressure is the indication of how much flow of fuel and air is going though the engine's intake system. Because the amount of fuel and air going through the intake is reduced if the throttle setting is left alone when ice is restricting the flow, the gauge will show a decline in pressure within the intake system, just as if the throttle setting had been reduced.

So, watch for small incremental decreases in manifold pressure. If you see a decrease, suspect carb ice and react. You prevent carb ice the same way as with a fixed-pitch propeller, by knowing when to anticipate its formation and preventing it with the judicious use of carb heat. When you see ice developing by noticing unintended decreases in manifold pressure, get the heat on.

USE OF CARBURETOR HEAT

We've been saying that the best way to cure carb ice is to prevent it. That's the best technique. But no matter how weatherwise or mechanically inclined you are, there will be times when ice will develop and you need to cure it.

Read your airplane's POH for specific advice on how to use the carb heat. What follows is generic advice, and your technique ought to follow whatever the POH has to say.

If you own your own airplane, think about investing in a carburetor-air temperature gauge (CAT). This is a wonderful little device. A probe in the carburetor throat senses the temperature of the airflow at the place where ice can form. The reading is displayed on a small dial in the cockpit. Knowing the carb's internal temperature takes most of the guesswork out of preventing ice formation.

If you fly IFR and own your own plane, a CAT should almost be considered a required instrument. Flying IFR puts you in the clouds with the water vapor; in fact, the humidity inside a cloud is already at 100 percent. That's why the cloud has formed. Plus, as an IFR pilot, you'll fly in lots more weather where the water-vapor content of the air is very high, at or near 100 percent. Rain, fog, low clouds, drizzle, and other similar manifestations of visible moisture exist in conditions that are prime for the formation of carburetor ice. As this chapter is being written, I'm looking out of my office window to see a wonderful IFR day: clouds so low that the downtown-building tops are hidden in them, drizzle, about a mile visibility, and temperatures in the 40s. I wouldn't relish flying a carburetor-equipped airplane today without a CAT installed.

The carb heat control works by closing a flapper plate in the carb-heat box, which is installed in the flow of intake air just upstream of the carburetor. The flapper plate closes off the normal source of outside induction air and routes air into the carb that has come from a shroud around the exhaust pipe. This air is very hot and raises the temperatures inside the carb to the point where ice can't form. And if you catch the icing early enough, it will melt ice that has already formed.

While we're on this subject, you should know now why it's important to ensure that the exhaust system is tight and free of leaks. The cabin heater works in much the same manner as does the carb heat. There is a control box with a flapper plate that closes off the normal source of outside ventilating air and causes heated air to enter the cabin. The cabin air is heated by passing first through a shroud around an exhaust pipe, and then into the passenger cabin of the airplane. If there are any leaks in the exhaust system, deadly carbon monoxide can mix with the heated air and be directly introduced into the cabin environment.

I handled a legal matter where a student pilot was on a long cross-country flight when trouble struck. The last thing the pilot remembered was cruising along at about 3,500 feet. After that, he remembered waking up in the seat of the airplane after crashing into some woods. With a stroke of divine intervention or extremely good luck, he suffered only some superficial cuts, one broken ankle, and a few broken ribs in the accident. The exhaust system of the airplane was leaky and carbon monoxide leaked into the cabin as he turned on the cabin-heat control. He didn't even know that he was overcome by the fumes and lost consciousness. Thanks to the stable flying qualities of the trainer he was flying, the airplane flew itself right side up in a shallow descent until it hit the woods. I don't think that many of us would want to bank on similar odds.

One old rule of thumb that has been taught for decades is to not apply partial carb heat. Rather, pull the control all of the way out and apply full heat. If you don't have a CAT, that's still good advice, unless the airplane's POH says otherwise. If you apply partial heat, particularly in cold weather, it's possible that you can warm up the carburetor to the point where ice crystals that would have otherwise flowed through it would melt and then refreeze as carb ice. You won't do any harm by using full heat when it's not actually required, but you could unintentionally cause a problem by using partial heat. If you've got a CAT, then you can use only the amount of carb heat needed to raise the temperature inside the carburetor outside the danger zone, as shown on the gauge.

When you apply carb heat, something else is also going on that might require other adjustments on your part. Hot air is less dense than cold air; therefore, when you introduce hot air into the fuel-air mixture, the mixture goes rich. There is more fuel now in the mixture because the amount (density) of the air in it has been reduced. That's why you see a power drop when you test the carb heat during the runup before takeoff. The engine is producing less power with the less-dense air, and you see that effect through lowered RPM.

If you're going to keep the carb heat on for more than a few minutes, readjust the mixture to account for the hotter air. Releaning will restore some but not all of the power loss. The hotter air is less dense, and the engine behaves as it would if you climbed to an altitude where the air was similarly thinner. If you're using carb heat in the traffic pattern, releaning is seldom needed because you're operating at low power anyhow.

Once you've applied the heat, don't get into situations where you need full power. One, the engine can't produce it; two, if you apply full throttle with the heat on, the engine will run rough. That's why your primary flight instructor taught you to first turn off the carb heat before you applied full power when you were doing touch and goes. When I was doing primary instruction, I always suggested that a pilot remove carb heat just before the flare, about 100 feet in the air. That way, if anything developed that necessitated an immediate go-around, full power was available, and the student didn't have to remember to get rid of the heat first. By removing the heat that late in the approach, the odds were slim indeed that any ice would develop in the few seconds before the landing or the go-around.

AIR-INTAKE ICING

Air-intake icing is not the kind of ice formation that we've been discussing. It's really a form of airframe icing, which is covered in a moment. When you're flying in conditions that result in ice adhering to the airframe, there's always a good chance that it will form around the air intake, from which the normal supply of air comes for the engine's normal use. Airframe icing can develop when carb ice doesn't, and vice versa.

If you fly an airplane that has a fuel-injected engine, intake icing is your biggest concern. Fuel-injection systems aren't subject to internal icing like carburetors are, although there has been some discussion over the years to the contrary. Some folks feel that fuel injection is susceptible to internal icing in extreme conditions. You should seek the advice of a competent mechanic and maybe even an engineer if you think about flying in the worst icing-potential conditions. I have never encountered it in a fuel-injected engine, but I haven't gone out of my way to find it either.

There is a cockpit control called "alternate air" in airplanes equipped with injected engines. This control operates another flapper door that allows the engine to draw its intake air from inside the cowling. Alternate air can provide the engine with a source of intake air when the primary intake is blocked with ice, a failed air-cleaner filter, or any other obstruction. The pilot uses the alternate source if airframe ice obstructs the normal air intake on the outside of the cowling.

Very few fuel-injected airplanes have a fixed pitch propeller, so we'll assume that any airplane you fly with an injected engine will also have a constant-speed prop.

There are two indications of ice in the air intake. First, you'll notice a drop in manifold pressure as the ice blockage builds because the supply of air will be diminished and the engine will produce less power. This is very similar to a clue provided by a carbureted engine.

Second, you'll probably see ice forming on other parts of the airframe. If you see or otherwise detect ice building up on any part of the airframe, be ready for the air intake to get blocked. Open the alternate-air source at the first sign of intake blockage. Don't wait until the ice plug is so big to risk engine failure.

The pilot generally doesn't have to worry about ice when injected engines are flown in VFR weather away from visible moisture and in temperatures where airframe icing can't occur. That's one advantage of fuel injection and one of the many reasons for the increasing popularity of this more modern system of supplying fuel to the engine.

AIRFRAME ICING

Icing on the airframe of an airplane is deadly. The severity can't be overemphasized. Any accumulation is a situation that must be dealt with immediately. What course of action the pilot takes depends upon many factors, including but certainly not limited to whether the airplane has any ice-protection equipment. Before a review of airplane equipment and what to do when icing starts to form, here is a refresher regarding what causes ice to form.

Supercooled water and other prerequisites

Air always has some water in it. Normally the water in the air is in a gaseous state, and we refer to it as water vapor. Water vapor will change to the liquid state at a certain temperature (determined by atmospheric conditions) and become visible. That temperature is the "dew point." When the dew point is lower than the ambient temperature, the vapor remains a gas, and we don't see the water molecules in the air. When so much vapor is contained in the air that the air can't hold any more, the humidity has reached or very nearly approached the 100-percent level.

When humidity hits 100 percent, dew point and temperature will be the same, and water vapor will start becoming visible. We might see it as fog, clouds, rain, drizzle, or other forms. Airplanes can fly just fine through most visible moisture as long as the temperature at the flight level is warm enough that the water doesn't freeze. When the ambient temperatures are cold enough that the water in the air is already frozen, it generally won't adhere to the airframe; hence, structural icing isn't generally a problem in those conditions. Unless you're flying VFR through light rain with accompanying excellent visibility, almost all flight through visible moisture will be IFR.

Water can exist in the liquid state at temperatures below 32°F. It's called "supercooled water." The science behind this phenomenon is complex, but for our purposes we only need to know that supercooled water can be present even though the temperature outside the airplane is below freezing. When a droplet of supercooled water hits the airplane, the surface tension on the outside of the droplet breaks. Because the airframe is cold and at or below freezing if the ambient temperature is likewise, the droplet freezes to the airframe upon impact, and ice forms.

We're going to ignore the friction heating that occurs on the leading edges of the airframe because it's insignificant at lightplane speeds. Even though the space shuttle gets red hot from friction as it reenters the atmosphere, you won't gain any similar effect in a small airplane. At speeds faster than about 400 knots, ice seldom adheres to airframes, but you're not going that fast either. When your light airplane goes through the applicable atmospheric conditions, ice will form on it.

Airframe icing can also occur when the clouds or other visible moisture and the surface of the airplane are at a temperature slightly warmer than freezing and the water isn't supercooled. As water droplets hit the airframe and splatter, they cool slightly. Expect airframe ice in temperatures as warm as about 34°–36°F.

Classifications of ice

Ice that forms on the structure of the airplane falls into three classifications: *rime, clear*, and *mixed*. Rime ice is cloudy in appearance due primarily to the fact that it contains air entrained within the ice. Clear ice is smooth and much more transparent than is rime because it has little if any air trapped inside. Mixed ice is a combination of rime and clear types.

Rime ice is probably the most common of the three types. It is usually found in stratiform clouds but can happen in cumuloform as well. Any amount of any type of ice on an airplane is dangerous, but if an icing encounter is unavoidable, rime would be preferred. Because of the air trapped within the ice accumulation, rime ice adds the least weight to the airplane, compared with an equal thickness of clear or mixed ice sticking to the structure. But rime ice can form into weird shapes and can even produce a "horned" appearance as it forms into two protrusions from a leading edge, one protrusion above the other.

Clear ice is the most dangerous. It is more pure, lacking air entrainment. Clear ice weighs almost as much as an equal volume of water, about 64 pounds per cubic foot. When encountered, clear ice can build up very rapidly. The formation is physically harder (denser) than other ice and more difficult for pneumatic boots to break off. Clear ice is most common in cumuloform clouds, but it also can occur in stratiform.

Mixed ice can have characteristics of either rime or clear ice, depending upon which type is predominant in the mixture of the two. Regardless of cloud types in which you're flying, watch out for mixed icing.

While not a true type of airframe ice, frost also produces most of the detrimental effects of ice. Frost isn't encountered in flight, except in rare circumstances. Frost forms on a parked airplane and results in a flight hazard or emergency because a pilot was either ignorant of its potential for disaster or too lazy to clean it off before takeoff. Regulations prohibit operation of an aircraft with frost adhering to the surface of the airframe.

Why ice is dangerous

Accumulations of ice on the airframe do three things, none of which is positive: airfoils change shape, weight is added, and drag increases.

Any amount of ice on the wings, tail surfaces, or propeller changes the shape of the affected surface. By changing the shape, ice changes the airfoil and alters its characteristics. Ice never accumulates exactly the same way twice, so when you're flying an airplane that is carrying any ice, you've unwittingly become an experimental test pilot.

Nobody knows what shape the airfoil will take as ice builds. As the accumulation progresses, the shape of the wing is constantly changing. No engineer has been able to test the new airfoil's characteristics. No one knows its handling qualities, stall speeds, stall characteristics, or any of the other performance parameters. Fly an icy wing and you're on your own to discover it all.

Ice adds mass to the entire airframe where it adheres. Mass equals weight; therefore, an airplane encountering ice gets heavier as the ice grows. Ice is heavy. Water weighs about 64 pounds per cubic foot, and recall that clear ice will be very close to the weight of water. Rime and mixed ice will be a little lighter, but not by much. Let's do a little math. There are 1,728 cubic inches in a cubic foot $12 \times 12 \times 12 = 1,728$.

If your light single has a wing span of about 40 feet, which is fairly typical, and the fuselage is about 48 inches wide, you have 36 feet of wing leading edge. Assume that ice accumulates 6 inches above and below the exact centerpoint of the leading edge; also assume that the ice is 1 inch thick. The calculation of ice buildup on the wing is $12" \times 1" \times 432" = 5,184$ cubic inches, or 3 *cubic feet*. Those 3 cubic feet added 192 pounds to the airplane's weight.

But you're not done. Think about the ice clinging to the nose, the wing struts, the fixed landing gear, and the tail. You could easily double the weight of the amount on just the wings and end up with the airplane about 400 pounds heavier. Many light-planes don't even have a cabinload weighing that much when the tanks are full of fuel.

Ice also adds drag. As the buildup occurs, the drag penalty increases. Ice is also accumulating on the propeller, which is losing its efficiency and producing less thrust. As the airplane weighs more, you have to increase the angle of attack to produce the extra lift to carry the added weight. Higher angles of attack mean higher induced drag, which is a by-product of lift. More drag requires more thrust to overcome the drag. The vicious circle has no end, not at least until the pilot loses control.

DEALING WITH ICE

When any ice starts to accumulate on the airframe of an airplane that is not certified for flight into known-icing conditions, the pilot has only one course of action, and that is to get out of there immediately. Most VFR pilots have very little experience in dealing with ice and have never been trained to handle it. Ice can occur during VFR flight because you don't have to be in the clouds in order to encounter it. Flying through rain, in the right conditions, can be as bad or worse than flying through ice-laden clouds.

Freezing rain and sleet occur when there is a temperature inversion, which occurs when the temperature of the air at some height above the ground is actually warmer than is either the ground or the air at lower altitudes. Freezing rain is just about the worst thing that you can meet in an airplane, except for a sudden structural failure of the airframe or penetrating a thunderstorm. If you are flying through a layer of air when the outside temperature is close to freezing, yet you notice that rain is ahead, turn around NOW.

If your airplane is going through air at or below the freezing point, the airframe is at the same temperature. When a rain droplet hits the structure, it'll freeze solid on impact. More than likely, clear ice will form rather than rime or mixed. Your troubles double; the ice is forming faster than you can blink an eye and the ice is the heaviest possible type. The only avenue of escape is to do a 180° turn and get out of those conditions as quickly as you can.

Some of the aviation pundits advocate climbing into the warm air from which the rain is falling, which would stop the additional accumulation of any ice. This theory has a couple of potential pitfalls. First, rain falls out of clouds, and if you're a VFR pilot, the warm air might be in the clouds where you don't belong. Second, all the time spent climbing is time spent in the ice, and if you can't get into that warm air, you have to spend more time in the icing conditions trying to get back down and out of them. For the VFR pilot, forget about climbing out of freezing rain. Rather, turn around and beat a fast track out of there at the first hint of freezing rain.

Most of the ice encountered by airplanes forms when flying through clouds. The VFR pilot doesn't fly in that environment, so you shouldn't have an icing problem, unless it's with freezing rain. But if you do, you need to remember a few facts and suggestions and just maybe ignore some of the older myths about dealing with ice.

Recent studies have come a long way toward understanding some of the less obvious hazards associated with airframe ice. If an airplane encounters ice while climbing or if a pilot immediately starts a climb to escape icing conditions, additional problems are generated. When a wing and a tailplane start icing in a higher angle of attack (AOA), more ice will build up than if the wing were in more level flight or at a reduced AOA.

Ice accumulates the fastest around what is called the "stagnation point" of an airfoil, where the flow divides as some of the air travels over the upper surface and the rest goes under the wing. When the AOA is increased, the stagnation point moves farther aft, and so does the region of ice accumulation. This causes the wing to become cambered on its bottom surface because the ice buildup's bulge is located beneath the leading edge. In low-wing airplanes, this point is also out of the pilot's range of sight.

When the undersurface is cambered, lift goes to pot. Due to some of the physical laws of flow separation and the inertia of particles in a flow field, the water droplets actually strike the wing behind the stagnation point when the wing's AOA is high.

For some of the same reasons, devices like antennas and tail surfaces with small radii on their leading edges collect ice even faster than the wings.

One of the age-old pieces of advice that every aviator has heard is to first try to climb out of ice, accept what you've got, and get into the colder air at higher altitudes where ice won't be likely to form on the airframe. In light of the recent advances in understanding how ice accumulates on the lifting surfaces, perhaps this isn't such a good idea. In my experiences with ice, I've always preferred to turn around and simultaneously descend if altitude permitted. Most of the time you'll find warm air below, not above you. I'd rather get out of the icing conditions and also get down into air warm enough to stop any further accumulation and perhaps even start melting off what's already built up.

It is usually preferable to climb a few hundred feet if you can and get out of the clouds into clear skies. You should know where the cloud tops are whenever you are IFR. If no pilot reports are available, ask the controller for cloud-tops information that might be available from airplanes higher than you, including jets. The ice will probably start to slowly disappear regardless of the outside air temperature when the sun starts to shine on it; "sublimation" is the name that scientists have coined to describe a solid's passing directly into the gaseous state without going through the liquid state first. If the weather conditions are clear on top, and if there is no higher overcast above you, the sun will speed up sublimation in most circumstances.

The most important thing to remember about flying an airplane with any ice accumulation is to keep the airspeed up. The altered wing will surely stall at a certain speed that is faster than what you would normally expect, but again, no one knows for sure what that speed will be. When an ice-laden wing does stall, the event is often violent and more than one crash has ensued after a stall in icing conditions. One such accident happened in 1992 when a Beech Duke went out of control at 13,500 feet and entered a spiral dive from which the pilot was never able to recover. A similar incident happened to another Duke in 1980. This pilot suffered a control loss at 19,600 feet but was high enough to regain control at 2,000 feet and live to tell the story. It was a wild ride for 17,600 feet.

One manufacturer has come out with recommended minimum airspeeds for flight in icing conditions for its twin-engine airplanes that are approved for flight in known-icing conditions. It's highly doubtful that you'll find any such advice in the POH of a light single-engine airplane. The best approach would be to fly as fast as you can, particularly when you descend and get nearer to the ground where there isn't much altitude in which to recover from a violent and unexpected stall.

Be careful about extending flaps if you're carrying any ice. Flap extension in most airplanes requires the tail to produce more downforce in order to keep the airplane trimmed. If the wings have any ice on them, the tail will too. Because the cord of the horizontal stabilizer is substantially shorter than the wing's cord, the same amount of ice will be more detrimental to the tailplane. Also recall that the tail's leading-edge radius is sharper than the wing's, which encourages even more ice to form on the tail. Tailplane stalls have been at least implicated in several crashes that occurred while airplanes with ice accumulated on the airframes were slowing to approach or landing speeds.

If the tail loses its effectiveness or stalls, the nose will pitch violently down, and recovery will most probably be impossible. Keeping the airspeed up is about the only way you can hope to keep the wings and the tail doing their respective jobs until you can get out of the icing conditions. Remaining at higher speeds is even more crucial if you have to land with any ice still adhering to the airplane.

Another problem when landing an icy airplane: The windshield will probably be ice-covered too. Lightplane defrosters are anemic at best and aren't designed to heat the windshield adequately to melt ice off the exterior. Most barely remove fog and mist from the inside. While you might be able to fly with the windshield obstructed with ice, landing is another matter. Those of us who first learned to fly in older tail draggers, where we had to look out the side to see the ground, might know what it's like to land without seeing out the front; it's not pleasant when you're neither accustomed to it nor expecting it.

FROST

Frost on the wings and other lifting surfaces acts upon them in the same way as ice does, but to a different degree. A light coating of frost looks benign enough, but it can be a trap for the unwary. Even though there isn't enough mass to have much effect on the airplane's weight, all of the other detrimental effects are still present.

Accidents due to frost on airplanes usually occur during takeoff. The wing's shape is altered enough, even with just a skim coating of frost, that the stall speed goes up, and the wing's ability to produce lift goes down. The surfaces of the wing and tail cannot "enjoy" the normal smooth airflow over them because the frost disrupts flow, increasing drag and degrading lift.

When a pilot tries a takeoff with a frost-covered airplane, no one can tell for sure what lift will be produced at what airspeed. Most of the time, the airplane fails to either lift off at all or becomes airborne only to be unable to climb at a high enough rate to clear an obstacle. Sometimes the airplane won't even climb out of ground effect. Then the accident happens.

Every pilot has heard or read that all frost should be removed from the airplane before flight is attempted. Yet every winter season we see these needless accidents. Do what needs to be done to prevent such an occurrence; put the airplane into a heated hangar to melt off the frost or wait until the ambient temperature rises sufficiently to get the job done.

If you put your airplane into a heated hangar, there is one additional hazard to be aware of and prevent. When the frost starts melting, it will naturally become water. The water will slowly flow off the upper surfaces of the wings and down through the hinges and control components for the ailerons and flaps. If you take the airplane back out into the cold before all of this water is dried completely off the airplane, you run the risk of ice forming and blocking or jamming the controls. This possibility noticeably increases if you've put the airplane in a hangar to melt off a substantial covering of snow or ice.

Dry the airplane thoroughly after the visible ice, snow, or frost has melted. That might mean leaving it in the hangar for a while, perhaps a few hours longer than it takes to just melt off the frozen covering. Delaying a departure is better than the alternative if any water refreezes when the airplane goes back outside or shortly after takeoff when you climb into colder air. Allow plenty of time for the airplane to dry out completely. Plan ahead. Put the airplane in a heated hangar far enough ahead of your anticipated departure time that you aren't hurried to take off before everything has warmed up, the snow or ice is gone, and the airplane is thoroughly dry.

ICE ON THE GROUND

If you fly in colder climates, you will have to deal with ice and snow on the ground at airports. Since the combination of salt and aluminum is one of the most corrosive mixtures known to man, airports don't salt runways and ramp areas the way that highways crews salt the roads. Occasionally you'll find an airport that will use sand on a runway, but sand can wreak havoc on turbine engines and propellers, so sand is not used much anymore. Most airports do a very good job of cleaning snow and ice from the surfaces where airplanes operate. But plowing alone cannot remove all snow and ice without the aid of ice-melting chemicals. Because the chemicals aren't used at airports, pilots have to deal with ice on the ground.

Most pilots will associate ice on an airport surface with the same hazards that are present when driving a car on ice- or snow-covered roads. For sure, they're right; however, problems inherent to operating airplanes from icy surfaces have no correlation in automobile driving.

No airplane steers on the ground with the accuracy or positive control of a car regardless of whether the season is winter or summer. Airplanes are made to fly, and most of them make miserable "cars" for the short times when they are moving on the ground. Nosewheel steering is imprecise, and even more care has to be exercised when the taxiway, ramp, or runway is slippery. Lightplane brakes are not as good as car brakes, so don't think that your airplane can stop on an icy surface as well as your car. Even on the slickest surfaces, automobiles have brakes on all four wheels. Lightplanes have only two wheels with brakes, and the footprints of those little airplane tires don't begin to have the same friction components against the surface that car tires do. Pilots lose sight of these facts every winter at several airports across the country and run off the end of a runway that appeared to be plenty long enough for a landing.

You might face a distinct problem in trying to find a space to do the normal runup. Don't wait until you get to the usual place near the departure end of the runway only to find out that the surface is too slick for the brakes to hold while you apply runup power. You have two other choices. First, if the entire airport is still slippery, let the engine warm up on a tiedown spot, then tie the airplane down, chock the wheels, and do the runup right there. (Make sure the "blast area" is not pointed at people, airplanes, or other objects that might be injured or damaged by debris.) Second, if the taxiway is clear enough that you can taxi fast, a runup can be performed by applying runup power during taxi. Don't prolong the runup, and watch your taxi speed; again be aware of reduced braking power.

An icy runway makes for a real roulette game during takeoff and landing if there is any crosswind. The airplane will weathervane into the wind because the wheels don't have enough friction with the runway surface to prevent it until the aerodynamic flight controls become effective during the takeoff roll or after control effectiveness is lost upon landing. When an airplane is weathervaning on ice, you're sailing, not taxiing or flying. When landing, use the proper crosswind deflection of all flight controls until the airplane comes to a crawl, if not a complete stop. Patches of ice on the runway are troublesome during a normal crosswind takeoff or landing because the airplane tires will do fine on the dry areas and lose traction on the icy spots. Crosswind operations on any runway surface that is slippery are risky affairs and should be avoided.

Every private pilot had to learn soft-field takeoffs and landings during training and probably demonstrate that ability during the flight examination. Simulating a soft-field takeoff or landing on a normal runway is a poor second to doing it for real. If there is any snow or slush at all on the runway that you'll be using, carefully review the POH's recommendations for soft-field operations. Tricycle-gear airplanes are much more prone to difficulty in these conditions than taildraggers, and because most of us fly the "milk stools," we have to be aware of the problems.

The nosewheel is an inherently weak and unstable device. The trick is to keep it out of the snow or slush as long as possible upon landing and to get it up off the surface as soon as possible during a soft-field takeoff. Even if your airplane doesn't normally use flaps for takeoff, and most lightplanes don't, the POH might recommend a certain amount of flap deflection during a soft-field takeoff so the nose can be raised sooner and at a slower speed. Nosegear failure is a real threat anytime that you take off from or land onto a soft field. If the nosewheel digs in, the strut or its mountings might bend or break and fold the gear under the nose.

A soft-field landing needs to be made at the slowest possible airspeed and with the tail as low as possible. The key is to reduce the stresses on the nosegear. You accomplish that by keeping the nosewheel out of the muck as long as possible. Be careful about the depth of snow, slush, or mud. In most lightplanes, I'd think long and hard about flying when snow, mud, or slush is more than about 1 inch deep, unless the POH had other recommendations.

If you are going to fly in the winter, remove the wheel fairings. Even if the takeoff is uneventful, it's very likely that slush, snow, or mud will lodge in the fairings. As you climb into colder temperatures, any such accumulations will freeze rock solid, potentially seizing a wheel. You don't want to land with a wheel that can't rotate. The same can go for the brakes on the main gear. Allow the wheels to rotate after takeoff to clear as much snow, ice, or mud as possible. If you fly a retractable-gear airplane, delay gear retraction beyond the point where you probably normally tuck the wheels away. So doing allows them to spin as long as possible and reduces the amount of muck that might get into the wheelwells. Retracting the gear while the tires are still rotating allows the dirt and snow to be slung into the wheel wells. While not common, a large accumulation of frozen muck inside the wells could possibly prevent normal extension of the gear at the end of a flight.

Flying in the winter climes offers unique challenges to all pilots, but especially to those who don't live where winter blows and snows. If you live in a region that is not blessed with snow and cold, be extra careful about conditions that you normally don't encounter. Winter flying can be a gorgeous experience in crystal-clear air and conditions where density altitude isn't a problem most of the time. Everything about aviation involves some sort of compromise; just don't compromise safety, especially through lack of training and experience.

9
Thunderstorm encounters

THUNDERSTORMS PRESENT SEVERAL SEVERE AND POTENTIALLY LETHAL hazards to aircraft and their occupants. We all naturally think of the turbulence to be found inside a thunderstorm cell, but we fail to often consider the other dangers of flirting with thunderbumpers. In addition to the violence inside of the storm cloud, the environment near the storm can be wrought with heavy rain, hail, and vicious winds. Let's first talk about the less often considered effects of flying in the vicinity of thunderstorms, and then we'll cover the dark day when you might actually tangle with the inside of a cell.

THUNDERSTORM DYNAMICS

Every pilot has seen the typical diagram of a mature thunderstorm with the vertical currents of air displayed at the edges and in the core of the storm cloud (Fig. 9-1). These movements of air in and around the thunderhead directly or indirectly account for all of the miseries that thunderstorms visit upon aviators.

For a thunderstorm to develop, the main requirement is a lifting force, which lifts unstable air. The upward force can come from thermodynamic heating, wind patterns, or frontal movements. The end result is the same; moist and unstable air gets lifted, and

Fig. 9-1. *Common makeup of a thunderstorm.*

the cycle begins. As the air goes up, it sucks more air into the storm. At the edges of the cloud, particularly in a strong thunderhead, there are heavy downdrafts of air as the cooler air descends to be warmed again and repeat the up-and-down cycle. The boundary areas, or shear areas, between the updrafts and downdrafts inside a thunderstorm can produce turbulence that will literally tear any airplane apart.

As the moist air in the center of the storm is lifted upward, often to heights exceeding 40,000 feet and many times even higher, the moisture eventually condenses out of the atmosphere. Because the cloud and storm reach such high levels, where the temperature can be 30 or 40 degrees below freezing, the water vapor condensing out of the air most often produces hail as the condensed water droplets freeze solid. Most of the time, the updrafts are so strong that a small hailstone doesn't weigh enough to initially fall out of the updraft, but it gets recycled a few times, alternatively falling to the lower parts of the thunderhead, then being uplifted again. During each cycle, the hailstone grows in size as more water vapor condenses around it, freezes, and makes the stone larger and heavier. Eventually, the size and weight of the stone are sufficient that it does fall out of the thunderstorm, and we see hail on the ground.

HAIL

Hail can also be thrown out of the top of the visible thundercloud. While you certainly can't fly near the tops of thunderstorms in a lightplane, you must be aware that the threat of hail extends beyond the visual boundaries of the storm cloud. When tossed out of the cloud, hailstones will fall to Earth like little bullets. If they are large enough, they will be more like large-caliber ammunition or small artillery shells.

An encounter with hail will be something that you'll never forget; it can destroy an airplane quickly. The first threat is to the windshield. Lightplane windshields are neither designed nor tested to withstand rock-hard pellets or baseball-size hailstones being impacted against them. If you're flying along at only 100 knots, the impact force of a hailstone striking the windshield is tremendous, and that pounding can cause windshield failure in a few seconds.

There are many reported instances of airliners and other high-performance jets suffering windshield failure from hail. These airplanes are tested for bird strikes into the windshields; your lightplane isn't tested. Yet even the much higher standards of strength to which they are designed, built, tested, and certified weren't enough to withstand a beating from hail. The danger to the windshield from a hail encounter cannot be overemphasized.

Even if the windshield survives, many parts of the airplane will be rendered into junk very soon after you fly into hail. The wings, fuselage, and tail leading edges will probably look like someone worked on them for several hours with a hammer. The propeller will suffer similar damage. There are stories of airplanes making it through hail, only to be totalled when the extent of the damage was carefully reviewed afterward. Stay out of hail at all costs.

RAIN

If the conditions aren't right for hail, thunderstorms still produce large quantities of rainfall. The rain will be intense but probably of short duration. Duration is relative in discussions about flying in and around thunderstorms. While a 20-minute downpour might be short for someone inside a building, the time would be an eternity for a pilot caught in it.

Normally, airplane engines run just fine in regular rain. But there is a breaking point where you're asking an engine to ingest more water than it can withstand and keep on purring. The torrents of rain inside a thunderstorm might be at that point. Sometimes the use of carburetor heat, which causes the normal air intake to be bypassed, can help. If the air is taken in from inside the cowling rather than through the regular outside impact source, the amount of water going through the engine will decline to a point where the engine can possibly still run. Maybe it'll help; maybe it won't.

Almost all lightplanes leak water into the cabin to some degree. If you fly through rainfall as intense as you'll find in a thunderstorm, you'll see how leaky yours really is. Be prepared to get drenched. While it's not fatal to get wet, large amounts of water pouring in will compromise your ability to deal with the situation and will probably increase whatever level of panic factor you're already coping with. The amount of water coming in might work its way into the instrument panel, causing the loss of the avionics as they get soaked.

WIND

Recall that wind currents are the culprits that cause all of the hazards associated with thunderstorms. (Turbulence inside the thunderstorm formation is covered in the discussion regarding flying through an inadvertent thunderstorm encounter. The present concern is the danger posed by winds outside the thunderstorm formation.)

Because the thunderstorm is an "engine" that is cycling vast quantities of air into, through, and out the cloud, it creates strong winds while sucking in air. Similarly high winds accompany the discharge of air out of the storm cloud. Even if you never enter the actual thunderhead, you can still have the ride of your life if you encounter these peripheral wind currents.

Never try to fly under a thunderstorm, even if you can see through to what looks like bright sky on the other side of it. The updrafts and downdrafts around and beneath the cloud are so severe that you could suffer several different results. First, the updrafts could actually suck you up into the cloud before you could react to establish a descent that was fast enough to counter them. And in so doing you might have to dive at such fast airspeeds that the combination of approaching the structural limits of the airplane and the turbulence of the situation overstresses the airframe beyond what it can withstand.

At the edges of the storm, where the airflow can be either up or down, the winds will cause a high level of turbulence. If you're trying to sneak under a thunderhead at a low altitude, it's entirely possible that a strong downdraft could slam you into the ground because the airplane doesn't have the climb rate to even remain at a level altitude in face of the powerful downdrafts. It's very difficult to conceive of winds creating updrafts and downdrafts this mighty, but they are there.

When you circumnavigate an isolated thunderstorm, allow at least 20 miles between your airplane and the visible storm cloud. Back 20 or 30 years ago, many writers used to say that 15 miles of lateral clearance was enough. But as we've advanced in the study of thunderstorms and their dynamics, we've learned that isn't sufficient. Twenty miles is now considered to be the minimum separation, but even more makes sense if the storm is a whopper. If you want to fly between two storms, be especially careful. Allow 40 miles between them, and fly between two storms only if they're isolated. It's entirely possible that the two thunderbumpers are moving at different speeds and getting closer to each other, and your "valley" could close up on you before you get through.

VFR pilots successfully fly around thunderstorms all of the time. I'll do it several times each summer. What I won't do is push the lateral clearance limits just described. You have to watch how the storm situation is developing. In many parts of the country, it's common to see isolated thunderheads that can be avoided by flying around them. But if you see any multiple storms building, expect them to build and get closer together as they grow and mature. When storms are actively breeding, there'll be more where they came from.

DEALING WITH THE THUNDERSTORM ENCOUNTER

Chapter 2 covered some discussion about off-airport landings, particularly those dictated by a progressive engine failure. Becoming trapped in an area of thunderstorms with no way out is another good reason to consider an off-airport landing. Landing in a field with the engine running normally is by far preferable to the alternative of flying inside one of the storms.

You might not be able to tie down the airplane after the landing; therefore, the airplane might yet be damaged by surface winds associated with the storms. Even if the airplane is damaged during or after the off-airport landing, your chances of survival are probably much greater than if you had flown through the cell or cells.

Every year, several well-intentioned pilots find themselves inside a thunderstorm. It happens mostly to IFR pilots who are flying in the clouds and encounter an embedded thunderstorm that has formed in or near a frontal boundary and is surrounded by other clouds. An embedded storm is masked by layers of surrounding clouds. It happened to me.

One summer morning I needed to fly my Aztec only about 100 miles to see a client. There had been lots of thunderstorm activity the night before. I thought that in the morning hours the thermal activity hadn't built to the point where renewed storms were a problem. I was wrong. A stalled cold front was lying parallel to my route of flight. The takeoff was uneventful. I entered the clouds about 1,000 feet above the ground, climbed out of them at about 4,000 feet, and flew on top until the time came to descend for the IFR approach to the destination.

The airport was served by a VOR approach. Approach-control radar at a bigger airport about 20 miles away served the little airport. When I left 4,000, I was solidly in the clouds, still quite a few miles from the destination. While the controller vectored my Aztec to the VOR where the inbound leg of the approach began, I entered a cloud as black and dark as any night has ever been. All was quiet for a few seconds.

Then the hammers of hell started pounding the airplane. The turbulence intensity strained the limits of controllability, and the rain was probably similar to standing under Niagara Falls. I immediately started a 180° turn, which might not have been the smart thing to do. During the few seconds, which seemed like hours, that it took to get out of the cell, the airplane was pitched and rolled all over. I didn't fear that as much as I just wanted out of there. Several years of aerobatic training and teaching aerobatics lessened the dread of unusual attitudes, even on the gauges. In just a short time, it was over.

During the turnaround, I told the controller what was happening and told him that I was turning around—I did not ask for permission. When I inquired if he was painting any precipitation on his scope, he said that I would have to go through the corner of a cell to make the approach. I informed him that no instrument approach would justify my flying through or near any cell. I flew over to the big airport, landed without incident, and called the controller on the phone and suggested that in the future safety would be well served by warning a pilot about a cell that could be seen on ATC radar. The meeting was canceled. I flew home VFR a few hours later when the front had finally moved out of the way, carrying the thunderstorms with it.

That evening's news reported that a tornado struck a small town in the morning hours. After getting out the charts and noting the relative times, the tornado was about 10 miles away from the thunderstorm on the approach path to the small airport. I know of no airplane that has ever come out of a tornado intact.

Certain details of the escape have been omitted, such as slowing down and flying attitude. Let's look at the conventional wisdom for escaping a thunderstorm.

First, fly attitude and forget airspeed and altitude indications. Because of the turbulence and vertical wind currents inside the cell, you can't maintain altitude anyway, and trying to will just put more stress on the airframe when it's already being sorely tested. The airspeed is going to bounce around for the same reasons, so don't chase it either. Keep the wings and nose level by flying the attitude indicator, and do your best to fly a straight course on the directional gyro. Without question, your survival depends upon staying upright with the wing and nose attitudes as level as possible.

Most knowledgeable instructors and other pundits advise against changing course inside the storm. When you are exposed to this kind of danger, the important factor is the time of the exposure. Changing course has three potential drawbacks. One, there is no guarantee that the new course will get you out of the cell any quicker than going straight ahead. Two, it takes time to turn, and that time will be spent in the cell, enlarging the window of vulnerability. Three, turning requires banking, which increases the potential for upset, and it detracts your attention from primary attitude control.

If your seat belt and shoulder harness aren't tight, cinch them up. It's very likely that the turbulence will be bad enough to bang your head on the roof. You can't fly if you're not firmly in your seat. Passengers should also tighten their belts and harnesses. Anything loose inside the cockpit, such as a binder of IFR charts, Thermos bottle, overnight case, and the like, should be secured. Flying objects within the cabin would only impede your attempts to maintain control.

If your airplane has an autopilot, turn it off immediately. Autopilots can't cope with the rapid updrafts and downdrafts, wide air-pressure changes, and turbulence inside a thunderstorm. The autopilot will only chase headings, altitudes, and roll rates. That stands a very good probability of overstressing the airframe to the failure point. As the autopilot is hopelessly trying to keep up with all of the variables, it will be running the electric trim too. An autopilot can't react like you can; it doesn't know when to leave good enough alone and ignore altitude and minor attitude variations.

Set your power for what it takes to produce flight at turbulence-penetration speed, or if that's not given in your POH, for the airplane's maneuvering speed. If you've trained yourself with the professional attitude of which we've been speaking, you already know the necessary power setting to achieve this speed, and you can adjust to it without having to guess. There are many situations in handling emergencies where preparedness and advance knowledge pay off and can save your life. This is one of them. It's vital to get the airplane slowed down to the proper speed.

Most POHs for older lightplanes don't quote a turbulence penetration speed, but all cite you to a maneuvering speed. Maneuvering speed is the maximum speed where any full and abrupt control movement won't damage the airframe because the G loads that the airplane can withstand aren't exceeded. The G loads will be exceeded if the airplane is flying faster than maneuvering speed (V_A). V_A is a usable speed inside a thunderstorm because at V_A the wings will stall before the updrafts and downdrafts can exert enough Gs to break things, or at least that's so in theory.

But if you slow below V_A, you lessen the amount of turbulence needed to induce a stall. That might seem OK, but it isn't. You need to keep the airplane under control, and if the wings are constantly stalling when they could be flying, you don't have the needed margin of control. Flying at or just slightly slower than V_A is one of the keys to survival. If you're going faster than that, you greatly increase the chances of a structural failure.

If the POH does specify a turbulence penetration speed, use that airspeed.

You will likely see intense lightning flashes. If it's at all dark inside the cell, and especially at night, turn up the cockpit lights to their full brightness to minimize the blinding effect of the lightning. At least do what you can to prevent being temporarily blinded by the flash. Turn off the rotating beacon or strobes because the pulsing light reflections inside the cloud would contribute to the onset of vertigo.

If you're talking to ATC, tell them of your emergency at once. This serves two purposes. First, there is no way that you can maintain any assigned altitude, and they need to know it. Second, you're going to need emergency services once you're out of the thunderstorm cell.

As soon as you do get out of the cell, land at the nearest airport. There is a high probability that the airplane is somehow damaged, even if it's not immediately apparent from your vantage point inside the cockpit. You can't see the prop and nose of the airplane and maybe not much of the tail. Internal wing or other structural problems aren't discernible until a qualified mechanic examines the airframe. If you are working ATC, tell the controller that you want emergency handling to the nearest airport. Fly no faster than V_A during the rest of the flight because you don't want to take any more chances of the airplane's coming apart.

WIND SHEAR NEAR THUNDERSTORMS

Let's finish the discussion of thunderstorm encounters with a subject that has been relatively unknown to lightplane pilots. Wind shear describes the phenomenon encountered when wind speeds or directions change dramatically over a very slight altitude gradient. If you're performing a takeoff or a landing approach in the vicinity of a thunderstorm, a significant wind shear is a distinct possibility.

The presence of high winds around the edges of thunderstorm cells has been established. Downdrafts coming out of the storms flatten out near the ground, and this airflow is perceived as a surface wind. Winds in excess of 35 knots are common around thunderbumpers, and velocities as high as 50 knots are not rare. These winds encompass a relatively small area; therefore, the difference is usually quite high between the normal wind conditions present on a given day and the wind speeds and directions that are generated due to the thunderstorm's effects.

A wind shear will be present anytime that the wind has a major change in either speed or direction over a small surface area. That's why you should expect wind shear anytime that you're flying within at least 20 miles of a thunderstorm. Wind shear has caused airline accidents that have killed hundreds of people. Fortunately, the death toll attributed to general aviation aircraft wind-shear encounters hasn't been so significant, but only because smaller airplanes can generally deal with the problem better than can heavier aircraft.

The typical wind shear scenario goes something like this. An airplane is on a stabilized final approach. Sometime during the last stages of the approach the pilot notices that the airspeed starts falling off and that the angle of descent starts increasing. If the pilot quickly deals with these changes in the airplane's performance, the approach can often be salvaged. If corrective action isn't taken when appropriate, the airplane flies into the ground.

Yet many pilots don't understand why the airplane does what it does in this situation. We've all been taught that the airplane's airspeed is irrespective of wind. That's true in almost all conditions but isn't exactly so when the wind's speed or direction changes suddenly and greatly. If you're flying an approach into a 30-knot headwind at 75 knots airspeed, your airplane is traveling across the ground at 45 knots, which we'll assume is well below its stalling speed if that speed were the airspeed instead of the groundspeed. When the wind suddenly decreases, let's say to 15 knots, there is 15 knots less air flowing across the wings and producing lift. So the airplane's airspeed is temporarily reduced by the 15-knot drop in the wind's speed. Now you're flying at 60 knots, and that's what you'll see on the airspeed indicator.

When the wind suddenly decreases like this, the airplane has to accelerate to make up the difference. You need to speed up by 15 knots because that's how much the airspeed has quickly dropped. All of this happens in a few seconds, and that's why it's so crucial. Instead of an approach speed of 75 knots, you're suddenly faced with going 60. When the approach speed is reduced this much, the only result will be an increase in rate and angle of descent until you add enough power to get the speed restored or drop the nose to do the same thing. If the deceleration is great enough, the airspeed could drop below stalling speed.

If you're low enough on final, dropping the nose might not be possible and still be safe. Adding power is often the only way out. Piston engines react to throttle inputs fairly rapidly, and the propeller is a very effective means of transferring that increase in power into thrust. That is the reason that lightplanes can usually deal with a wind shear encounter without a poor result. Turbine engines, even the new fanjets, don't respond as fast to increased throttle, so it takes longer for a turbine-powered airplane to accelerate out of the wind shear. Also, the heavier the airplane, the longer it takes to gain speed because you're moving so much more mass. Since lightplanes are light, they regain lost speed more quickly.

The reverse can also occur. You can be flying an approach to landing or a departure leg immediately after takeoff in a steady-wind state and without warning encounter an area of much higher winds; the airspeed will temporarily increase. Because the result will be an improved climb rate if taking off or a flatter approach if landing, this situation isn't as dangerous as encountering the shear on final.

Be ready to deal with wind shear, and don't delay making the power and airspeed corrections that are called for. If you take too long to recognize what is happening and then muddle over what to do about it, you might find yourself in the trees, power lines, or on the ground, short of the runway. If you're in the neighborhood of thunderstorms, anticipate the fact that wind shear is probable. We humans can always deal better with what we're expecting, rather than what surprises us. If you suspect that wind shear might be present on your approach, or if you were warned about the possibility by ATC, increase your approach speed by as much as is necessary to deal with it.

Pilot reports will often indicate the airspeed loss that was suffered by another aircraft while on the approach. Fly faster than the normal approach speed by at least the amount of loss reported by other pilots. At larger airports, the FAA is installing much better equipment to warn of the presence of wind shear. Never take a wind shear advisory from the tower lightly.

Wind shear can also be the product of a rapid shift in the direction of the wind without a change in its velocity. When the wind quickly shifts, it will be perceived by a pilot in an airplane in the same manner as if the speed had either increased or fallen off. Sometimes the effect of a shift in wind direction can be even more pronounced than just a velocity change. If you have a steady 30-knot headwind on a final approach, as in the previous example, and the wind shifts 180° but remains constant in speed, your airplane has flown through a shear of 60 knots.

An airspeed of 75 knots can become 15 knots in a very few seconds. If you encounter this, you're obviously going to stall if you don't increase and maintain the airspeed above stalling speed. You're going to have a very short period of time to recognize the loss of speed, figure out why, and cram the power in. Since virtually all lightplanes take off with full power, don't be hesitant or bashful about applying power. Add enough throttle to get the job done, and do it quickly. Whenever you think that you might be in a shear area, add as much extra airspeed to your normal speed on final as is practical. We're not advocating coming down the final approach screaming at V_{NE}, but use good judgment. If you're unsure, err on the conservative side by carrying too much speed. A go-around is far preferable to crashing short of the runway.

If you're making an approach onto a runway of marginal length, maybe you shouldn't try it in conditions when shear is a possibility. Short runways dictate against fast approach speeds, and slow speeds mean trouble if you encounter shear, especially when low to the ground where you can't aggressively lower the nose to help accelerate. Don't compound your problems. Most accidents are the product of several little foibles compounding themselves into a set of circumstances that the pilot either doesn't recognize or can't solve. Eliminate as many potential problems areas as you can from every flight, and learn to deal with those that you can't.

Thunderstorms are deadly to all classes and sizes of aircraft. My best friend in college became an air traffic controller and worked in an air route traffic control center. When we would visit and share war stories, he told me several times how utterly amazed he was at the number of lightplane pilots who flirted with thunderstorms. Some would even intentionally penetrate storms instead of going around them. He and I still fly. Some of those pilots aren't with us anymore. The risks are so obvious and lethal that any pilot with any wits doesn't venture anywhere near thunderstorms.

10
Loss of communications

MOST MODERN FLYING INVOLVES THE USE OF SOME OF THE AVIONICS found in almost all airplanes active today, except for the antiques and a few classics. Chapter 5 dealt with the loss of electronic aids to navigation. This chapter covers the loss of the ability to communicate with ATC. In IFR flying, loss of voice communication is an emergency, and there are specific rules and procedures to overcome that failure. When operating under VFR, loss of communications isn't a real emergency, but it can be disconcerting. Let's first talk about the problems and solutions when you are on a VFR flight, then we'll cover what to do when the comm radios fail under IFR.

LOSS OF COMMUNICATIONS UNDER VFR

A VFR pilot needs to talk to ATC when taking off from a controlled field, flying through any Class B, C, or D airspace, or when landing at an airport with an operating control tower. For takeoff or landing, every pilot must be aware of the light-gun signals used by the tower to communicate with a no-radio airplane (Fig. 10-1). Study the chart carefully before any planned no-radio operation when light-gun signals will be expected.

ATCT Light Gun Signals
Meaning

Color and type of signal	Movement of vehicles equipment and personnel	Aircraft on the ground	Aircraft in flight
Steady green	Cleared to cross, proceed or go	Cleared for takeoff	Cleared to land
Flashing green	Not applicable	Cleared for taxi	Return for landing (to be followed by steady green at the proper time)
Steady red	STOP	STOP	Give way to other aircraft and continue circling
Flashing red	Clear the taxiway/ runway	Taxi clear of the runway in use	Airport unsafe, do not land
Flashing white	Return to starting point on airport	Return to starting point on airport	Not applicable
Alternating red and green	Exercise extreme caution	Exercise extreme caution	Exercise extreme caution

Fig. 10-1. *The light-gun signals used by ATC towers when the pilot of an aircraft cannot establish two-way communications because the transceiver is inoperative or the airplane is not so equipped.*

No-radio departures

If you plan to take off without a radio from a controlled field, you should call the tower on the phone first and see if ATC can accommodate you. Nothing requires ATC to permit a no-radio takeoff, so they might restrict the time that you can leave. If the traffic is heavy, or if there are IFR aircraft either departing or arriving, you probably won't be allowed to leave on a moment's notice. Be patient and understanding, and you'll most likely be worked into the flow when you can be safely handled. Due to restrictions in the controller's handbook, ATC can't have any IFR traffic in certain areas of its airspace if a no-radio aircraft is nearby.

I've had occasion to depart many a controlled airport without a comm radio and have never been refused. I have been asked to delay my leaving for a short while, and I always cooperated. Remember that you're the one asking for something that ATC doesn't have to give you. Prepare the request with that attitude, and the odds are very good that you will be accommodated.

For departure, you'll be told in the phone conversation with the tower what your taxi instructions are and what runway to expect. When you get in the airplane, the ground controller will use the light gun to clear you to the runway. Light-gun signals should be memorized, but don't hesitate to have a color-coded chart of light-gun signals out where you can quickly refer to it if need be. Don't become a jam in the gears of smooth traffic flow.

Once you get to the runway, do your normal runup, then turn the airplane into a position from which you can see the tower. Not much is more frustrating to a controller than sending light-gun signals to an airplane when the pilot can't see them.

After takeoff, execute the pattern departure that is approved for that airport. If you want a nonstandard departure, or if you have any questions, clarify all variables during the telephone conversation with the tower before you head for the airplane. Because you can't talk to anyone from the cockpit, get everything established in your mind as well as the controller's mind before you start to taxi. When you get underway, it's too late to sort out any misunderstandings.

LOSS OF COMMUNICATIONS EN ROUTE WHILE VFR

Many airplanes fly cross-country flights everyday without radios. The problems precipitated by radio failure occur when a pilot who is accustomed to having communications capability suddenly loses it, particularly if already inside Class B, C, or D airspace. You cannot legally enter one of these three classes of airspace without a functioning two-way radio unless you have advance approval from ATC. If the radio conks out after you've already entered one of these areas, you have to deal with it appropriately and legally to avoid hassles for either the controller or the pilot.

When you first called the controller for either permission to enter, as in Class B, or to advise of your intentions before getting into the airspace class, as in C and D, you should have told ATC where you're headed. The controller will have given you an altitude and route to fly in Classes B and C. If communications are lost after that point, follow that assigned route, and stay at the assigned altitude until it's practical and normal to begin your descent for landing, assuming that you're landing at some airport within that airspace. If you're only transiting through the airspace, stay on the route, and at the altitude you were given until you are out the other side. The only deviations that you should make from your assigned route and altitude are those required to stay out of IFR conditions, avoid other aircraft, and to keep from hitting anything else.

Entry into airspace Classes B and C requires a functioning Mode-C encoding transponder. With this device, the controller will know your altitude. As you descend for landing, if that's what you're doing, the descent won't come as a surprise to the controller, and the radar screen will indicate altitude changes. If only the transmitter is lost, continue to listen for the controller's transmissions. Often you will be asked to squawk ident as a method of acknowledging ATC instructions, so pay attention. If you can't hear anyone talking to you, go ahead and make calls to the controller as you start the descent because you might have only lost the receiver or the cabin speaker. Don't automatically assume that you have lost all of the components of the communications radio installation. Transmitters, receivers, and speakers can and often do fail independently.

Many pilots have taken to wearing headsets, which are more reliable than cabin speakers. I prefer to wear foam ear plugs and still listen to the cabin speaker because I wear a size 8½ hat and find most headsets uncomfortable. But I still carry a headset or earphones for the day when the speaker fails, which it has on several occasions in my years of flying lightplanes.

There are headsets that do not encompass the entire head but just wrap around one ear and have a little microphone that is placed in front of the mouth. I've used these comfortably; try one if you've also found that large headsets are as uncomfortable as putting your head in a vise. Cabin speakers are frail devices, and can fail from a multitude of causes, usually old age. If you don't like the big headsets, at least buy a set of inexpensive headphones. With the proper adapter for the plug, you can even use household stereo headphones in an airplane.

Watch out for a stuck mike. If yours sticks in the open position, a carrier wave will be transmitting constantly, blocking the entire frequency. You should hear a little "click" as you activate the mike, and if you don't, yours might be stuck open. If you never hear anyone respond to your calls, suspect your microphone. Check for the click sound, and if you don't hear it as you try to transmit, pull the mike cord out of its socket, so you don't jam the channel. Since most airplanes are equipped with two navcoms, turn off the one that you have been using, and try the other. If the loss of communications prevails after you try the second radio, use another mike. Your headset mike might be the culprit, so unplug it and revert to using the airplane's hand-held microphone. If you don't carry a headset on board, always carry a spare mike. If you use a headset, it will be the additional microphone. Thinking ahead, anticipating what components might fail, and carrying appropriate and practical spares will eliminate many communications failures.

VFR ARRIVALS WITHOUT RADIO COMMUNICATIONS

If you need to land at a controlled airport without benefit of a radio, you need to basically follow the departure procedures in reverse. Land at an uncontrolled airport near the controlled field where you want to go, and call the tower on the telephone. Once again, ATC has no obligation to permit a no-radio arrival, but most controllers are extremely helpful, especially if you're headed back to your home base or going to an avionics shop for repairs. You might be asked to wait a while if traffic is heavy, or if the controlled field has some upcoming IFR departures.

Try to time your arrival for periods when the airport isn't laboring under the heaviest traffic peaks. If your destination is an airport that normally caters to business aircraft, early mornings and late afternoons are often the busiest times when the airport is a beehive of activity. If you are headed for an airport that generally serves recreationally used aircraft, don't plan to arrive without a radio on a beautiful Sunday afternoon in the spring or summer. Again, a little common sense used in preplanning your flight to fit into the program at the destination will make things go much more easily for you, the controllers, and the other pilots flying to and from the airport.

During the phone call, you'll be told how to approach the traffic pattern, what runway to use, and what pattern to fly. When you receive light-gun signals, the standard method of acknowledging them is to rock your wings. Remember that the controller's vantage point might be a mile or two from your position in the pattern, so rock the wings vigorously. Little banks of 15° or 20° might not be discernible from the tower's viewing angle.

Losing radio communications during VFR operations should not cause anyone any consternation. Know what to do and what the light-gun signals mean, and plan ahead. Then you can fit into the flow and probably complete your flight uneventfully.

LOSS OF COMMUNICATIONS UNDER IFR

Losing the ability to communicate when flying IFR is quite a bit more serious than if it happens where you're operating under VFR. But if you know and follow the procedures in the regulations and in the *Airman's Information Manual*, the flight can be finished without undo problems. Let's look at a few different situations and examine first the time when you might be on an IFR flight plan and clearance, but you're not in actual IFR weather. Section 91.185 of the FARs governs all of these situations. FAR 91.185(a) provides:

Unless otherwise authorized by ATC, each pilot who has two-way radio communications failure when operating under IFR shall comply with the rules of this section.

Then FAR 91.185(b) says:

VFR conditions. If the failure occurs in VFR conditions, or if VFR conditions are encountered after the failure, each pilot shall continue the flight under VFR and land as soon as practicable.

Let's analyze what this regulation means.

A great majority of the actual time that aircraft spend flying under instrument flight rules is actually flown in VFR weather conditions. Many pilots, especially if they fly high-performance airplanes, file IFR for every cross-country flight regardless of the actual weather conditions. Even if the weather is IFR at the airport of departure or at the intended destination, there is always a good chance that some portion of the trip will encounter VFR conditions. This section of the regulations is directed precisely at those times when a pilot, having filed IFR and while operating on a clearance, is really flying in VFR weather at some point either at the time the radios fail or afterward.

FAR 91.185(b) requires the pilot to stay in VFR conditions once they are encountered. You are prohibited from flying back into IFR weather, even though you're on a clearance. Obviously, if your encounter with VFR weather is only momentary, and if you can't stay VFR, this section won't apply. An IFR aircraft that has suffered a communications failure presents a tremendous inconvenience to ATC and a safety hazard as well. The controllers can't control your routing or altitude; vectoring is also impossible. All they can do is wait and hope that the pilot knows what to do next.

For that reason, the regulation dictates that you stay VFR if you can and land as soon as practicable. The requirement to land gets you on the ground and out of the ATC system. Other IFR operations can return to normal, and the controllers won't have to deviate other aircraft, hold them, or take the other measures that have to be taken to deal with an airplane in the system that can't talk to anyone.

The modern IFR system is built around radar and two-way communications between controllers and pilots. When radar or radios fail, the entire system goes into slow motion.

The landing requirement has a little vagueness to it. The regulation says to land as soon as practicable, not as soon as possible. There is a difference between what is practicable and what is possible; many things are possible that aren't necessarily practicable. The *Airman's Information Manual* gives the FAA's view of this difference in a note that says,

> . . . It is not intended that the requirement to 'land as soon as practicable' be construed to mean 'as soon as possible.' The pilot retains (the) prerogative of exercising . . . best judgment and is not required to land at an unauthorized airport, at an airport unsuitable for the type of aircraft flown, or land only minutes short of (the) destination.

Notice that AIM says that you aren't required to land only minutes short of the destination, but doesn't say how many minutes. Don't think that you should continue flight for 50 or more miles if an appropriate airport is close to your position at the time of the radio failure, unless you're in a very fast airplane. ATC wants you down on the ground for good reason. Continuing the flight would tie up the entire ATC system in the area. You would present a safety hazard to other IFR aircraft, particularly if radar contact is lost and the controller can't see you on the radar screen.

If you bypass a suitable airport in VFR conditions, you could become the subject of the FAA's enforcement scrutiny. I'd land at the nearest airport where a safe landing could be made. For sure, that landing would be "as soon as practicable." Upon landing, I would call an FSS and tell the specialist what happened, and I would request that the appropriate ATC facilities be notified that I had landed.

Unfortunately, two-way communication failures also occur when the airplane is in actual IFR conditions and when no VFR weather presents itself to the hapless pilot. In this scenario, FAR 91.185(c) comes into play. It's a long section, which is quoted in its entirety and then broken down and analyzed.

> (c) *IFR conditions.* If the failure occurs in IFR conditions, or if paragraph (b) of this section cannot be complied with, each pilot shall continue the flight according to the following:
> (1) *Route.* (i) By the route assigned in the last ATC clearance received;
> (ii) If being vectored, by the direct route from the point of radio failure to the fix, route, or airway specified in the vector clearance;
> (iii) In the absence of an assigned route, by the route that ATC has advised may be expected in a further clearance, or
> (iv) In the absence of an assigned route or a route that ATC has advised may be expected in a further clearance, by the route filed in the flight plan.

(2) *Altitude.* At the highest of the following altitudes or flight levels for the route segment being flown:

(i) The altitude or flight level assigned in the last ATC clearance received;

(ii) The minimum altitude (converted, if appropriate, to minimum flight level as prescribed in Section 91.121(c)) for IFR operations; or

(iii) The altitude or flight level ATC has advised may be expected in a further clearance.

(3) *Leave clearance limit.* (i) When the clearance limit is a fix from which an approach begins, commence descent or descent and approach as close as possible to the expect-further-clearance time if one has been received, or if one has not been received, as close as possible to the estimated time of arrival as calculated from the filed or amended (with ATC) estimated time en route.

(ii) If the clearance limit is not a fix from which an approach begins, leave the clearance limit at the expect-further-clearance time if one has been received, or if none has been received, upon arrival over the clearance limit, and proceed to a fix from which an approach begins and commence descent or descent and approach as close as possible to the estimated time of arrival as calculated from the filed or amended (with ATC) estimated time en route.

That's a long-winded set of requirements, but each is necessary, as we shall see. If you're an IFR pilot, you need to know this regulation by heart because you probably won't have a copy with you when the need for it arises. Now, let's break it down into understandable steps.

First, if you can't comply with (b), which means that you're not in VFR weather or don't encounter VFR weather, you're expected to continue the planned flight. Remember that you're in IFR weather and ATC doesn't want you to make just any IFR approach to some airport somewhere and in the process lose any idea of where you are. ATC wants you to fly to your destination, and if you miss the approach there, continue to your filed alternate airport. You also need to be aware that this regulation is written to allow for a nonradar environment, in case radar contact with your airplane is lost or if the radar on the ground fails. A no-radio airplane creates havoc to the controller's handling of other traffic, and ATC has to be able to at least estimate your position from the information about aircraft type, airspeed, route, destination, and alternate that you gave in your IFR flight plan, and then estimate where you're going and when you'll be there.

How do they do that? You fly the route(s) that the regulation requires, that's how. It's easy if you are on the en route phase along airways or on a direct routing with onboard navigation such as RNAV, loran, or GPS. You just fly the route specified in your IFR clearance that you initially received, unless it's been amended. Fly by that route until you reach your clearance limit, which is most often your destination airport. If you have a different clearance limit short of your planned destination, stand by for an explanation.

When you're being vectored, you are always told by ATC the airport, fix, route, or airway toward which the vectors are designed to take you. If the radio calls it a day before you get to that position, just continue on a direct route that will take you there from the point where the radio failed.

Sometimes ATC will not assign a precise route to somewhere, but will give you a route to expect. If you lose the ability to communicate while being vectored under this circumstance, follow the routing that you were told to expect. Rarely will you not have an assigned route nor will you have been told to expect any certain routing. If that's the case, revert to the route that you put in your flight plan and fly it. This gets you to the clearance limit. The choice of altitude(s) to fly is next.

There are three possible choices of altitude, depending upon where you are and what ATC told you before the radio quit. You are to fly at the HIGHEST of the possible choices. That altitude will probably change as you proceed from one route segment to the next.

Look at your IFR chart, and see what the minimum en route altitude (MEA) is for that portion of the flight where you currently are located. Fly at the MEA unless ATC has assigned you a higher altitude for that segment or has told you to expect higher in a further clearance. If you were told to expect higher in a given distance or period of time, climb to that higher altitude when you have flown the referenced distance or flown the stated number of minutes. That's all there is to it. If the MEA goes up to an altitude above what you were assigned or told to expect by ATC, always fly at the MEA.

Clearance limits are places where your IFR clearance theoretically ends. You are almost always cleared to your destination airport, particularly if it's served by an IFR approach. If you were initially cleared to the destination, and assuming that your clearance wasn't amended by ATC, this section doesn't really apply to you. With an airport as your clearance limit, you're expected to proceed to that airport to which you were cleared, shoot an IFR approach, and land. If the weather is below minimums and you miss the approach, you're then required to go to your filed alternate and land there.

Occasionally you'll receive a clearance limit short of your destination, such as an airway intersection, VOR, or NDB. If you lose communications with this kind of clearance limit, your life gets a little more complicated. Still, it's not an incomprehensible task if you study what you're supposed to do before you have to do it. When you have a clearance limit short of an airport, you probably will have received an expect-further-clearance time from the controller. If you arrive at the point of your limit early, fly a standard holding pattern until the expect-further-clearance time comes.

If you arrive on time or late (or at the conclusion of the holding pattern), when the expect-further-clearance time comes, you start taking appropriate action. If the clearance limit is a fix from which an instrument approach begins, start the approach procedure. If you never received any expect-further-clearance time, you should hold there until your estimated time of arrival (ETA) as disclosed on your flight plan or as amended and communicated to ATC, then begin the descent and approach at your ETA.

If the clearance limit is a fix that is not the start of an approach, you have to reach such a fix at the appropriate time. You figure that time in a similar fashion as if the fix were an approach-starting point. If you received an expect-further-clearance time from

ATC, leave the clearance limit at that time. If you arrive early, hold until the expect-further-clearance time; if you arrive late, proceed immediately.

If you never received an expect-further-clearance time before the radio packed it in, leave the clearance limit headed toward a fix from which an approach will begin. When you get to the approach fix, see how your ETA is coming. If you're on time or late, start the descent and approach. If you're early, hold at the approach fix until the ETA, then start down for the approach.

When you think about these procedures from a logical point of view, they make common sense. ATC wants you to go where you're going by the most sensible route, the assigned route, if applicable. ATC wants you high enough to stay out of the rocks. And ATC wants you to make your approach to land on time. If you keep these goals in mind, it's much easier to understand the regulation, keep its requirements organized in your mind, and follow them.

The way to keep fresh on this emergency procedure, like most of the rest of them, is to practice. During recurrent training or on your next BFR, ask the instructor to give you a problem with a simulated loss of communications. Then keep one other course of action at hand. If you've lost communications, you most likely still have operating VOR receivers. ATC can transmit over the VOR frequency, unless it's a no-voice VOR. Turn up the VOR receiver volume, and you might well hear controllers talking to you. If they ask you to acknowledge transmissions by turning, squawking ident on the transponder, or whatever, do it. You're communicating again and the problem is solved.

If you fly IFR, buy a hand-held radio. It would cost not much more than $500 or so and would solve all of these problems; however, their reception and particularly transmission ranges aren't as great as avionics installed in the panel. If you own your own airplane, have an avionics shop install a cable from the outside antenna to the inside of the cockpit. You can plug the hand-held into the normal antenna and greatly increase its range. In the event that both panel-mounted radios fail, get out your hand-held and attach the antenna cable. If the hand-held isn't transmitting or receiving, the problem is probably a broken off or failed external antenna.

Revert to the "rubber ducky" antenna that came with the hand-held. You might have to wait until you get closer to an ATC facility to reestablish communications, but you won't be in a world of silence for the rest of the flight. Because battery power is consumed at a much higher rate when transmitting as opposed to only receiving, tell the controller that you are using a battery-powered hand-held radio. Explain that you would like to keep your transmissions to a minimum in order to extend the battery's life. Naturally, a hand-held is of no use whatsoever if the battery or batteries aren't charged. Make sure everything is charged up, including spare batteries, before every flight.

USE THE TRANSPONDER

If you lose communications capability while IFR, the AIM says to set your transponder to code 7600, which is designated as the code for loss of communications. Stay on

7600 for the remainder of the flight. Every center and terminal radar facility that is in radar range will understand the situation and keep other IFR traffic safely separated from you.

KEEP TRYING

If you lose communications with the controller with whom you are working, don't give up on trying to reestablish contact. First, switch back to the previous frequency that you were using. The problem could be with ATC's radios, not yours. If that doesn't work, switch to the FSS frequencies and try calling them. Occasionally a center or terminal radar facility will suffer a power outage. You won't be able to talk to them on any of their channels, but you still could raise a flight service station. An FSS can then relay instructions or reroute your flight through a terminal facility or neighboring center that is still on the air.

Many an IFR flight has been successfully completed without voice communications between the aircraft and ATC. Before radar coverage was completed, IFR pilots flew quite often in nonradar environments, which was the next best thing to not being able to communicate because the controllers couldn't tell where we were anyway. You know the "secret" to successfully handling this emergency is training and mental attitude, which will most likely get you out of other trouble as well. Know what to do, train for it, and then do it.

11
Partial-panel flying

IN THE TYPICAL LIGHTPLANE INSTALLATION, THREE OF THE FLIGHT instruments used for IFR flight are gyroscopic instruments: the attitude indicator (sometimes called the artificial horizon), the heading indicator (sometimes called the directional gyro), and the turn coordinator (or turn and bank indicator in older airplanes). These instruments derive their proper display because at the heart of each is a gyroscope spinning thousands of revolutions per minute, giving the instrument a stable platform for its frame of reference. Usually, the attitude indicator and directional gyro (DG) are driven by either vacuum or positive air pressure produced by either a vacuum pump or pressure pump driven by the engine. The turn coordinator is most often electrically powered.

In addition to these gyro instruments, the instrument pilot uses instruments that derive readings from certain air pressures outside and sometimes inside the airplane: airspeed indicator, altimeter, and rate of climb indicator (often referred to as the vertical speed indicator and abbreviated VSI).

The gyro instruments can and do fail because they are mechanical devices that depend upon either other mechanical gizmos (a vacuum or pressure pump) or the aircraft's electrical system for their power to operate. Generally, the failure mode of the gyro instruments rests in their relative power sources. Either the vacuum or pressure pump gives up the ghost, failing the attitude indicator and DG, or there is an electrical problem that manifests itself in a failure of the turn coordinator. (From here on, "vacuum pump" will refer to either a true vacuum pump or the positive-pressure pump used primarily in Beechcraft products. From an operational point of view in the cockpit, there isn't any difference between them.)

The instruments do wear out like anything else mechanical, but they usually do so gradually. The pilot can notice that the heading indicator is beginning to precess more than normal or that the attitude indicator fails to properly stabilize and always lists to one side after engine start. When you see these symptoms developing, don't do anymore IFR flying until you have the affected instrument overhauled or replaced.

When the attitude indicator or DG suddenly fails, most often it's a dual failure because the vacuum pump failed. For decades, lightplanes were equipped with vacuum pumps that had a lubrication system oiling the rotating vanes of the pump, which derived oil from the engine and circulated it through the pump body. These units were called wet pumps because they were wet with oil. They worked fine, had some advantages, and some disadvantages. The biggest problems with wet pumps were that they are heavy and were often a source of oil leaks, dirtying the inside of the cowling. The greatest advantage of them was that they had a long service life, were dependable, and went to pot over a long enough period of time that they seldom failed suddenly. A pilot could tell of impending trouble because the vacuum gauge would show less and less vacuum, usually over several flight hours, until the pump quit entirely.

Now most all airplanes made since the late 1960s use a dry pump. With the advent of Teflon and other materials that don't need outside lubrication when they rub against each other, the vacuum pump changed. Dry pumps have vanes with these manmade materials at the outer edges where the vane tips are in contact with the cylindrical pump body as they rotate; hence, the pumps no longer need oil lubrication because the vane tips are self-lubricating. With a dry pump, you don't need the oil plumbing that was required in a wet pump installation, and dry pumps can be made quite a bit lighter than the former generations of wet pumps.

However, there's no free lunch. With the benefits that we gained from dry pumps, we also got two very bad side effects. When they fail, they usually do so suddenly and without warning. Add to that the fact that the service life of a dry pump can be very short, sometimes as little as 500 hours. The old wet pumps usually lasted for the overhaul life of the engine. From a purely personal viewpoint, I've always felt that the switch from wet to dry pumps was a case of "fixin' what ain't broke." But dry pumps are with us to stay, so unless you fly an older airplane, you've got to cope with them.

For seven years, my wife and I owned a 1959 Piper Comanche. It was a decent old airplane, but it had its maintenance problems and costs like anything else that old. But it never had a vacuum pump failure in all of those years because the airplane had a wet pump. A few of my buddies were very proud of their newer steeds, until they got the opportunity to do some partial panel flying for real when their new dry pumps suddenly packed it in during flights in actual IFR.

Before delving into the art of flying without benefit of the gyro instruments, let's consider standby vacuum systems, which come in two basic kinds: a second (standby) pump and a system that derives vacuum from the intake manifold of the engine.

Standby pumps are probably better, but you might not be able to install one in your airplane either conveniently or affordably. Many modern high-performance airplanes, especially those equipped with deicing boots, have a second factory-installed pump that is driven by the engine, the same as the primary one. Other manufacturers have designed a second pump that is electrically driven, and sometimes these are mounted in the tail area far away from the engine. If you're lucky enough to fly an airplane with two pumps, count your blessings. Of course, most twin-engine airplanes have a vacuum pump driven by the respective engine in each nacelle.

It's very difficult to put a standby pump in an airplane that isn't equipped with one from the factory. It can be done, but often the cost and complexity are prohibitive. For these planes, consider installing the type of secondary vacuum source that taps into the engine's intake manifold. When the primary pump fails, the pilot can activate this standby system and continue to power the gyro instruments with the suction that is created inside the intake manifold as the engine runs. But there's a problem here too.

In order for the intake to produce usable suction, there must be at least about 4" of mercury differential pressure between the outside ambient air pressure and the manifold pressure. Manifold pressure increases with throttle settings and is measured in inches of mercury, the same as ambient air pressure is. On the ground close to sea level, you'll see the manifold pressure gauge on the panel indicating about 30" when the engine isn't running. That's the ambient pressure. When you start the engine, the manifold pressure immediately goes down. When you're idling, the manifold pressure will indicate somewhere around 10" or 12", so there's about 18" or 20" of difference between MP and ambient pressure.

Recall from basic atmospheric science that at the altitude normally flown by lightplanes, ambient pressure decreases very close to one inch of mercury per thousand feet increase in altitude; therefore, if ambient pressure is 30" at sea level, it'll be somewhere around 20" at 10,000 feet. Because there has to be that differential between ambient pressure and MP of about 4" minimum, you couldn't use the intake-type of vacuum source if the manifold pressure setting were any greater than about 15" or 16" at this hypothetical 10,000. If you climb higher, say to 15,000 feet, you'd need to have the manifold pressure down around 10" or 11" to create the necessary differential. A manifold pressure that low is probably too low to be able to fly at a level altitude and at anywhere near a normal cruise airspeed.

If you opt for an intake-manifold standby vacuum system, you can't use it much above about 10,000 feet and still produce much engine power. That usually isn't a problem over flat terrain, but if you fly a lot of IFR where lofty altitudes are necessary to comply with MEAs through mountains, this system won't help on route segments that high. Still, any standby system is better than none.

RECOGNIZING THE PROBLEM

When you review accident reports frequently, it's uncanny to see how many pilots have failed to recognize that a flight instrument is inoperable; sometimes two instruments were inoperable. Apparently their training and instrument flying skills were wanting. Let's see how this confusion can settle into a pilot's mind.

When one gyro fails

A proper scan of all of the instruments in the panel is the foundation of instrument flying and is a skill the instrument pilot possesses or did have at one time. Just looking at the instruments isn't a scan in the sense of proper instrument flying. Scanning is the practice of gathering a totality of information from all of the sources available in the panel. No single instrument in a lightplane provides the pilot all of the information necessary to fly IFR.

When a pilot fails to recognize the failure of an instrument, he or she is starting down the road to disaster. Confusion can quickly set in, robbing the pilot of common sense and the ability to analyze the situation and deal with it. Scanning techniques have to be constantly practiced so you can tell the whole story from all of its various component sources. When one piece of information doesn't seem right, it's time to relax, think, and use some judgment.

If the attitude indication shows a bank to one side, yet the DG is not rotating, you've got a conflict in the stories being told by these two instruments. We all should know that airplanes normally turn when banked, unless opposite rudder pressure is applied to prevent a change in heading. Look at the turn coordinator. Where is the ball? If it's in the middle, the airplane is in normal coordinated flight. What is the little airplane symbol in the turn coordinator showing? Or if you have the older style turn-and-bank instrument, is the needle centered or off to either side? If the ball is centered and the airplane symbol or turn needle is also in the middle position, you're neither turning nor are you holding cross-rudder pressure against a bank.

The attitude indicator isn't telling the correct story. Something is wrong. Now figure out what it is. Three sources indicate that the airplane is in coordinated flight and not turning. The DG indicates straight ahead, which is backed up by the turn coordinator's indications. The ball shows that the airplane isn't cross-controlled. When three versions of a story are identical and one is not, believe the three. Now you know that the attitude indicator is on the fritz and is to be ignored throughout the remainder of the flight. The attitude indicator won't cure itself, so put it out of your mind.

You're not finished. What does the vacuum gauge show? If vacuum pressure is normal, you may now assume that only the attitude indicator has failed. If the vacuum gauge shows that the vacuum is gone or is very low, you know to suspect the vacuum pump. When the pump goes, all of the instruments that it drives go with it. That means that the DG will soon "go south" along with the attitude indicator.

Anytime that you have reason to doubt the veracity of the attitude indicator's display, suspect the DG too. The DG's gyro might spin down more slowly than the attitude indicator's gyro, and the DG could appear to be functioning normally at first blush. When the DG finally does give it up altogether, it might spin wildly for a few seconds or "freeze" on some current heading. You won't know in advance which will happen. If the DG goes crazily spinning, you know for sure that something is haywire, which can be confirmed by looking at the zero reading on the vacuum gauge. If the failed DG doesn't spin and instead stays on a heading that you appear to be maintaining, you could be turning unknowingly at a hefty rate. That's just another reason to include the vacuum gauge in your routine instrument scan.

The turn coordinator is driven by a different source than the DG and attitude indicator. In almost all modern airplanes, the turn coordinator is electrically powered, so it continues to function properly following a vacuum pump breakdown. If the turn coordinator does go out and starts giving either false or no indications, fall back to the DG and attitude indicator to see what's going on. Remember that the ball portion of the turn coordinator is a gravity instrument and needs no power to work. Even when the turn portion of the indicator, either the airplane symbol or the needle in a turn and bank indicator, stops functioning, the ball still works just fine. If the cause of the turn coordinator failure is in the airplane's electrical system, you'll probably already know it because other electrical devices will be dropping offline or the ammeter will be showing quite a rate of discharge. If the problem is only in the actual instrument, you'll have to go through the crosscheck scan to determine that fact.

The key to recognizing the failure of an instrument or all of the gyro instruments is to remember that no single instrument tells the whole story about what the airplane is doing. We've talked about how to crosscheck for turn or bank indications with other instruments to determine if the airplane is banked, turning, or both. Use airspeed indicator, altimeter, and the rate of climb indicator (the VSI) to crosscheck an indication that the nose is either up or down. If the attitude indicator says that the nose isn't level, something else must happen as a result. Anytime that the nose attitude isn't level, the airplane will climb or descend and lose or gain airspeed. Unless the power setting is changed significantly, an airplane cannot undergo a change in nose attitude without a corresponding change in some other flight parameter.

An airplane with surplus power in a nose-up attitude will climb; the climbing attitude will also result in a drop in airspeed. This crosscheck should be easy. If the nose has risen, all of the air-pressure instruments will let you know it. If the nose is still level, the airspeed will remain stable, the VSI will be centered on the zero indication, and the altimeter will not be changing. Then you know that the attitude indicator isn't telling the truth.

Conversely, when the nose is lowered, the airspeed will increase, the altimeter will show a descent for a short time, and the VSI will be pointing down. Look for the secondary indications of a low-nose attitude. If the indications aren't present, if the airspeed is stable, if the altimeter reading isn't changing, and if the VSI is again on zero, the attitude indicator is providing false information. Three very reliable instruments are refuting the story that you are being told by a gyro instrument that is much more likely to fail. Suspect and then ignore the attitude indicator.

The combinations of potential instrument failures and appropriate crosschecks to verify the failures are virtually endless. But you don't need to engage in memory exercises. If you learn how to use all of the pieces of the story to figure out the whole, you can quickly and easily tell what is wrong, to what extent, and what instrument to then suspect and ignore.

FAILURE OF AIR-PRESSURE INSTRUMENTS

The primary instruments normally installed in lightplanes are referred to as air-pressure instruments: airspeed indicator, altimeter, and VSI. Each instrument operates by using air that is either rammed into it (airspeed) or static (altimeter and VSI). Mechanical breakdowns inside these instruments are extremely rare. What does happen to cause one or more of them to go haywire is a blockage of the air source needed to function properly.

The airspeed indicator works by comparing the pressure of the air rammed into it through the pitot tube with the pressure captured on one side of a diaphragm. As the ram-air pressure increases (more air is forced through the pitot tube from faster speed), the diaphragm moves. The diaphragm is connected mechanically to the needle on the face of the instrument, and the pilot sees airspeed changes according to movement of that needle. If the pitot tube or the static-air port for the airspeed indicator becomes blocked, the indicator won't function correctly.

These blockages often occur on the ground before the flight is even begun. Various bugs, like wasps and other flying insects, love the pitot tube opening as a home. If you get a nest built in there, it's the same as stuffing the opening with bubble gum, and no ram air will get in. People have accidentally bumped into pitot tubes and bent them, crushed them, and broken them completely off. Pilots have forgotten to remove the protective sleeves that cover the tube, so it might as well be blocked.

If there is a blessing in disguise for this type of airspeed failure, it is that the problem will show up immediately, even during the takeoff run. While I agree with instructors who teach pilots to take off in single-engine lightplanes without reference to a specific rotation or lift-off speed, I do think it's a good idea to scan the airspeed indicator during the takeoff. If the indicator isn't showing an increase in speed, abort the takeoff if there's room to do so.

After liftoff, most pilots will start using the airspeed to settle into the climb. If you see a zero indication or some other wild number, it shouldn't be too hard to determine that the airspeed isn't working correctly. Sometimes when a pitot gets blocked, the instrument will go to crazily high-speed indications, resulting from the needle's actually going on the negative side of zero. Your options at this point are reduced to one—fly the pattern and return for a landing. A functional airspeed indicator is required by the FARs, even for VFR flight.

Every pilot ought to be able to fly an airplane without an airspeed indicator, regardless of whether he or she has an instrument rating. Every primary training student of mine flew a complete traffic pattern from liftoff around to landing with the airspeed indicator covered. Even though that wasn't partial-panel flying as we use the term relating to instrument pilots who suffer instrument failures, it was an introduction to the process. Instruments don't know whether a fully trained and competent pilot is in the airplane or one who just passed the private pilot flight test. Instruments can fail with anyone in the pilot's seat.

If you're instrument rated and making a takeoff into low IFR weather, you better have included the pitot in your preflight inspection. Operating under Part 91 of the FARs, you can legally (not necessarily sensibly) take off when the weather is zero-zero. If you engage in this version of Russian roulette, check the pitot and make sure that the airspeed indicator is working properly during the takeoff run.

If the pitot tube is clear and unobstructed at takeoff, about the only way that it will get blocked in flight is from ice. (Refer to chapter 8 for a refresher on airframe icing.) If the airplane starts to encounter ice, one of the first things to happen will be the blockage of the pitot tube. Don't fly IFR without a heated pitot. Pitot heat should be turned on as soon as you enter visible moisture or clouds when the temperature is conducive to icing. Normally, VFR pilots don't encounter airframe ice because they don't fly in clouds.

Altimeter problems usually result from a blockage of the static air vent. The altimeter is nothing more than a barometer that measures the density of the outside air. If it can't get outside air to measure, it doesn't work. Always crosscheck the altimeter after liftoff to see if it's showing an altitude gain in the initial climb. If it doesn't, fly the pattern and land. It is also legally required for VFR flight, as well as obviously being crucial for IFR.

If the static-air vent is blocked, the VSI will not function properly either. Losing the VSI should not be crucial for a proficient IFR pilot, and that loss should be close to meaningless for a VFR trip. Know where the static port is on the airplane that you fly. It might be on the side of the fuselage near the front, near the tail, or on the back side of the pitot tube. Look at it carefully before any flight, but use even more prudence if you're about to launch under IFR.

Flying IFR without an airspeed indicator is possible, but it's no fun. I've been there. Back in the late 1960s, I got a load of ice on a Piper Arrow that did not have a heated pitot. Airspeed, altimeter, and VSI were lost. In addition, the separate pitot that fed data to the automatic landing gear extension system iced up, and at 8,000 feet, down came the gear. That system sensed lack of speed from the lack of ram air into the pitot tube dedicated to the automatic gear sensors that began to lower the landing gear when slow speed was sensed.

I descended out of the ice into a warmer layer, and the problems disappeared within a few minutes. But for a while, I only had the gyro instruments to keep things in check. Many airplanes have an alternate static source to use in case the primary static port gets blocked. The Arrow didn't. If you are in a similar situation, there is one last-ditch method of restoring static air if the airplane doesn't have an alternate source. Break the glass face out of one air-pressure instrument, and allow the pitot static system to draw static air out of the cabin.

If you have to resort to breaking the glass out of one of the instruments, think about the fact that you stand a very good chance of physically damaging the instrument in the process. You might well break the indicating needle, smash the dial, or otherwise ruin the instrument. So, break the glass in the VSI, not the airspeed indicator or the altimeter. You can do without the VSI much more easily than either of the other two.

FLYING WITHOUT A PRESSURE INSTRUMENT

It's probably harder to fly in the clouds without a pressure instrument, excepting the VSI, than it is to get along without the vacuum-driven gyros. Airspeed and altitude are necessary bits of information, and there really aren't any good backup sources of this information. If the airspeed breaks, and the altimeter is still with you, it isn't too bad. Controlling the airplane by a combination of attitude and power setting should get the job done. You can "backup" by looking at the altimeter to make sure that a descent isn't going too fast. A functional VSI is also a backup.

This book has repeatedly stressed in several situations that a proficient pilot knows the airplane. Part of knowing the airplane is also knowing what combinations of attitude and power produce what results. Flying an airplane in all of the realms of flight boils down to managing the multiple combinations of attitude and power. Certain attitudes, with certain power settings, always produce the same results, unless weight or some other variable factor is grossly different. Every instrument student that I trained learned to fly all phases of flight, including approaches and landings, with the airspeed covered.

If you know what attitude and power combination produces a rate of descent that you want, you can shoot a near-perfect ILS without any airspeed indication at all. The same goes for climbout, cruise, descent, and the traffic pattern. I always told students to view the airspeed indicator as a secondary source of data and to use it just to assure themselves that things were okay. Attitude and power are primary.

If the altimeter is out of commission, you might have a more serious problem when IFR. Maintenance of proper and safe altitudes is one of the more crucial facets of IFR flying. Assuming that the gyro instruments are working, you should be able to maintain the airplane reasonably level and suffer only mild rates of altitude change. If you've trimmed the airplane for level flight before the altimeter failure, you ought to be able to fly for quite a while without any appreciable altitude change, unless you get into turbulence.

But you can't stay in cruise forever; you have to descend and land somewhere. Because this is a real emergency under IFR, let the controller know what's wrong. The Mode C transponder can be a lifesaver in this circumstance because its readout on the controller's screen can be relayed to you in cruise and during the descent. Again, if you know attitude flying, you know the combinations of attitude and power settings to use for all types of descents and approaches.

A GPS receiver can be a backup altimeter because it's capable of displaying altitude. The GPS works by receiving signals from a constellation of 24 satellites. The memory of the GPS unit knows how high these satellites are above the earth, and by measuring the time it takes the signals to travel from the satellite to the airplane, the unit can calculate how far you are from the altitude of the satellite. Since that data alone is pretty useless, the GPS receiver does the math and displays the aircraft altitude above sea level.

FLYING AFTER GYRO FAILURE

When pilots talk about partial panel flying, most all are referring to coping with a failure of the vacuum-driven gyros. They're right. This failure mode is the most common disruption in the operational world of IFR flying. I know several pilots, some of whom have ATP certificates, who have never had an engine even hiccup, but who have suffered at least one vacuum pump failure. Gyro instruments do fail, but usually they die a slow death and give the pilot plenty of warning. They can be replaced or overhauled long before they become unusable.

With the dry vacuum pumps installed in most newer airplanes, a pilot isn't so lucky. When they go, they do so right now with little or no warning, and the pilot is faced with getting out of the situation without an attitude indicator or DG.

If you're going to do much IFR flying without a backup vacuum system, buy a vertical-card magnetic compass. The old, standard "whiskey" compass is close to worthless in any turbulence. It bounces around with its readings sometimes swinging through an arc of 90°. While the vertical-card compass is still a long shot from a DG, it's far more stable than the old-fashioned fluid-filled compass that it can replace. It's considerably more expensive, but in my mind well worth it.

We've already talked about the necessity to recognize an instrument failure in progress. When gyros quit after a vacuum-pump failure, you should have noticed the problem before the instruments finally keel over. The vacuum gauge should be a part of your instrument scan, and it deserves at least a glance every couple of minutes. The gyros in the attitude indicator and DG take a few minutes to spool down completely after they lose their vacuum source.

Perhaps you've noticed a grinding noise from the panel when you finish a flight and shut down the engine. More than likely the noise was from the bearings in one or both of those instruments as they coasted down from their operating RPMs (tens of thousands RPMs). If you fly an airplane that makes this noise, don't operate it under IFR. Bearings that start to grind aren't far from failure. Overhaul or replace the affected instrument(s) before any further IFR flights.

The problem with the coast-down period after a pump breakage is that the indications aren't reliable. This is a particularly vulnerable period of a few minutes when the instruments might seem to be working normally but aren't. Include the vacuum gauge in your regular instrument scan to avoid blindly following invalid indications from dying gyro instruments.

Once you see that the vacuum isn't there anymore, forget using the gyro instruments powered by vacuum pressure, usually the DG and attitude indicator. Some pundits advise instrument pilots to carry the little covers that instructors use to blank these gauges when practicing partial-panel flying. That might be somewhat severe, but go ahead and do it if you are the type of individual who can't ignore something and, in essence, see straight through the now-failed instruments.

When the attitude indicator and DG are useless, you're flying partial panel. It isn't too hard to do. The biggest impediment is probably fear, which can be managed with training and mental attitude. Just remember that back in the 1930s and into the 1940s pilots intentionally flew IFR without the two lost gyros because those instruments were just then coming into vogue. Your have two goals. Keep the airplane under positive control, and navigate to the nearest VFR weather or suitable airport with an instrument approach and land.

The turn coordinator takes on a prime role in controlling the wing attitude. Any bank produces a rate of turn, unless you counter it with opposite rudder. If you keep the ball centered, you won't be crosscontrolling. I advocate flying the needle with your feet and allowing the bank angle to follow along. As long as you don't overcontrol, you can keep the turn needle centered or airplane symbol level with very minor control inputs. Trying to fly straight by using ailerons will be sloppy and will require constant coordination of the control wheel and the rudder pedals. Walking the turn needle or airplane symbol with rudder pedals is easier for most pilots.

During training sessions, try it both ways: controlling the turn needle with just your feet and then with coordinated use of ailerons and rudder pressure. Determine which is easier for you, but do it on several occasions before you make up your mind. Some pilots find it better to use the coordinated method, but the majority of folks whom I've trained or flown with like the rudder technique. Decide for yourself. Regardless of which way you do it, keep the control inputs small and the pressures slight.

The nose attitude is obviously controlled with the elevators via the control wheel. This might be the hardest part of the job because you don't have a gyro instrument to assist. While you're in level flight, the primary instrument for nose attitude becomes the altimeter, backed up by the airspeed indicator. At normal cruise airspeeds, any meaningful deviation from a nose-level attitude will show up in an increase or decrease in altitude. The altimeter will trigger your attention before the airspeed changes enough to warn you. Again, keep the control inputs small and the pressures light. If you were trimmed for level flight before the gyros packed it in, you shouldn't have a great deal of trouble maintaining a nose-level attitude.

Another problem arises when it's time to transition from level flight to either a climb or a descent. During the transition, the airspeed indicator becomes the primary source of pitch information because the altimeter is in a state of constant flux. If you know your airplane like you must to be a safe instrument pilot, you can do these maneuvers without much sweat. To descend, reduce power to the value that you would normally use for a cruise descent. Then watch the airspeed; as it starts to decrease, lower the nose just a little. Your goal during a cruise descent is to lose altitude and maintain an airspeed close to cruising speed.

Adjust the pitch attitude with slight pressures on the control wheel to keep the airspeed where you want it. Crosscheck the VSI and altimeter to make sure that your rate of descent is near when it should be. Make minor adjustments with the wheel, and leave the power alone. Naturally, if there is a gross deviation from the desired descent profile, you might have to fiddle some with the throttle. But it's much easier if you have less to do and change fewer of the airplane's performance parameters. You can control the airspeed much better with the wheel alone. When you reach the altitude to which you are descending, increase the power to the cruise setting. Then raise the nose as the airspeed increases, but don't allow it to increase much. When you're back to level flight, revert to the altimeter for primary pitch information.

Climbing on a partial panel is done the same way. From level flight, increase power to the cruise-climb value. Raise the nose ever so slightly, watching the airspeed, to establish the normal airspeed for cruise climb. During the climb, the airspeed indicator is your primary source of pitch information. If you're climbing at a speed that is too slow, lower the nose a little. If the speed is too fast, raise the nose. Near the target altitude, lower the nose a little, and let the airspeed build. Check the altimeter to stay level. As the airspeed increases to cruise, reduce the power to the cruise setting, and your climb is finished.

When you lose your gyro instruments, the key to understanding what is happening is to know which instrument is primary and which instruments are secondary in the various phases of flight. Know what is supposed to be stable and what should be changing. In level flight, everything should be indicating stable. When the airplane is climbing, the airspeed indicator becomes the primary instrument for pitch attitude because it should settle into a stable speed while the altimeter is naturally winding up. The same is true in a descent, except for the altimeter's unwinding. The primary instrument in any given situation is the one that ought to be giving stable and constant indications backed up by instruments that are showing changes.

WHERE TO GO

As soon as you realize that you are going to be faced with flying partial panel, declare an emergency to the controller who is working your flight. All bets are off for completing your planned route. Your job becomes staying alive and landing at a suitable place.

If there is VFR below or comfortably above the altitude that you've been maintaining, get out of the clouds. If the cloud tops are uniform and within easy reach, I'd request a climb to VFR on top. At least the aircraft-control emergency is over for a while, and you can settle down and plan where to go in some semblance of comfort. The same goes if you can descend to VFR conditions below the clouds. VFR below the clouds is the obvious choice because you can then proceed to the nearest airport and land without having to fly partial panel again or shoot an instrument approach procedure to get down.

Let's assume for the rest of the discussion that you can't get out of the clouds because ceilings are too low to permit safe VFR flight beneath them and you can't get on top. Throughout a flight, every competent instrument pilot stays aware of where the airplane is at all times and what airports are nearby. Remember that you might need to divert and forget the rest of your flight. Instrument failure is only one of many reasons to divert, in addition to electrical problems, an engine about to quit, a low-fuel state, pilot illness, or any of the other problems covered in previous chapters.

Immediately tell the controller that you want to deviate. Depending upon how bad the weather is, you need to make some choices of where to go. If you can get to a close airport with an ILS, that becomes your obvious choice. If the ceilings below you are relatively high, say about 800 feet or higher, you would break out during any type of approach high enough that your palms shouldn't get too sweaty. Flying an instrument approach on partial panel will be the toughest part of the ordeal.

So, if the weather is low, try to avoid flying an approach with a lot of maneuvering, like an NDB or VOR approach, if an ILS isn't too much farther away. If not an ILS, I'd rather shoot a VOR approach than an NDB. The mental math that you have to do to make a good NDB approach can cause a brain overload during this emergency time, unless you're very proficient at partial panel work and NDB approaches. If you have an IFR-approach-certified GPS receiver, then you can consider shooting an approved overlay approach.

If you're in radar contact with an ATC facility, ask for vectors toward the airport that you chose. Tell the controller that you need "no gyro" vectors. Controllers are trained to assist pilots who have lost their gyro instruments. Instead of getting instructions to turn to specific headings, as you do in normal vectoring, the controller will handle you differently. You'll be told to make standard-rate turns (to the doghouse on the turn needle), in whichever direction the controller says. To start a turn, ATC will say "Begin turn." When the controller wants you to stop turning, you'll hear "Stop turn." In that manner, you can be vectored without having to figure out when to stop a turn by trying to follow the bouncing magnetic compass.

Most airports with radar approach control facilities also are equipped with approach surveillance radar (ASR). An ASR radar can be adjusted so the controller's screen display is tremendously enlarged and concentrates on the environment of the approach to a given runway. It's a poor cousin to the old precision-approach radar (PAR), or ground-controlled approach (GCA), as military pilots called it. PAR and GCA have virtually been phased out of service since the late 1960s. When they were around, the controllers could see both the airplane's position relative to the final approach course and its altitude relative to the glide path. GCAs were great; you could make an approach to ILS minimums and even right down to the ground in an emergency, but the controller could only handle one airplane at a time, so they couldn't be used at high-density airports for routine approaches.

ASR shows only azimuth, so the controller can't precisely see your altitude. The advent of Mode C transponders has helped because the controller can see your transponder's readout to the nearest 100 feet. But that isn't a tight enough tolerance for precision approaches. So, the minimums for an ASR approach are in the 600-foot ceiling range, the same as other nonprecision approaches. I like the idea of an ASR approach if I were faced with getting down on partial panel because I wouldn't be concerned about trying to determine heading using only the magnetic compass. Somebody else has reduced that part of the workload.

Most airports that have ASR also have an ILS, but the reverse statement cannot be made. If you chose a destination that has an ILS, ask the controller if ASR is also available for an approach to that runway. If it is, ask the controller to monitor your ILS approach using the ASR equipment. Conversely, you could ask for a primary ASR approach and back it up with the ILS equipment in your airplane. Whichever combination you like, the point is to put together all of the available resources to enhance your odds of successfully making a partial-panel approach.

CONCLUSION

Partial panel flying isn't as tough as it might seem if you practice. Too many instrument pilots get into trouble due to pure lack of proficiency. I've flown with instrument-rated pilots who only fly without gyros during a biennial flight review, if they get a concerned instructor to administer it. Only a few of them and sometimes none of them have shot an IFR approach without the vacuum instruments. If you don't have a standby vacuum system in your airplane, the odds are good that someday you'll be faced with flying partial panel. Unless the weather is good beneath you, you will then have to shoot some kind of approach in order to get down.

Without denigrating advances in technology, every instrument pilot should be cognizant of the failure rates of modern-day dry vacuum pumps and be prepared to deal with the inevitable probability of a pump failure. This is one of the emergencies when proper training, continued proficiency, and the right mental attitude can convert a life-threatening situation into not much more than an inconvenience that only requires a diversion to another airport instead of completing a long IFR flight. Training, practice, and a cool head will carry the day.

12
Some other happenings and suggestions

MOST ACCIDENTS ARE THE PRODUCT OF A SERIES OF SMALL ERRORS, confusing events, and pilot-induced problems that culminate in bent metal or injuries. The "size" of the problem doesn't necessarily dictate either its importance or its potential for disaster if not managed correctly before mushrooming or combining with other problems. This last substantive chapter takes a look at problems that can cause concern for lightplane pilots. While these occurrences aren't of a sufficient magnitude to justify a chapter separately dedicated to each one, they can still be serious.

BLOWING A TIRE

Because light airplanes don't have to go at very high speeds on the ground during either the takeoff run or landing roll, tire blowouts are not a common malady. The materials and manufacturing techniques used in making airplane tires have improved in the past few decades, so we have better equipment these days than did former generations of pilots. But tires still do occasionally fail, and when they do, a tire blowout can be serious.

Just as with most emergencies, an ounce of prevention is worth a pound of cure. Every pilot can do several things to take care of airplane tires and diagnose when one might be about ready to fail, and proper technique in everyday handling of the airplane will make tires last a lot longer.

During the preflight inspection, really inspect the airplane. Too many pilots limit their normal preflight to checking fuel and oil levels and a casual walk around the airplane to make sure that there aren't any dents in it. A proper preflight is more detailed. The entire landing-gear system—struts, brake lines, brakes, and the tires—ought to be thoroughly examined. Checking the tires of a fixed-gear airplane with wheel fairings can involve a little work, but not nearly as much work as retrieving an airplane from a ditch or the mud alongside a runway if a tire blows.

If your airplane has wheel fairings, you'll have to inspect the tires in stages. In most installations, the wheel fairing will leave about 20 to 30 percent of the total circumference of the tire exposed to view; the rest will be hidden inside the fairing. You'll have to inspect what can be seen at first sight, then use the towbar to pull or push the airplane a few inches and reinspect the portion of the tire now exposed. Repeat the process until you've seen the whole tire on each side and on the nose.

Don't pull the airplane by the propeller, which is both dangerous and improper. Use a towbar. Pulling an airplane by the propeller could cause an unintended "kick over" of the engine if the magneto grounds are defective. Additionally, pulling the prop can cause stress in the blades, leaks in the hub of a constant-speed propeller, and cracks in the spinner. All of these areas of damage are the result of pilot abuse when they are caused by using the propeller as a towbar.

Look for two things when inspecting a tire: tread condition and signs of obvious damage to the tread or tire casing including the sidewalls. Lightplane tires can typically be safely used until the tread is worn down quite a bit. Because many pilots normally don't depend on an airplane's tire tread to the same extent as an automobile, you'll see many airplane tires used until the tread is almost gone. That's okay as long as the tire is replaced before the tread is completely worn off, especially in the lightest of airplanes.

While you're checking the tread, look for flat spots where more tread is gone than generally has worn off over the rest of the tire's surface. If there are some flat spots in the tread, use these spots as your determinate for when the remaining tread is no longer sufficient. If the tread has completely worn off in one or more places, it's time for a new tire.

Flat spots in tires are almost always the result of pilot abuse. How many times have you seen a pilot make a sharp turn on the ground by locking a brake, blasting the power, and "horsing" the airplane around? I would venture that we've all seen that kind of abuse all too often.

When you need to make a sharp turn, allow the airplane to roll just a little bit, as much as possible within the confines of the area where you have to make the turn. Letting the tire on the inside of the turn roll any amount without total lockup will greatly reduce the amount of wear put on it. If you lock the brake altogether, you're abrading that tire against the pavement and really increasing the wear rate.

Better yet, think ahead, and don't routinely allow yourself to get in the position that demands this kind of ground handling. Keeping the inside brake from being totally locked will also reduce the amount of power that you need to get the turn accomplished. In turn, less power will lessen the chances of damaging the propeller from loose objects, like gravel, that might be on the parking ramp or taxiway.

While you're looking at the tires during preflight, also watch for any cuts and sidewall damage. The tire might have plenty of tread, but any slits or other cuts in the portion of the tire that come into contact with the ground should be regarding as a no-go item. The physical strength of any tire, airplane or automotive, is severely compromised by cuts. Sidewalls take a significant amount of the loads placed upon tires in normal operation, so inspect them too.

Look for cuts, significant areas of scuffing, and for checking in the sides of the tires. Cuts and scuff marks indicate abuse. The sides of the tire aren't as thick as the bottom tread areas, so any damage here should be checked by a mechanic before further flight. The rubber in tires is subject to rotting. Usually this will show up as small checking cracks in the sidewalls. If you see any, have a mechanic check that out before you fly.

When an airplane is owned and flown exclusively by the owner, the tires will often last so long that sidewall deterioration dictates replacement of the tire before the tread is worn out. Most private owners probably tend to fly more cross-countries and do fewer takeoffs and landings in every 100 hours of flying than pilots of airplanes in rental or student-training fleets. If you own the airplane, you might never wear the tread off the tires before they need to be changed. Rental and training airplanes spend a good portion of their lives doing touch and goes, which wears off the tread much more rapidly.

The best way to stretch the life of tires is to fly the airplane correctly. Remember to eliminate those sharp turns on the ground that tear the tread off a tire very quickly. In addition to proper ground handling, two things can be done during landing to extend tire replacement intervals.

First, don't land and use aggressive braking unless it's really needed. Recall that airplane tires are small and have a much smaller footprint in contact with the pavement than car tires. When you ask that little tire to absorb lots of braking effort, you're putting that force upon a very small area of rubber. Most flat spots in the tread are the result of overly enthusiastic braking or turns on the ground done with a locked brake.

Second, think about what happens to the tire as you touch down. During the final approach, until the tire makes positive contact with the runway, it is completely motionless. Then in a split second it has to get its rotational speed up to whatever the touchdown speed is. Again because airplane tires are so little, they have to rotate at far more RPMs for a given forward speed than do the much larger tires on a car. Each time that you land, you scuff some tread off as the tire goes from stationary to landing speed in less time than you can bat an eye. You see the puffs of smoke from the tires of a landing airliner because the touchdown speed is so high.

Land as slowly as is safe, consistent with the wind conditions each time. Tire wear will increase exponentially with any increase in landing speed. Almost all fixed-gear single-engine airplanes should be stall landed if the wind allows. There is no good reason to touch down any faster in slight winds or if the wind is down the runway. In the days when pilots learned to fly in tailwheel airplanes, everyone learned how to stall land because the bouncing from landing too fast taught you the proper technique very soon. Because most pilots who have been trained since the 1960s have learned in tricycle-gear airplanes that tolerate sloppier piloting, many pilots don't make stall landings anymore.

If you want to extend the life of tires, start doing your landings right. You'll get another benefit from landing as slowly as possible; you won't have to use the brakes as much and maybe not at all on a normal-length runway. Your brakes will last longer, and you won't be wearing flat spots in the tires either. I've always liked the old notion that runways are made to land on, not fly over, so I like to land as slowly as I can and as near to the approach end as is safely possible. I reduce the chances of tire failure. I am going slower if it does happen. And I have more runway remaining to deal with it. As a plus, wear and tear on brake linings is reduced, which extends their life.

Always use the center of the runway for takeoff and landing. You don't know which tire might blow. The middle of the runway improves your odds of staying on the hard surface if a tire fails on either side. Touching down on one side or the other of the runway centerline can spell real trouble if the tire that is closer to the pavement's edge blows out. They paint a centerline down the middle of the runway for good reason.

When a tire blows, it will tend to pull the airplane toward the side that failed. Keep going as straight as you can by using the flight controls to simultaneously steer and unload the blown tire. Unless you're in a strong crosswind, use the ailerons to immediately reduce the load on the failed tire by turning the control wheel away from that side. If the left tire blows, go to full right-aileron travel. If you've landed correctly at or very near to a stall, there isn't enough lift remaining in the wing to raise the tire off the ground, but you can significantly reduce the load and therefore also reduce the friction that is pulling toward the side with the blown tire. Because the airplane is still going fairly fast when touching down, that's the time when a tire will most likely fail if it's going to blow at all. Quick use of the ailerons might save the day.

As forward speed decreases to the point where you lose any aileron effectiveness, the airplane will want to swerve toward the failed tire. No doubt you've already been steering with the nosewheel to keep things straight, but now you will probably need to use differential braking on the good side to keep from running off the runway. It's okay to let the airplane drift somewhat toward the blown tire. How much drift depends mainly upon the width of the runway. If you steer with the nosewheel and apply differential braking, you should be able to stay out of the weeds or mud.

If you fly a low-wing airplane, you need to be aware of where any obstacles are located. When a tire goes flat, you'll lose several inches of wingtip-to-ground clearance. If the airport has highly placed runway or taxiway lights, there is a greater chance of hitting one with a wing after a tire has blown. The same caution should be exercised if there are any snow piles or other hazards alongside any paved area.

Don't get too aggressive with the nosewheel. Remember that it is the weak link in the landing-gear system. It is possible to apply so much nosewheel steering that you bend or break the structure, especially if you get too excited at high speed. When you're still traveling down the runway fast enough that the ailerons are effective, be careful not to get too heavy with the nosewheel steering.

If you need to unload the forces on the nosewheel, use up-elevator control. Most pilots of tricycle-gear airplanes don't pay enough attention to when to use elevator to keep the nosegear from being overstressed. If you are taxiing in a strong tailwind, you might need down-elevator to take some load off the nose. Review the diagram in the POH to show the correct positions of flight controls when taxiing in high winds.

If you have advance warning that a tire might be flat, another technique might make the upcoming landing more controllable. Try to select a runway where there will be a crosswind blowing from the side where the *good* tire is located. Use the wing-down method of approach and landing. The normal procedure for such a landing will automatically unload the failed tire because you'll be applying aileron into the good side and away from the side with the flat tire. Plus, as you slow down and lose aileron effectiveness during the landing roll, the crosswind will have another positive side effect.

Airplanes weathervane into any crosswind. Recall that the nose wants to swing into the wind as the crosswind acts upon the fuselage and vertical tail surfaces. This weathervaning tendency will aid a little in counteracting the yaw force that the failed tire will be putting on the airplane. You'll still have a significant pull toward the bad side, but every little bit helps when it comes to overpowering that swerving tendency and keeping the airplane under control.

If the wind is really strong, try landing into it because the airplane's groundspeed at touchdown will be minimal anyway and that will help you keep the airplane under control. Plus, when the wind is strong, a crosswind landing will probably be rougher and the wind gusts might drive you down onto the bad tire, exacerbating your troubles. Choosing the best wind condition is another decision that can only be made by the pilot. All circumstances will never repeat themselves, so you have to use your best judgment in light of the scenario that presents itself at the time.

BRAKE FAILURE

The brakes on an airplane can fail in two modes. One side or both sides can either lock up or not produce any braking effort at all. Just as for tire failure, a good preflight inspection goes a long way toward preventing problems with the brakes. Combined with maintenance when needed, proper inspections can eliminate most brake failures.

When you inspect the brakes, you're looking at three things: hydraulic lines, pads, and discs.

Check the hydraulic lines that extend down the landing gear legs. Examine the fittings that are usually present at the upper ends where they exit the fuselage or the wing and at the bottom ends where they couple to the brake calipers. Brake fluid is red in color. If you see any stains around the hydraulic fittings, that means that the stained fitting is leaking. A very small leak might be safely deferred until you finish a flight, but always have a mechanic take a look. Because of the high pressures exerted on these fittings during braking, a little leak now might progress to total failure the next time that you get on the brakes.

See if the lines themselves appear solid. Look for cuts or holes in them. Also see if the braiding around the outside of the line is worn. Any of these defects in the brake lines can spell trouble if the affected spot ruptures and disrupts the application of hydraulic pressure from the brake pedals in the cockpit to the calipers on the wheels. Any brake-fluid leaks in the cockpit should be checked by a mechanic before any flight.

Look at the edges of the brake pads, which are a part of the calipers (Fig. 12-1). If you're not a mechanically inclined type of individual, ask a mechanic to spend five minutes with you and show you these components. It does no good to inspect, if you don't know what you're seeing. Ask your mechanic how thick the edges of the brake pads ought to be. Usually you should see at least $\frac{1}{8}$ of an inch of pad thickness, but sometimes more is required, depending upon the airplane involved. These pads wear down over time. If you try to fly after they have reached their minimum thickness, you risk severe damage to the brake discs. Most brake pads contain rivets that are countersunk into the linings. The rivets will grind into the brake disc faces if you allow the linings to wear down and expose the rivet heads. A very expensive disc will be trashed if you let the pads go that long.

Fig. 12-1. *Always include brakes, wheels, and tires in a thorough preflight inspection.*

Examine the discs for the rivet damage, warping, and cracks. The face of the brake disc should be smooth and shiny. If your airplane doesn't have chrome or stainless-steel discs (most don't), you might see a very thin coating of surface rust if the airplane has been sitting for a while. A small amount of rust is not a problem. But if the airplane isn't hangared and sits for protracted periods of time between flights, the rust can easily progress to the point where it pits the surface of the discs. Pitted discs should be examined by a mechanic.

Pitted discs create three more troubles. The brake pads will wear much faster than normal. The pad material will abrade much more quickly as it rubs against a pitted disc than it does when applying friction to a clean, undamaged disc. Plus, the pitting compromises the structural integrity of the disc, making the disc more prone to cracking or breaking. Pitted discs also don't provide as much braking force as undamaged discs.

See if the disc is nicely round and not warped. Discs usually get warped through abusive braking. A warped disc will not produce the braking force of an undamaged disc, and it can cause excessive tire and wheel bearing wear. If the disc is slightly warped, a mechanic might tell you to go ahead and fly the airplane, carefully monitoring the condition, and getting it in for repairs soon. Let a competent mechanic make this call, it's not for the pilot to decide.

Make sure that there are no cracks in the disc. Never fly an airplane that has a cracked brake disc (or drive a car with one either). Get it repaired immediately. Any crack in a disc can quickly propagate and lead to disc breakage. The affected wheel would probably lock up, which isn't very desirable during a takeoff run or a landing roll.

Do all this during the preflight and you will eliminate almost all causes of brake failure, assuming that everything checks out all right. It will be a rare event if the brakes do give you any trouble. A thorough preflight would include a check of the brake-fluid reservoir. Most of the reservoirs in lightplanes are easily accessible. Pipers for the most part are the easiest to check because they use a little metal can attached to the firewall as the fluid container. Unscrew the top, look in, and you've checked it. Cessna and other manufacturers' products can be more difficult. Read your POH to determine where the reservoir is in the airplane you fly.

There isn't much you can do about a failure of the brakes that results in the total absence of braking effort. This mode of failure is almost always the result of either a ruptured brake line, which lets all or most of the fluid escape, or it comes about from a small leak that depletes the supply of fluid over time. Good preflights are essential for innumerable reasons, such as detecting leaks.

Proper landing technique will alleviate the potential for an accident if you suffer total brake loss. Land slowly at or near stall, and don't fly over the runway but land near the approach end. You will have the entire length of the runway to get slowed down. You want to be going as slowly as possible if you depart the pavement. Shut the engine down when you realize the brakes have failed. An idling engine still produces some thrust through the propeller, and the stopping distance will decline if the engine isn't running. You'll do far less damage to an engine that is shut off if the nosegear collapses and the prop hits the ground or the runway.

Most likely, any brake failure will occur on just one side, not both. You can still use a small amount of braking force on the good side, countering the swerving tendency with judicious nosewheel steering. If you try this, it's a delicate balancing act. Nosegear structures can't withstand very much sideward stress. Aggressive braking on the good side and standing on the rudder pedal to steer in the opposite direction might fold the nosegear underneath the airplane. Be careful and brake very cautiously.

A brake that locks up on one side almost always happens upon landing. Remember the earlier discussion about removing wheel fairings in the winter? Snow, slush, and mud can accumulate inside the fairing, then freeze in the colder temperatures aloft and form an iceball around the brake caliper and disc. The ice can also seize the tire solid inside the fairing, which will produce the same result. Corrective action can be taken if you quickly recognize a locked brake.

Raise the wing on the affected side by using aileron input just as you would for a blown tire. The point is to unload the failed side as much as possible, and thereby decrease the amount of friction that side is applying to the runway. Perhaps the tire on the locked side will blow, and perhaps it won't. You are probably better off if it does because the wheel will then slide to some extent. If the tire remains intact, you will more than likely leave the runway. Do your best to minimize the swerving with nosewheel steering, but avoid breaking off the nose strut. This is one time that you can't totally overcome the negative effects of the malfunction. At least running off of the runway isn't life threatening unless there is an obstacle adjacent to it.

Any crosswind from the good side of the airplane can assist in controllability whether the known problem is a failed tire, locked brake, or broken disc. In the case of either a failed tire or locked brake, don't overdo it and go out hunting for a howling or gusty crosswind. A steady crosswind within the allowable crosswind component for your airplane will help maintain control during the landing roll. Moderate your desire to land with a crosswind if the wind velocity is high. Landing straight into a strong wind will produce a very slow groundspeed at touchdown, and the landing will most likely be smoother than fighting a heavy crosswind. Again, use your judgment after you have become aware of all the relevant facts and have analyzed them. When you land with either a failed tire or brake, do a stall landing, so that you make contact with the ground at the slowest possible speed.

CHECK YOUR ELT

Every airplane that is used for cross-country flights is required to be equipped with an emergency locator transmitter (ELT). Surprisingly few pilots really know much about ELTs or how to check them.

An ELT transmits a signal on both international emergency frequencies of 121.5 and 243.0 MHz. The signal makes a "whooping" sound that is very recognizable. There are authorized procedures to check an ELT, and you ought to do a test once in a while. Whether you have a portable ELT in the airplane or one that is mounted to a bracket somewhere in the cabin, take it out. Either carry it yourself or send it to an avionics shop because most shops have a shielded area where the ELT can be activated without sending the emergency signal outside the building. An ELT that is permanently mounted in the airframe can be tested in the airplane, but only on the ground. You may also test a portable ELT if an avionics shop is not convenient.

Tests are authorized during the first five minutes after every hour and at no other time. Realize that you are working with an emergency alerting device, so the regulations are written with a view toward minimizing the time that any ATC facility that hears a signal might suspect that a unit is being tested. When a test is conducted at a controlled airport, call the tower and explain that you plan to test an ELT. Make this call a few minutes before the hour, and let the tower know precisely when to expect the unit to be activated.

When the appointed time comes, within that first five minutes after each hour, tune your communication radios to 121.5 and activate the ELT by switching it to the "test" or "on" position. You should immediately hear the wailing, whooping sound. You are allowed to keep it on for only three sweeps of its signal, and that is plenty to tell if it's working. Then immediately turn it off. Call the tower and ask if they heard it. The reason for the second tower call is to check the ELT's antenna. Despite a broken connection between the ELT and its antenna, you might still hear the whoops through the airplane's comm radios due to the close proximity of the ELT to the receiving antenna while the ELT's signal actually isn't getting out much farther. If the tower heard it, you can assume that it's functioning normally.

Most ELT batteries have to be replaced every two years. Quite often the replacement date for the ELT batteries doesn't coincide with the time of the annual inspection of the airplane. The mechanic who does the annual is supposed to enter the ELT battery replacement date in the logbook when the annual is performed. Most of the time the entry is made, but the pilot either isn't advised of it or forgets. Make it a part of your conversations with whomever does your maintenance to make sure you know when the ELT battery needs changed. Flying with an expired battery is a regulatory violation, and if you ever get ramp checked by an FAA inspector, you might get a rude surprise if yours is out of date. More importantly, an ELT can save your life, and its ability to transmit for as long as it can is diminished without a legal battery. ELTs are great devices. As a Civil Air Patrol search pilot for many years, I've had several occasions to hear them for real.

Also test for inadvertent activation. When you finish every flight, tune the transceiver to 121.5 MHz for a few seconds. You will know immediately if the ELT is accidentally transmitting. Turn it off. If the ELT switch is faulty and doesn't deactivate the ELT, take the battery connections loose to disable it. From personal experience, I can tell you that CAP search crews don't like phone calls at 3 a.m. to go fly in the cold or the wet only to find an airplane securely tied down or in a hangar with its ELT blasting away. If you can't find the battery connections or for whatever other reason you can't get it turned off, at least telephone the nearest FSS or other ATC facility and let them know about your predicament. You don't want to precipitate any needless activation of the Search and Rescue (SAR) system.

During cross-country flights, do your fellow pilots a favor. Occasionally listen on 121.5. After testing your ELT and learning what the signal sounds like, you'll recognize one if you hear it while airborne. ELTs normally have a line-of-sight range, and if you're flying very high, you can hear the transmissions from quite a long distance. But if an airplane has been forced down in a valley, terrain might block its signal. Even though satellites listen for ELTs, several are heard each year only by overflying aircraft monitoring the emergency frequency. Be sure to tune your radio away from 121.5 before transmitting.

Upon hearing an ELT, notify ATC or an FSS immediately. Report your altitude, position, and heading when you first heard the signal. Also report how strong the signal was and how long you were able to hear it. Relate any effects upon the signal during any position or heading change; did the signal fade in and out, grow weaker, or grow stronger? Information of this nature helps SAR better pinpoint an area to search.

MARGINAL VFR WEATHER

While flying in marginal VFR weather isn't really an emergency, it can by a scary endeavor for some folks. A few considerations and tactics can reduce the fear factor. Most of all, keep in mind the sobering statistic that flying in reduced visibility is the greatest killer of pilots in lightplanes. Don't fly in marginal VFR weather that has the potential of deteriorating further. There are times when marginal weather is stable, but there are many more occasions when it is not.

When the ceiling lowers, you have to fly lower. With a lower flight altitude, you cannot rely on VOR navigation as much because the reception range decreases, perhaps remarkably so, compared to what you might be used to if you usually fly cross-countries at fairly high altitudes. Unless you have a GPS or perhaps a loran (as long as the loran transmitters remain in operation), you are compelled to navigate the old-fashioned way, a skill that might be rusty. If the visibility is really marginal, down to around 3 miles or less, most pilots won't feel comfortable trying to find their way by dead reckoning alone and will need to use a good degree of looking out the window and flying mainly by pilotage.

Roads, railroads, and rivers make excellent paths to get from one place to another in these conditions. Don't be afraid to admit to yourself that you need an extra margin of security in your navigating. When the weather is low, you don't want to get lost because your available means of getting found are reduced in poor conditions; however, there are hazards lurking that you need to remain aware of and avoid.

If you are flying above a road at a minimum legal and safe altitude, remember that commercial radio stations are built with comparatively easy access to the transmitter site. Keep referring to your current sectional chart and making sure that the area is free of towers near the road. Give it a wide berth if you are in an area with a tower or towers. Most towers are supported by guy wires that might extend on a slope toward the ground quite a distance horizontally from the tower structure itself. Missing the tower only to get entrapped by the guy wires would be unfortunate.

If no obstacles are shown near the road, still be cognizant of power transmission lines that cross highways. In some parts of the country, they can be several hundred feet above the ground and will not be visible even in the best weather until it's too late to avoid them. If you see a supporting tower off to one side of the road, be sure that you are safely above the top of it. A small static wire runs from one tower to the next; the static wire is above the main lines that carry the electricity. All too many pilots have cleared the main lines, only to be snared by the static wire.

If circumstances permit, fly along the right side of the road. Many parts of the world drive cars on the right side of the road: therefore, many pilots have relatively powerful instincts to "keep right." Whether it is on a roadway, sidewalk, or hallway in a building, most people will naturally favor the right side of a pathway. Pilots flying down roads, railroad tracks, or rivers tend to also "keep right" in airplanes. Give yourself every edge possible to avoid a midair collision.

The rules for VFR flight are different for helicopters than they are for airplanes because the helicopter pilot can slow to a creep if necessary to see and avoid obstacles. While you can't fly at 30 knots in an airplane, you can slow down significantly from your normal cruise airspeed. If the clouds are low or the visibility is murky, reduce speed. Extra time to see and avoid hazards is your greatest ally when you're stuck in marginal weather. This time is dramatically increased if you slow down.

The FARs allow helicopters to fly VFR in about any kind of weather. The only real requirement is that the pilot limit forward speed to a point where obstacles can be seen and avoided. If you are tooling around in low weather, be vigilant for choppers. They can operate on special VFR clearances into airports where fixed-wing special VFR is prohibited. Helicopters are hard to see in good weather because only the fuselage is visible, and the fuselage usually isn't very large to start with. Keep your eyes open and your head on a swivel.

INADVERTENT STALLS AND SPINS

In a recent survey of over 1,000 general aviation pilots conducted by a major aviation trade organization, a surprisingly large number of pilots admitted to having inadvertently stalled an airplane. Because the facts and opinions that are concluded from any survey depend on how the questions are devised and how the person replying perceives the question, you may draw your own conclusions about how many pilots do accidentally get into stalls. I could answer that question both ways. While soaring in thermals, which is normally performed at an airspeed just above stall, I will let a sailplane brush up against the edge of a stall quite often. It will buffet some, and if I'm in a playful mood, I'll let the nose break every now and then. Does that mean I'm one of those who inadvertently stall? Or did the question that was asked on the survey imply an affirmative answer only if the pilot was caught completely by surprise?

Regardless of how you would view the query, too many pilots have gotten their airplanes into stalls without intending to come even close. Worse yet, several pilots are killed every year by accidental spins, usually begun very close to the ground. An unintentional stall should not be a big deal, if it isn't followed by a spin. Primary training teaches students to recover early and with minimal loss of altitude. Done correctly, the recovery from complete stalls in lightplanes can be accomplished with no more than 100 ft. of altitude loss at the most. You should be able to do it with almost no loss. But when a spin develops, that's another story.

Ever since the spin training requirement was eliminated from the private pilot training curriculum (before most of us learned to fly), instructors, safety experts, and writers have been debating the wisdom of reintroducing spin training. Some take the view that the best spin training is learning to recognize and recover from stalls so that a spin never develops in the first place. Others feel that because virtually every airplane can be spun, it is a flight regime to which a pilot ought to be exposed and learn to handle. I'm in the second camp.

If your philosophy is to learn everything that you do as completely as you can, and try to be the best at it that you can be, I'm at a loss to understand why people want to avoid spin training. Especially when you see the stall/spin accident numbers, which are appalling, I will never understand the thinking that safety is enhanced by relying only on good stall recognition and recovery techniques to prevent spin accidents.

When I was a flight instructor working my way through college in the middle 1960s, I had a lesson I'll never forget. I was teaching an older gentleman to fly; he was not particularly quick in his progress, but he was steadily coming along, primarily through determination. He had about 5 to 10 hours of solo time when he came back from one local-area flight as white as a sheet with his legs literally shaking as he walked into the FBO's office. I asked him what was wrong, expecting to hear that he had become airsick. The tale was far more harrowing.

He had been practicing stalls up at a safe altitude. He decided to do a departure stall, which is those days were taught with full power. When the Cessna 150 stalled, he didn't catch the wing drop, and it entered a spin, according to him, faster than he knew what happened. He said that he sat there, petrified, as the world became a whirling dervish in the windshield. When he realized that the ground was coming up, he reached up and put his hands on the headliner and braced his feet against the cockpit sidewalls, waiting for the impact. Without knowing it, he had done the right thing. The 150 stopped spinning, and my student then recovered from the dive. I bet it was a shaky ride back from the practice area to the airport.

I never soloed another student without first doing at least a couple of spins to show him or her what one was like and how to recover. In preparation for the flight test, I would subsequently teach him or her how to enter and recover from spins without assistance from me. Very few accidental spins occur when the airplane is high enough to recover on its own, as it did for my fortunate grandfatherly student. I know of no student of mine who was ever scared out of flying or who became a reckless "cowboy" by being exposed to spins. I've kept track of a good many of the people whom I taught to fly in 22 years as a flight instructor, and I honestly don't know of any who have had a stall/spin accident.

Read your POH. There are some techniques for spin recovery that are fairly generic for all lightplanes, but each might have its own peculiarities. All single-engine airplanes must endure spin testing as a part of their certification by the FAA. Read and adhere to what the manufacturer has to say about how to get out of a spin. The factory test pilots have done innumerable spins and experimented to find the best recovery technique. What follows is only basic in nature and must be supplemented or supplanted by the POH's dictates.

A spin will only develop after the wings have stalled. When you are in a spin, you have two tasks to perform: stop the rotation and get the wings flying again. Spin recovery follows that order. If you know for sure which way you're spinning, apply full opposite rudder to stop rotating. If you're not absolutely sure which direction the airplane is spinning, neutralize the rudder pedals, and the rotation will stop of its own accord, albeit that it will take a little longer than if you are able to use full rudder against the spin. The great majority of modern airplanes have to be forced to stay in a spin; therefore, they will recover when the positive rudder input is removed, which was continuing the rotation.

When the rotation stops, briskly but only momentarily apply full-forward control wheel or stick. This breaks the stall, reduces the angle of attack, and restores proper airflow over the wings. Finally, recover smoothly from the ensuing dive, and don't overstress anything by "honking" back on the wheel to get the nose level. Take it as easy as altitude and airspeed allow.

Without doubt, accidental spins are most deadly when they occur at very low altitudes, when there might not be sufficient height to recover regardless of the pilot's proficiency at spin recovery. This event usually happens in the traffic pattern when a pilot allows an airplane to overshoot the turn from base leg to final. Rushed to complete the turn and get lined up with the runway, the inattentive pilot applies too much rudder, starting a skid. If the airplane is also low on final and the pilot pulls the wheel back too much and stalls the airplane, all of the elements required to initiate a spin are already at work. The airplane "snaps" into a spin in a microsecond. Watch your technique, and don't fall into this trap. If you're low enough when it happens, there is no way out.

DECLARE AN EMERGENCY

When any in-flight emergency occurs, your first job is to deal with it. When you have been able to take the first steps toward recognizing the fact that an emergency is upon you, don't hesitate to declare that state of affairs. For some unknown reason, pilots are routinely hesitant to declare an emergency. That delay often makes the situation worse for all concerned.

Throughout this book, I've tried to mention, where appropriate, the services that ATC facilities can provide to a pilot in trouble. But if you don't ask, they'll never know. Or if they do find out, it might be after a problem has needlessly magnified itself. The paperwork that is entailed after the conclusion of the emergency is no excuse to deny yourself the value of ATC assistance. In the few occasions that I've had to personally avail myself of ATC help, controllers have bent over backwards to provide whatever assistance they could. Controllers are as vigilant about safety as are we pilots, sometimes even more so; many of them are aviators. Whenever they can do something to prevent an emergency from snowballing or to alleviate an emergency already in progress, they do it.

The word MAYDAY is the international distress signal that will be recognized everywhere. PAN-PAN are the words to use to signify a problem that is not yet life-threatening or control of the airplane hasn't been lost, but the situation might soon become a full-fledged emergency. If you establish contact with any ATC facility following either a MAYDAY or PAN-PAN call, transmit the following information:

1. Aircraft identification and type.
2. The nature of your problem.
3. Current weather conditions.
4. Pilot's intentions or request.
5. Present position and heading. If you are lost, tell them your last known position and heading, and when you were over that position.
6. Your altitude.
7. Fuel remaining in hours and minutes.
8. Number of people on board.
9. Any other useful information, such as aircraft color, and what equipment you have on board.

If you're already squawking an assigned transponder code, leave it set there until you're told to change. If you are not working any ATC facility when the emergency begins, squawk 7700 as soon as you can. That will light up every radarscope in range of your transponder. The controllers will be alerted and will be expecting a MAYDAY call from you. If you are communicating with ATC before the distress happens, go ahead and make your MAYDAY call on the frequency in use. In the event that you're not already in contact with ATC, don't waste time by trying to look up a frequency for the facility that you are trying to call; get on 121.5 MHz without delay.

If you are going down over land or water, give the controller the most information that you can to assist the search aircraft that will be dispatched. At a minimum, include the following:

1. The status of your ELT.
2. Any landmarks that you can see.
3. The color of your aircraft.
4. What emergency or survival equipment that you have on board.

If your ELT is of the type that can be activated from inside the cockpit, turn it on, regardless of whether you've talked to anyone yet. If the satellite can hear a few sweeps of the ELT, you are far more likely to be positioned by it accurately. Don't wait until you are on the ground to turn on the ELT; if the forced landing doesn't go well, the airplane might end up inverted, breaking off the antenna. If you are forced down in hilly terrain, the ground might shield ELT transmissions that won't be heard by either the satellite system or a search aircraft. Turning your ELT on while still in the air gives you the best chance that it will be heard.

If you make a forced landing, get out of the aircraft and remain safely clear of any wreckage until all possibility of fire or explosion passes. Then stay near it. An airplane is always easier to see from a searching aircraft than are people wandering around. If you must leave the wreckage for any reason, no matter how close you think you are to civilization, leave a note behind as to the direction you went, where you thought you were going, and the date and time that you headed out.

Also make an arrow on the ground with tree branches, stones laid out, or something else that won't disappear. Point the arrow toward the direction that you are going to walk. If the ground is covered with snow, don't depend upon an arrow made by trampling in the snow to stay visible very long. It probably won't be seen at all from a search aircraft, and it will disappear if any more snow falls or drifts in the wind. With the proper information, any search parties that find the airplane will have some idea of where to continue looking for you.

PILOT ILLNESS

One emergency that we don't think too much about is what happens if the pilot gets sick or becomes incapacitated. A recent FAA survey of accidents over a six-year period documented only seven accidents caused by pilot physical incapacitation. This number is statistically insignificant, but regardless of whether the number is only one, pilots ought to do what is reasonable to prevent any. This certainly does not justify raising the physical requirements for general aviation pilots to the level required of astronauts, but there are a few things to consider.

Don't fly when you're sick. That sounds simple enough, but there is more to it than the obvious. Few pilots would attempt flight when deep in the throes of illness; however, the physical effects can linger on after the worst of a cold, the flu, or some other common problem leaves you. A nuisance of a stuffy nose can become a debilitating sinus headache or eustachian-tube blockage at altitude. I've flown as a passenger on airliners in this condition, and I was glad that I wasn't in one of the front seats. An accident occurred several years ago when a Naval aviator rammed an airplane into the stern of a carrier while attempting a landing. The pilot was taking over-the-counter antihistamines for a simple head cold, and the drugs were blamed for the tragic result of that flight.

Before flying while taking any drugs, prescription or over-the-counter, call your aviation medical examiner for advice about whether you ought to fly. If the examiner you see for your routine aviation medical exams won't take personal phone calls from patients, find another one. You might get a bill for the consultation, and that is appropriate. Better to pay a few dollars for professional advice than chance it on your knowledge of what is acceptable. Consider everything to be unacceptable until approved by an aviation medical examiner.

There is another way to prevent the slight chance of a fatal accident if you do become incapacitated in flight with a passenger on board. Obtain elementary training for a spouse, child of reasonable age, business partner, or whomever flies with you on a regular basis. The training would provide a nonpilot with enough experience to take over control of an airplane, navigate, and communicate to land at the nearest airport of decent size. Most people can learn these few skills on a weekend. The emergency flight might not be very precise, and the landing probably won't be textbook perfect, but there have been instances of passengers with this minimal level of training getting an airplane safely on the ground. My wife and daughter are already pilots; otherwise, they would be appropriately trained.

Whenever you feel ill during a flight, land as soon as possible. A sour stomach might be the precursor to food poisoning or incapacitating nausea. A case of common diarrhea might be manageable on the ground, but it might have fatal effects in an airplane if you can't keep your wits about you to fly.

Also be aware that the FARs prohibit flying during any period of illness or injury that would be disqualifying if you were to then seek a medical certificate. In fact, your certificate is automatically suspended during those times. Even though you might have several months to go until the normal period of validity runs out, you don't technically have a valid certificate when you wouldn't otherwise pass the exam.

THE PILOT'S EMERGENCY AUTHORITY

FAR 91 states:

> In an in-flight emergency requiring immediate action, the pilot in command may deviate from any rule of this part to the extent required to meet that emergency.

This language is plain and simple. When the need is present, do what you have to do to meet an emergency. Don't worry about whether reasonable actions that you take comply with the regulations. Handling the emergency is paramount. If you are IFR and working a controller's frequency, it's your call whether to ask for something different from your current clearance, or to tell them what you are about to do.

The need might be immediate if an altitude change is required. In that case, tell the controller that you are leaving the assigned altitude and whether you are climbing or descending. Report the altitude toward which you're headed. Request the altitude change if the situation isn't so dire as to require an immediate climb or descent, but be sure to explain why you need the change.

The same basic guidelines are applicable to heading changes. When in dire straits, turn and tell them. Request a deviation before it becomes an emergency if you have advance warning, such as seeing a thunderstorm ahead. ATC will do everything it can to help you, but in turn, help the controllers by making the request as soon as that need becomes apparent. Don't be timid or bashful. Do what needs to be done.

FAR 91 also gives the FAA the right to ask you for a written explanation of what happened and why you needed to deviate from any regulatory requirements. Like many other things about flying, I'd rather deal with this task from a desk days after the emergency instead of worrying in the air about the ramifications of not adhering to some regulation if in doing so I prevented an accident or incident. I've never known a pilot who had a true emergency who suffered later at the hands of the FAA, unless the problem was the result of some incomprehensible pilot action or omission. FAA inspectors are for the most part aviation professionals who understand what faces a pilot in extremes, and they seldom second guess any action that you have taken to get out of a life-threatening situation.

KEEP FLYING

No matter how bad things seem or become, keep flying the airplane. Panic and the surrender to events that it causes will deal you a deadly hand as quickly and more certainly than about anything that can happen to the airplane. There are amazing stories of pilots who have lived through midair collisions, catastrophic structural failures, and other seemingly hopeless trials. One thing they all had in common was that none of them gave up; they all kept flying the airplane.

One of my close friends had a wing spar break in a twin-engine freighter. The broken wing deflected upwards by as much as 2 feet at the wingtip. He told me about it in person, rather than my learning about the emergency by reading an accident report. There was no accident because he is a well-trained professional pilot who kept his cool. He didn't subject the airplane to any additional stress than was absolutely necessary for the descent and landing. He put it on the runway so gently that the broken-spar condition did not worsen under the load of the weight on the landing gear.

I know several pilots who have come out the other side of a thunderstorm that was embedded in a cloud layer. Each one successfully fought back any panic and flew the airplane. Everyone has the pictures of World War II bombers that returned to their bases in England after having rudders, elevators, nose cones, and other airframe parts shot off. Pilots *flew* them back; the airmen did not merely hope to get a ride home. Just like they did, never give up.

13
Conclusion

HOPEFULLY THIS BOOK HAS ACCOMPLISHED ITS MAIN GOAL, WHICH HAS been to make every pilot who picks it up start thinking more about in-flight emergencies. That thought process needs to include not only mental rumination, but it then needs to be carried to the next step, which is action.

No amount of reading, talking, and thinking about how to handle emergencies will save your skin without more training. When combined with training and practice, it probably will. Once in a while the proverbial blind squirrel finds an acorn, and the best aviation analogy to that old saying occurs when the ill-trained and unprepared pilot survives some sort of emergency through luck alone. It does happen, but not often.

There are extremely few emergencies that cannot be managed to a safe and satisfactory ending. Certainly some events in aviation might be insurmountable, but no more real risk attends them than is present in many of our daily endeavors. Everything has some risk, even getting out of bed in the morning. The key to a long career as a pilot is eliminating those risks that can be avoided, regardless of whether one flies for a living, for personal transportation, or for sport. Then learning to manage the other risks that might arise completes the training circle.

Develop your mental attitude to the point where you see the regulatory minimums in pilot skill, aeronautical knowledge, and training to be no more than they are—minimums to get a license. Very few of us perform our jobs or practice our professions to the lowest degree of competency that are governed by prevailing regulations or standards. Why approach flying with that cavalier mentality?

Perhaps one of the best things about flying is that most everyone who does it is in love with it. When you really enjoy any activity, you've got a built-in motive to do it well and hone your skills at it. Approach aviation this way. Read the magazines, books, and anything else that you can get your hands on. Study the POH intently so that you really know every airplane that you fly. Make every flight count for something other than just getting you from one place to another. Train constantly. A training flight isn't only a flight with a flight instructor, but it is every flight where you increase or at least maintain your proficiency. Practice a specific aspect of aviating whenever you get in the airplane.

The odds are very much in your favor that you will enjoy decades of flying light-planes without encountering any of the emergencies discussed in this book, except that at sometime you might be unsure of your position for a little while. Preparation for the unlikely doesn't make it more likely to occur. In fact, the reverse is true. For in training for emergencies, you learn more about how to prevent them entirely or discern the warning signs that something isn't just right. Then you can do what it takes to manage an inconvenience before the situation degenerates and becomes dire. The airline training philosophy puts it best: When emergency procedures are well-learned, they cease to be emergencies and simply become additional procedures. If you make that a personal standard, you will perform to that same level.

I've been a very fortunate person. Almost every aspect of my professional, personal, and family life either has revolved around or does revolve around general aviation. I met my wife when I was a college student working as a flight instructor. My family has seen parts of the United States from a unique perspective that is only available to people who fly light aircraft.

But I don't feel as though I've lived a charmed life. There have been little happenings in airplanes, or the lack of happenings, that I can attribute to luck, but not many, and no important ones. No person is perfect, and we all make errors. The vital thing to remember about flying is that you might not get a second chance to relive selected escapades. Accidents in aviation are almost always the product of human oversight.

Machines don't err; people do. Sometimes the person who makes the miscue can be a design engineer, factory production worker, or mechanic. The sad fact is that these folks have a much better record of avoiding serious mistakes in their work than do the pilots who later fly what they have conceived, built, and maintained.

This book has covered some of the darker corners of aviation. There was no intent to scare anyone or drive anybody away from flying. We owe ourselves and all other pilots with whom we come in contact a duty to raise the safety of general aviation to new levels. Most of the technical advances in the industry have gone a long way to achieve more efficient, more comfortable, faster, and safer aircraft. But when it comes down to the final analysis, the pilot in command is ultimately responsible according to regulation and common sense for the successful outcome of any flight.

Be the kind of pilot with whom I'd let a member of my family ride. Know yourself and your airplane first. Then work on both to eliminate any areas of deficiency. When crunch time comes, if it comes, you have only yourself and the airplane to safely get out of whatever situation is confronted. A pilot who has trained, practiced, and retrained is the one I'm comfortable with. When you think about the complexities of airliners and corporate aircraft and conceive of all that could go wrong with such advanced machines, you should come to one stark conclusion.

The safety record of airline operators and corporate flight departments in the United States of America is no fluke. (Corporate aviation's safety statistics are very close to the airlines.) Pilots of these aircraft are among the best schooled in the world. They have practiced emergency procedures at every training opportunity. Sure, the pilots do have advanced simulators to perform emergency procedures that might be too risky in the actual airplane. But the airplanes that they fly present many more potential failure modes than the average lightplane.

If general aviation pilots would think, practice, train, and fly like a pro, the accident rate for light aircraft would subsequently drop. An airline-pilot friend always makes it a point to tell laymen who might have some fear of flying that he thinks about accidents and emergencies constantly; he never loses sight of the fact that from his vantage point in the nose of a jetliner, he'll probably be the first person at the scene of any crash.

You're in the same position in a small airplane. The life you save with adequate preparation, training, and practice will be your own. You're the pilot, and you'll always get there first.

Index

About the author

Jerry A. Eichenberger has written three previous books for TAB Books: *General Aviation Law*, *Your Pilot's License*, and *Cross-Country Flying*. He has written more than 100 magazine articles dealing with aviation law and aviation safety. His works are regularly featured in *Business & Commercial Aviation* magazine, which serves the corporate and commuter airline industries.

Eichenberger is a commercial pilot, rated for single and multiengine airplanes, helicopters, and gliders. He holds an airplane instrument rating and previously held a flight instructor certificate for 22 years. He is rated to teach instruments and to give instruction in single-engine and multiengine airplanes. Eichenberger has logged more than 4,500 hours.

He is a practicing attorney in the area of aviation law, representing manufacturers, maintenance facilities, flight schools, airlines, FBOs, airports, and individual pilots and aircraft owners. He is a partner with one of Columbus, Ohio's oldest law firms, Crabbe, Brown, Jones, Potts, and Schmidt. He remains an active general aviation pilot.

Other Bestsellers of Related Interest

ABCs of Safe Flying, 3rd Edition
—David Frazier
This clearly written pilot's guide describes the keys to competency as a pilot, the habits of safety, and the attitude of the professional. Also covers ground operations, airspace designations, Federal Aviation Regulations, navigational equipment, cross-country flights, pilot/controller cooperation, and aviation career opportunities.
0-8306-2089-3 #157718-1 $15.95 Paper
0-8306-2091-5 #157719-X $22.95 Hard

Avoiding Common Pilot Errors
—John Stewart
Teaches students and licensed pilots the correct procedures for operating in controlled airspace. Covers preflight preparation, communications, phraseology and word concepts, regulations and procedures, and more.
0-8306-2434-1 #155395-9 $17.95 Paper

Cockpit Resource Management: The Private Pilot's Guide
—Thomas P. Turner
A comprehensive guide to cockpit resource management and the key to becoming a safer, more proficient flier in the 1990s for both the private and professional pilot.
0-07-065604-5 $19.95 Paper
0-07-065603-7 $32.95 Hard

Pilot's Guide To Weather Reports
—Terry T. Lankford
How to obtain and understand FAA weather reports; use current and forecasted weather to plan the best flight route; and decide whether to put off the flight to another day.
0-8306-6582-X #156003-3 $19.95 Paper

Stalls & Spins
—Paul Craig
A practical guide to help private pilots and flight students meet new FAA requirements, this book demystifies stalls and spins. Readers gain a better knowledge and understanding of the aerodynamic principles involved, the psychological effects of stalling and spinning, the actions necessary to avoid disaster, and the spin characteristics of specific aircraft.
0-8306-4020-7 #013422-7 $18.95 Paper
0-8306-4019-3 #013421-9 $26.95 Hard

Stick & Rudder: An Explanation of the Art of Flying
—Wolfgang Langewiesche
The classic first analysis of the art of flying is back, now in a special 50th anniversary limited edition with a foreword by Cliff Robertson, leatherette binding, and gold foil stamp. Langewiesche shows precisely what the pilot does when he or she flies, just how it's done, and why.
0-07-036242-4 $50.00 Hard

How to Order

Call 1-800-822-8158
24 hours a day,
7 days a week
in U.S. and Canada

Mail this coupon to:
McGraw-Hill, Inc.
P.O. Box 182067
Columbus, OH 43218-2607

Fax your order to:
614-759-3644

EMAIL
70007.1531@COMPUSERVE.COM
COMPUSERVE: GO MH

Shipping and Handling Charges

Order Amount	Within U.S.	Outside U.S.
Less than $15	$3.50	$5.50
$15.00 - $24.99	$4.00	$6.00
$25.00 - $49.99	$5.00	$7.00
$50.00 - $74.49	$6.00	$8.00
$75.00 - and up	$7.00	$9.00

EASY ORDER FORM—
SATISFACTION GUARANTEED

Ship to:

Name _____

Address _____

City/State/Zip _____

Daytime Telephone No. _____

Thank you for your order!

ITEM NO.	QUANTITY	AMT.
	Shipping & Handling charge from chart below	
Method of Payment:	Subtotal	
☐ Check or money order enclosed (payable to McGraw-Hill)	Please add applicable state & local sales tax	
☐ VISA ☐ DISCOVER	TOTAL	
☐ AMERICAN EXPRESS Cards ☐ MasterCard		

Account No. ☐☐☐☐☐☐☐☐☐☐☐☐☐☐☐☐☐☐

Signature _____ Exp. Date _____
Order invalid without signature

**In a hurry? Call 1-800-822-8158 anytime,
day or night, or visit your local bookstore.**

Code = BC15ZZA